"We must speak the truth about terror. Let us never ~~~

outrageous conspiracy theories concerning the attacks of

September the 11th, malicious lies that attempt to shift the blame

away from the terrorists themselves, away from the guilty."

George W. Bush before the United Nations General Assembly,

Nov. 10, 2001

CONSPIRACIES, CONSPIRACY THEORIES, and the SECRETS of 9/11

MATHIAS BROECKERS

CONSPIRACIES,
Conspiracy Theories,
and the
Secrets of 9/11

Translated from the original German work,
Verschwörungen, Verschwörungstheorien,
und die Geheimnisse des 11.9,
the first of two books on 9/11 by the author.

Copyright © by Mathias Bröckers

All English Rights Reserved
& Published by
Progressive Press,
PO Box 126,
Joshua Tree, Calif. 92252,
www.ProgressivePress.com

ISBN: 0-930852-23-0. ISBN-13: 978-0-930852-23-8
Library of Congress CIP Data applied for
Length: 104,000 words
Translated by Simona de Logu and John Leonard
First Regular Edition printed June 2006
Printed in the USA

TOPICS:
The nature of Conspiracy. Its pervasive role in life and history.
Secret societies. Philosophy and fallacies of conspiratorial thinking.
A science of conspirology. World conspiracies. Skull & Bones Club.
9/11 and the rise of the Osama bin Laden-Al Qaeda conspiracy theory,
unsupported by evidence. Countervailing theories. WTC, Pentagon.
The Great Game. Drugs, finance, and the CIA. Oil, War and Peace.
Puppets of Empire in the Third World and Fourth Estate.

TABLE OF CONTENTS

Foreword to the American Edition

When I went over this book again in recent days, I was astonished, and even frightened, because in "normal" times – the past, when honest journalism and enlightenment of the public were virtues – the incredible scandal of this unsolved crime and its continued cover-up simply couldn't have been maintained for so long.

It is now more than three years since this book was first printed in German, and four years since I started writing the columns presented here. When published in September, 2002, it was an immediate best-seller, being the first – and for some time the only – book in German with a critical and skeptical approach to the "official version" of the events of 9/11, to the story-line trumpeted all over by the mainstream media.

When I wrote the first columns in the days after the attacks, I didn't expect they might be turned into a book or be translated in several languages, with an international impact. My thought then was: OK, I might be kind of an early bird in picking up and commenting on these inconsistencies and contradictions, but when my colleagues at the editorial desks of the main papers and broadcasters wake up, they will take over reporting and investigating the case. After a decade of work as a senior editor with Berlin's alternative daily paper *die tageszeitung (taz)*, I became a freelance-author in the early 1990's, writing books and working as a journalist for some of the major papers and radios.

So I was familiar with the media business, and had some good contacts there. But when I called the editors for some space or airtime in the weeks after 9/11, in one way or another I always heard the same: "Mathias, you may write about anything – but not about 9/11." So no critical question, by me or any other writer, appeared in the mainstream media at all – and this has hardly changed since. Instead, the legend of Osama and the 19 bandits has been ballyhooed and trumpeted over and over again.

This is exactly how brainwashing works, and the situation hasn't changed one bit with the publication of the 9/11 commission report in August 2004. By coincidence their report appeared on the bookshelves at the same time as the latest Harry Potter novel, and since it didn't answer any of the crucial questions, my *telepolis* review of it was entitled "Harry Plotter and the Boxcutters of Horror."

Many crucial points raised in David Ray Griffin's recent critique *The 9/11 Commission Report: Omissions and Distortions* (2005) are mentioned and discussed here in this book. They were already visible in the days and weeks after the atrocities; but there is no honest, investigative journalism in the mainstream anymore. Instead of the public, the media are serving business interests; instead of information they publish "infotainment"; and instead of checking corporate and government power, they are its propaganda tools.

The only way to escape the slimy bog of these Orwellian Truth-Ministries is to keep a golden rule firmly in mind: "Don't trust authorities. Think for yourself!" This book doesn't sell any "truth," let alone the "truth of 9/11"; it doesn't sell a theory of 9/11, and it's just the opposite of the label "conspiracy theory," which it got smeared with in Germany (and will be in the US too): it *analyzes* conspiracies and conspiracy theories in general, and those of 9/11 in particular. Not to convince the reader of any truth, but to show that there is no truth yet, that even the most basic facts of any criminal investigation are not clear at all. This alone should be enough to reach at least the goal of awakening distrust of the authorities of government and media – and if this book helps one or another reader to start thinking for her or himself, my expectations will be fully satisfied.

Mathias Bröckers

Berlin, September 2005

Introduction

This is a book about conspiracies. If that seems like something unpleasant, let me put your mind at ease: conspiracies are the most natural thing in the world. Their bad name, and the fact that most nations have passed laws against them, has nothing to do with the nature of conspiracy itself, but only with its misuse for criminal purposes.

This is also a book about conspiracy theories. They too are ill-thought of by many people today, but once again, this is for no inherent reason; the blame lies with their misuse for demagoguery and propaganda. Without suitable conspiracy theories, as we will see, one cannot begin to grasp our complex and intriguing world.

This is a book above all about the conspiracies and conspiracy theories of September 11th, 2001. If this date troubled you not only because of the burning collapse of the WTC itself, but even more because of the accused culprits, as broadcast from coast to coast, then at least for argument's sake, you might want to try and take an objective distance from a story, which has turned out to be nothing more than a pure, an unproven conspiracy theory, despite the biggest dragnet in history: that is, the official line. Today, there is as much evidence against the accused ringleader Osama bin Laden and his "Al Qaeda" band, as there was a few hours after the attacks: practically none.

This book is also a kind of diary of the "attacks" on the World Trade Center and the Pentagon. The shock of September 11th bowled me over in the midst of work on this book, crumpled it up, and unfolded it in a new direction. Instead of studying Conspiracy *in vitro* from historical and theoretical specimens, I could suddenly see it in action in real life, red in tooth and claw. As observer and researcher of the conspiracy phenomenon, I suddenly became a war beneficiary, a sort of ambulance chaser, as this catastrophe and its horrendous sequels unleashed an outpouring of ideal research material live on the screen. Starting on Sept. 13th, I published a running commentary entitled "The WTC Conspiracy" in the online magazine *telepolis,* www.telepolis.de, which is now presented here in print.

In this book I will not try to sell you my own conspiracy theory about September 11th. I can't promise simple answers, no perfectly fitting top on a bubbling kettle of contradictions, no rhyme or reason to patch over mountain ranges of discrepancies. But the reading may do this much for you: the propaganda menu that the cooks in Brainwashington D.C. are dishing up, with their waiters from the media on every channel, may no longer taste quite right. The ingredients may have a suspicious air to them, and you may start to ask questions and seek answers yourself. And if you are too shocked to know what to think about it, some of the most pressing "FAQ's" – "most frequently asked questions" about September 11th – are contained in this book.

This book is also an invitation to an Anti-Conspiracy Conspiracy – a conspiracy against a conspiracy. It is an attempt to adopt a conspirological viewpoint, understanding the cosmos as a bundle of probabilities, from which the individual action of perception draws reality. It is a plea to repatriate conspirology from its banishment as a dirty, messy theory of cognition, and to take it seriously as a critical, scientific tool of perception. A few centuries ago, it was naïve and superstitious to believe in invisible influences pulling the strings behind natural phenomena. In the future, it will be thought naïve not to suspect some string-pulling influences behind the simulated reality of the media...

> A few years ago, Council of the World Economic Forum co-chairman Maurice Strong told an interviewer the outlines of a novel "he would love to compose if only he could write." Each year, Strong explained as background to the novel's plot, the World Economic Forum convenes in Davos, Switzerland. Over 1,000 CEO's, prime ministers, finance ministers, and leading academics gather in February to attend meetings and set economic agendas for the year ahead. With this as a setting, he went on: "What if a small group of these world leaders were to conclude that the principal risk to the earth comes from the actions of the rich countries?... In order to save the planet, the group decides: Isn't the only hope for the planet that the industrialized civilizations collapse? Isn't it our responsibility to bring this about? ...
>
> "This group of world leaders," he continued, "forms a secret society to bring about an economic collapse. It's February. They're all at Davos. These aren't terrorists. They're world leaders. They have positioned themselves in the world's commodities and stock markets. They've engineered, using their access to stock markets and computers and gold supplies, a panic. Then, they prevent the world's stock markets from closing. They jam the gears. They hire mercenaries who hold the rest of the world leaders at Davos as hostage. The markets can't close..." The reporter airs his surprise, for Maurice Strong, co-chairman of the Council of the World Economic Forum, knows these world leaders. He sits at the fulcrum of power. He is in a position to do it. He finishes: "I probably shouldn't be saying things like this."
> *http://www.loccum.de/materialien/globalisierung/Krysmanski.doc*

H. J. Krysmanski is Professor Emeritus of Sociology in Muenster, with a specialization in Power Structure Research. He uses this anecdote to draw attention to a new aspect of globalization. A transnational power elite has arisen, which is much smaller in relation to the world's population, while much more powerful in comparison with earlier ruling classes, although this has hardly been noticed by the social and political sciences. The claim that a small club of hyper-capitalists secretly rule the world was ridiculed as a naïve conspiracy theory only a few decades past. Today, it is the reverse. In view of the global networks of finance and mega-corporations, anyone risks being laughed at who still believes unreservedly in metaphors like "free competition" and "market economics" – and does not see there on second glance, at the latest, the structure of a conspiracy.

Morbid forms of conspiracy thought seem to have served over the years to relegate the topic to a zone for paranoids and crack-pots, not to be taken seriously – let alone to make it a sober methodology, an aid to perception of reality, a skeptical science. A conspirological criticism would have taken note of the permanent factor of conspiracy in living systems – that is, to investigate the role of conspiracy in the evolutionary dialectic of competition and cooperation. Such a critical discipline would have been tasked with defining structures and models in the amorphous underworld of the struggle for mutual advantage, and could perhaps develop litmus tests to check the reality of conspiracy theories.

In this information age, conspiracies are to critical conspirology as "dark matter" is to physics, with conspiracy theories resting on indications and theoretical models of the state and workings of the hidden substance. Like neutrinos or other subatomic particles, the presence of the dark material of conspiracy is only proven indirectly: for as soon as they are observed directly and uncovered, they lose their conspiratorial character. The fuzzy relationships in quantum physics – the paradoxical cohabitation of particles and waves, of Schrödinger's cat and Einstein's mouse – seem also to apply to the observation of conspiracy systems. The more closely one focuses on one aspect, the more inevitably one loses sight of the rest. We will run up against this fuzziness again and again in this book, but to throw out the entire picture because of it were a mistake.

In the first part of the book we approach the subject from a great historical distance – two billion years, give or take a few aeons, with a flashback to the conspiracy of the bacteria, perhaps the only truly worldwide conspiracy ever. At the time, the rulers of the world of the age – single-celled bacteria – joined conspiratorially together to produce multi-celled creatures. Thus Bio-Conspiracy throws our current conception of the evolution of life pretty much on the junk heap, and unmasks Neodarwinism in passing as a conspiracy theory, too. Not only struggle and competition, in Darwinian terms, but two other principles as well – conspiracy and cooperation – saw to it that life could arise and flourish on this planet.

In the following chapters we draw in our historical scope considerably to shed light on human conspiracy in the last few centuries, on the structure and function of conspiracies and conspiracy theories – from Hitler and Stalin up to the covert business of the CIA, from the Knights Templar and the Freemasons to the Federal Reserve Bank.

The second part of the book then is devoted to "live reporting," and contains a conspirological diary composed of the articles that appeared in the online magazine *telepolis*, from September 12, 2001 through the end of March 2002. I have left these texts as far as possible in their original form, editing only minor errors and repetitions. Substantive corrections, additions and comments from a retrospective viewpoint are given in italics. The original publication date is given in the title and is significant in evaluating the contents. In the hysteria and media conformity of the days and weeks after the attack, my conspiracy-theoretical approach seemed shrill and shocking – an enraged colleague even called me a "flyspot on the wall" and wished me dead. But in retrospect, while preparing this book for publication, I was astounded how innocuous and almost obvious it all sounds in the meanwhile.

Perhaps it may have something to do with the "rear-view mirror effect," which the writer William Burroughs used as a metaphor for the mainstream of cultural consciousness, comparing it to a passenger in a car who sees the landscape only in the mirror. When something unexpected appears, he doesn't even notice it at first. What the forward-looking driver claims to see, he calls irrelevant. Only after the new thing finally appears in the rear-view mirror, and can no longer be denied, he says, "Oh we know all about that – that's nothing new."

That's just the effect I hope this book will have, and it is to be expected that some rear-viewers will label it as irrelevant, insane, and not to be taken seriously. I also hope that more forward-looking contemporaries will note, "This is nothing new" – and set to work on these well-known old facts.

Because everything is interconnected in the world of conspiracy, a few big things and a lot of little ones will be missing from my work. This is unfortunate but inevitable, and is simply a result of the limited intake and digestion capacity of my bio-processor. Nonetheless, to cite Burroughs again, only paranoiacs know all the facts – that is, a critically conspirological view, unlike the psychotically paranoid one, never produces a naïvely realistic image, but always a rather cubist or surreal, certainly a fragmentary picture.

In the third part of the book I have attempted such a sketch, and pulled my conspiracy-theoretical "field research" together, or rather, since conspiracy theories are always spaghetti theories – no matter which thread you pull, you get your fingers dirty – I have tried to orient myself somehow in this complex chaos. The attack on the WTC was an event of the century, which will occupy generations of historians and researchers. Still less than on the first day can I believe now that this was a "normal" act of terror. "The next steps the powers of world order take will show whether a motive really exists for this unimaginable, this staged catastrophe, like Pearl Harbor," I jotted on September 12. Since then, the motives have become so obvious, that I can easily imagine the unimaginable.

The complete non-result of the supposedly greatest dragnet in history, the non-investigation of the failures in intelligence and counter-terrorism, public opinion swept into a trance by war drums and incitation to panic, in short: the whole scenario of a bin Laden-al Qaeda World Conspiracy and the War on Terror hardly allows for any other conclusion than this: the catastrophe of September 11th was a carefully planned plot. Evidence that would hold up in court against the men behind the scenes is still as scarce as it is against bin Laden, but the suspicious facts, hints and motives of the suspects are by all means sufficient to be investigated by an independent tribunal.

One question would suffice for a start: If the CIA was not involved, what was it really doing instead?

One of the bloodiest conspiracy theorists of the last century, Josef Stalin, coined the definitive dictum of the paranoid style of government: "I trust nobody, not even myself." As a working hypothesis for handling conspiracy theories the phrase seems suitable, and I have tried my best not to trot like a donkey after the carrots that I hold before my own nose. Whereby I've also tried as well as I could to follow the golden rule of the cybernetic sage Heinz von Foerster: "Truth is the invention of a liar."

Notwithstanding, you will still find many such inventions in this book: words like "true," "really," "in fact," "certainly," pat abstractions and generalizations, like "the Taliban," "the CIA," "the USA," "the oil industry" – and I can only advise you, not to be ensnared by these lies. They are all just "inventions." Don't believe me at all, even when of course I claim that I've researched everything scientifically and conscientiously. And when you find yourself reacting at certain points and links of the narrative: "Yes, that's right, that's it, that makes sense!" then turn on your inward observer and ask the conspirological question No. 1: "And what is behind that?"

If this book leads, for a start, to a general uncertainty, then its enlightening mission will have succeeded by half. Yet its intention is not merely to dismantle, even when it *is* a mature achievement to open the gaze to the breadth, complexity and horror of fields of rubble, instead of fleeing into the comforting building blocks of black and white, good and evil, friend and enemy. The panic that the WTC attack was supposed to create, the fear that was fanned and spread by anthrax-laced letters or dozens of exploding mailbox-bombs in rural areas of the US, the hysteria that was awakened by warnings of "sleepers" and almost daily reports of new attacks: if the terrorists wanted to achieve anything, it was this fear; and if there is one thing the expert operators of mass influence and propaganda want, it is frightened, paralyzed herd animals, who have switched off their own individual common sense.

Here, too, the question is useful: "What is behind this?" Even the conspiracy-theoretical insight, "Somebody here is trying to scare people!" is often enough to banish fear. The haunted-house funride effect, the demystification of horror, the auto-immunization against fear is liberating – and it opens the eyes to peer behind the wings of the theater, at the manipulation, tricks and deception, at the Potemkin village of terror.

Sorcery and magic have not died out. The transformation of ideas – spirit – into reality – matter – belongs not only to the "Lord of the Rings" in our fantasy world, it happens in the real world as well. Talking crystal balls – TV and movie screens – murmur entrancing mantras, over and over; little sounds issuing from mouths – magical incantations – are applied to paper, and prayed to by the millions. And the wonder comes to pass: ideas are conjured out of thin air into reality. Empty words like "God," "Fatherland," "Civilization" and the like are loaded up and reach the full power of reality. Millions gather behind them, to bash each other's heads in for this or that slogan, until no stone is left upon another.

Note well: Andersen is now Accenture; french fries are rebranded freedom fries; "Operation Iraqi Liberation" (OIL!) was hastily renamed "Infinite Justice," then rebaptized as new, improved "Enduring Freedom" (how much longer will they have to endure it after passing the "Patriot Act?") And now on the market at a convenient outlet near you, in handy six-packs: "Axis of Evil."

Come and get it! Welcome to the ghost ride of the 21st Century! Think about it: Whoever creates chaos, wants control; whoever hammers fear in, has security for sale; where there is conjuring and abjuring the same formulae over and over, behind it is usually a conspiracy.

Fasten your seatbelts, ladies and gentlemen. World War III will be no picnic; keep eyes and ears peeled and expect the unexpected. Nothing is what it seems – it all appears the way it does, only because you let it. As in the ancient rule, passed down from Hopis to hippies, for overcoming this inertia and for reformatting perception and reality: *"Free your mind, and your ass will follow!"*

Google Twice Daily

Over the last decade the Internet has developed into a Meta-Medium containing all earlier media forms within itself. Mainstream broadcasters and broadsheets as well as the byways of alternative media and specialist journals – they are all here on the World Wide Web. Clarification and confusion, conventionality and cultism, conspirers and conspirologists coexist in a generally peaceful tumult. And they can all be got to by Googling. For documentation to follow up a lead or bolster a thesis, just type in two or three search terms and in a matter of seconds one is on the page.

But "finding everything" is also the problem with search engines.

How to sift chaff from wheat, sheer nonsense from serious reporting? One early indicator is the source, which shows in the domain address on the Google search results list. If it's an old acquaintance – BBC, CNN, *New York Times*, etc. – it can be assessed like any other "brand name" media reportage. With unknown websites, a glance at the presentation, the context of the sought material, and the masthead are things to go by.

In the emotionally wrought days right after 9/11, the tone chosen to present the horror gave a good idea of the quality and presence of mind of the authors and editors of web pages that were unfamiliar to me. For a firmer judgment of a source's reliability, "the proof of the pudding is in the eating" – that is, to at least read through the article and its back-up documentation. It is worth saving for thorough study later only when this test is passed without mishaps like missing documentation for major claims.

While the brand names of the media echoed in unison to the martial hymns of the Bin Laden Conspiracy Theory and Pentagon propaganda, "no-name" websites were the only scattered oases of what was known in peacetime as principled, independent journalism: asking questions, pointing out inconsistencies, and digging into background – the journalist's most basic duties. They were not and are not being fulfilled since 9/11 by those who are supposed to function as our Fourth Estate. The duties they owe to their readership, to their paychecks and to the Constitutional right of a free press have been taken on by underpaid and unpaid freelancers and free-thinkers in the galleries. When reading their alternative analyses and prognoses, their responsible and truthful web reports, even the most gullible believers in network and weekly news should have noticed how such pages were many times superior to the output of the media brothel.

The mainline media do the political work of an investigative backhoe in digging up the dirt on venial sins like intern-al matters of presidential sex or vacations on frequent flyer miles. Yet on the background to earth-shattering events like 9/11, their check and balance is missing – they are content to wrap up in the blanket of fog which systematically covers the olympian heights and underworld of politics.

The only escape from this pervasive brainwashing is to help oneself: to information.

Google twice daily, and make up your own mind – for reliable protection against infectious propaganda, virulent manipulation and the risk of chronic stupefaction!

Berlin, July 11, 2002

Mathias Bröckers

Acknowledgements

"The author's secret, so I've heard, is read two books, and write a third."

Er setzt sich an des Tisches Mitte – liest zwei Bücher, schreibt das dritte.

So easily as the poet Wilhelm Busch makes it rhyme was this book not to flow from my fingertips, and without the help and hints of many supporters, it could never have become a reality.

A special thanks is due to Florian Rötzer, Editor-in-Chief at *telepolis*, who stood by my "conspiracy-theoretical notes" from the very first episode, and allowed me absolute freedom as author. Considering how closely the media marched in lockstep, especially during the weeks right after the attacks, this attitude, which we journalists once took for granted, can not be too highly prized.

My friend Eberhard Sens permanently improved my rhetorical dribbling with his professional defense tactics as *advocatus diaboli*. That this virtual friend-foe relationship left the bonds of affection between us unchanged made him the perfect person to talk to. Even Eberhard could not stop me scoring against my own goal, but without his advice and help, it would have happened more often.

My friend Gerhard Seyfried came up with marvelous formulations like "Brainwashington D.C.," and his definitive diagram of the international conspiracy network (in the German edition) has given us perhaps the most important indication how we can face the gaping abyss that yawns here before us without immediately getting depressed: with laughter.

Thanks also to Alex Foyle, fellow thinker and reader who supplied me from Barcelona with many tips and links. The right link at the right time I often found especially from the following authors' websites.

Prof. Michel Chossudovsky, www.globalresearch.ca, Canadian political economist and author with many provocative and factual background analyses on imperialism and globalization.

Michael Rivero, www.whatreallyhappened.com, well-stocked with many up-to-date links – on what is really happening.

Alexander Cockburn, www.counterpunch.org, a left-libertarian online magazine with original opinion pieces.

Guerilla News Network (GNN), www.guerillanews.com, shines with background reports on the war on terror, war on drugs, and corporatism

Mike Ruppert, www.fromthewilderness.com, on 9/11 and the drug war.

www.antiwar.com, an iconoclastic online magazine.

www.bushwatch.com, with its daily critical press review.

Andreas Hauss, http://www.medienanalyse-international.de, the best site in German on the oddities of 9/11.

I was not able to read all of the thousands of postings and comments exchanged by *telepolis* readers in the "WTC-Series" forum, yet I thank them nonetheless for many good suggestions. Likewise the many e-mails I received but could not answer. This gigantic feedback supplied an inexhaustible source of motivation, without which I could not have hung on through the Sisyphus tasks of the last months.

To ferret out the information in this book, I needed no special connections, no Sherlock Holmes get-up, no clandestine stake-outs with under-cover agents or turban-topped terrorists. All my sources lay in the open. The only connection I needed to reach them was the Internet, and the services the search engine Google provided were priceless. "Our tools collaborate in our thought processes," noted Nietzsche once, as one of the first authors to use a typewriter. If that is so, then a great part of this book is owed to "Googling's" handiwork.

Nine summers ago, I had just finished the manuscript for the German edition of Jack Herer's *The Emperor Wears no Clothes: Hemp and the Marijuana Conspiracy*, when out of the blue, my father died – Walter Bröckers (1922 – 1993). He was a journalist who always encouraged me to express my point of view, even when he did not share it. He would have been the self same with this politically incorrect "fairy tale" about Emperor Bush II's new clothes. To his memory – to his fatherly as well as journalistic virtue of unconditional freedom of opinion – this book is dedicated.

PART 1.
EVERYTHING UNDER CONTROL

Until now, you have seen through colored glass, snatching at soap bubbles. You have taken the hilltop where your village church stands for the highest mountain in the world, because it was your highest point of view, and you were standing in the wrong place. Now stand over here, on the spot where We stand, and look up at the world anew – surprise! A different, new, more splendid world! Your homeland looks like a grain of sand, Europe, a molehill, and our great, world-shaking European events, the affairs of men, are reduced to an ant colony, almost completely lost in the enormous chain of the Universe, like a drop of water in the Sea...

Of course, you don't see the world as it is, but from your own standpoint, through glasses colored by your wishes, and you are too fond of this viewpoint to let it go. But make an effort, and we will show you the land where ugliness turns to beauty, and apparent disorder to the most perfect concord...

In your shameless self-complacency you set yourself up as the crowning aim of Creation, yet you and all mankind are only as good as the lowest, you are not the aim, but merely a part of the inexhaustible riches of Nature, just as you and your family are a subordinate part of civil society. One's standpoint is everything in this world, which head and heart follow compass-like, in happiness as well as sorrow.

Adam Weishaupt, Founder of the brotherhood of the Illuminati, 1786

"Question authority. Think for yourself."
Timothy Leary, 1967

Bio-Conspiracy

IN THE BEGINNING was Conspiracy. Individual molecules joined together in groups, the better to exploit the resources of our planet. Just when the first carbon bonds decided on this, how they went about it and how long it took them to succeed is not in the power of science to reconstruct exactly – only one thing is certain, that the result of this molecular conspiracy appeared around 3.5 billion years ago: single cells that could reproduce themselves... bacteria... Life! It seems certain, too, that it came about in a conspiratorial way.

Conspirare in Latin means literally to "breathe together," as in whispers, perhaps, although at the time of these first Biochemical Games, there was not yet any oxygen in the planet's atmosphere. But *Spiritus* means spirit as well as breath, and that conspiratorial spark must have been around even before the rise of oxygen – in the person of Secret Agent RNA, Mastermind of Conspiracy. Her partner DNA appeared soon after, and the two of them went forth and completely infested Planet Earth. No matter where RNA and her partner DNA originated, whether they are indigenous Earthlings, or alien conquerors: the genesis of these two supermolecules begins a new history on the Earth, the Conspiracy of Life.

Yet these two tiny Jane or James Bonds are no living creatures, but only chemical compounds. To accuse them of conspiratorial intent – of planning and intelligence – seems too bold; yet in the hindsight of today, everything points to a conspiracy. Be that as it may, during the following four billion years, the RNA conquerors leave no doubt of their intent. They settle every square inch of the dead Earth and its watery surface with what we call Life: bacteria, microorganisms, fungi, plants, animals and finally, human beings.

Until recently, the widespread view was that this was a process of pure chance, driven by the laws of nature and random mutations, resulting in new improved variations which caught on – a view which has been gravely challenged by newer theories of evolutionary biology.

How did life arise? Freeman Dyson[1] believes it happened by a "symbiosis" between RNA and a protein entity – although the concept of symbiosis, of living together, hardly applies to a mere acid like RNA and an equally lifeless protein. There was not yet any *Bios*, no life to put together. So the conspiracy concept seems to us more apt. Two units, the RNA-Agent and the protean protein, make an arrangement to survive in a hostile environment. And like any real conspiracy, the chemical conspiracy, which brought forth living creatures that could feed and reproduce themselves, also has its secrets. All our genetics and bio-technology have been unable to bridge the gap between chemistry and biology, the passage from dead carbon compounds to a living cell. How the acid molecule and the protein compound agreed to cooperate, behind the backs of all the other compounds, is unknown.

At first there were no living creatures at all with definite nuclei, only bacteria held together by thin membranes populated the oceans. They specialized on different resources, such as the plentiful sulfur, which they happily gobbled away at. Sooner or later of course the food ran out – yet the RNA-DNA-Protein-Trio was a jump ahead. The bacteria, which had been living in a wild free-for-all, joined together in groups, and gave up their individual existence for division of labor within a multi-celled creature.

According to the prevalent learned opinion in evolutionary biology, known as Post-, Neo- or Ultradarwinism, the performance of RNA and DNA is a simple copying trick, a mere mechanism with no room for mysteries, let alone conspiracy theories. In their view, the evolutionary factory that produces life on this planet is nothing but a gigantic copy shop, mechanically copying away under the eye of a blind watchmaker. There is no R&D department, and the secret, how complex living beings like Louis Pasteur or Robert Koch, the scientists themselves, were created from single-celled bacteria over a period of 3 billion years – this prescription is dumped by Neo-Darwinism on the scrap heap behind the copy shop – along with the mistakes, the defective copies or "mutations." Then, when market conditions are ripe, meaning the environment changes, the defective examples suddenly turn out to be the greatest hits, and go straight into mass production.

Darwin himself never denied that his Theory of Natural Selection left many questions unanswered and much work to be done, except that as a scientist he did resist "miraculous additions" to it. Nor was his contemporary, the Russian noble and intellectual Peter Kropotkin, interested in miraculous explanations. He was on a trip through Siberia and Manchuria after reading *On the Origin of Species,* and as he observed Nature, he noted a drive to cooperation countervailing to the merciless struggle for survival between the species. He wrote:

If we ask Nature, "Which creatures are cleverer, those which are permanently at war with each other, or those who give each other mutual support?" we immediately see that those animals which have adopted the habit of mutual assistance are doubtless the smartest and best adapted. They have better chances of survival, and develop to the highest degree of intelligence and physical organization known to their particular stage of evolution."[2]

Kropotkin's insight did not get very far. The ideas of a bohemian member of the anarchist movement and a scientific outsider were suspect enough anyway. Yet the title of his book of observations is a fitting description of the natural (and not at all miraculous) enhancements needed in order for Darwin's Theory of Natural Selection to explain evolution. If we concentrate only on competition in observing the workings of evolution, the opposite tendency of cooperation escapes our view.

As, for example, physicists can make experimental and mathematical tests of optical theory by assuming that light is made up of great numbers of light particles, the tabulations of the Neo and Ultra-Darwinists jump to the conclusion that competition and the random generator in the copy shop are exclusively responsible for the wonder of Creation. But light is a wave, too, that occupies space as a frequency and isn't really divided up in particles at all. To really understand the phenomenon of light, we have to understand its double character.

Evolution is equally paradoxical, based on contrary principles of competition and cooperation, simultaneously in effect although mutually exclusive. Yet there is a bridge between the two, a hidden, webbing and unifying principle shared by the two contradictory principles – it is Conspiracy. The conspiratorial instigation of symbiosis was the first link in the great chain of being. When the biologist Lynn Margulis[3] showed in the mid-60's that the first creatures with a cell nucleus arose from cooperation between bacteria, and that this "symbiogenesis" was the motor of evolution, it was pooh-poohed as wild speculation. Now her theory of cell development is in every textbook. That it completely undermines the ruling dogma of mutation and selection has gone almost unnoticed, however.

The conspiracy that RNA and protein launched has only one aim: to bring as much life into the world as possible. And since the plodding copy machine was not up to the task, and could never have made it unaided beyond the stage of bacteria, the cooperation principle kicked in to overcome the first great crisis of life on Earth.

Unlike the copying program, which is encoded in amino acids, the cooperation program is conspiratorial – without a script or code, without any material traces. And like any perfect conspiracy, we cannot uncover its structure by catching individual Mafiosi and forcing their confession. They themselves do not know the whole structure. At the most, they have heard something about it, but are only in contact with a few other brothers in their own area. The caterpillar can not understand the butterfly – and the flagellate protozoa of antiquity had no idea when they were inducted into these cells that 1.5 billion years later they would be stabled by male mammals as little thoroughbred spermatozoa.

English Darwinism reeks throughout of the dank stuffy air of over-population, that stench of poverty and cramped spaces of the under-trodden. But a natural scientist should rise beyond his human niche. In Nature, not scarcity but excess holds sway, wasteful even beyond reason.

Friedrich Nietzsche, *The Cheerful Science*

The conspirational side of evolution isn't recognizable on inspection of individual parts. It shows up when we look at the way they work together, at the overall interrelationships. "Life" first arose via the co-operation of lifelike things. Copying and competing for scarce resources can be conceived of as a completely soulless game, pure mechanics, tidy physics, with no "social work" involved – but not the beginnings of symbiosis, which first brought forth the higher species. Cooperation requires not only communication, but also conspiration: agreement, a shared idea, spirit.

From the dawn of time on Planet Earth, the microbes had conspira-torial possibilities, which we had no inkling of until a few years ago. We pride ourselves on telecommunications and data transmission equipment as great technical achievements, and on democratic elections as the pinnacle of civilization. But in fact, colonies of bacteria acquired such means 2 billion years ago. For a single bacterium, the ten meter long plankton carpet of his colony, undulating on the ocean waves, is as big as the Americas are to a man – yet the microbe in "Alaska" can communi-cate directly with his colleague in "Tierra del Fuego" to coordinate the behavior of the entire colony.

This process has been dubbed "quorum sensing," from the Roman legal concept of a quorum, the number of members who must attend a meeting to make binding decisions. The bacteria calculate their quorum by giving off a biochemical signal around them. When a certain threshold is reached, the chemical signal flows back, some genes are switched on and off, and the activities and reproductive behavior of the bacteria are changed accordingly, over their entire "continent."

What might a mite be

You tiny, unattractive mite! Which I could destroy – You too are one of my fellow creatures in the great ladder and staircase of Nature? Beings of my species say that you are so little, weak and insignificant, because you give no battle and win none, besiege no cities, write no trivia in quartos, don't understand the art of harnessing the hands of millions as means to satisfy your lusts, how to make your neighbor small, and yourself big at his expense. So they call you little, weak and insignificant. So am I also only a tool and means, like you? I, the King of Creation? For whom everything exists? – But you wouldn't be here at all, if you were not what you are. To us you are small, compared to us, your form is ugly, and your powers limited, because they are not ours.

But was I ever a worm, to know what goes on with and within you? You and all what is and is not mankind has no direct experience of what is Other, can not imagine, what powers and abilities are hidden in this or that form. The difference of your form from mine means that what goes on inside you is not the same as what goes on in a man; but is not proof that something even better might be going on within you. Perhaps it is an advantage to be a mite, and a dishonor to be a man, if it is possible for any station in Creation to be a dishonor.

Adam Weishaupt: "Greater Mysteries of the First Order – World Sage of Philosophy," in: Johann Joachim Christoph Bode, Journal of a Journey from Weimar to France in the Year 1787, *Munich 1994, pp. 361– 94*

These microbial media capabilities shed light not only on these not-so-primitive creatures, but also on the rise of all "higher" life forms. And this occurred entirely conspiratorially, so that the communication code was first broken only a few years ago. We now know that even the simplest life forms could communicate, and also that certain bacteria banded together about 2.5 billion years ago to constitute the first multi-celled beings – and that they have been working ever since to bring out ever more complex life forms.

In this respect the human brain is probably the most developed and complex colony that the microbe mind has yet created – so complex, that even its carrier, we human beings, can't understand it. "If our brain were simple enough for us to understand, we would be so simple that we couldn't understand it," as the brain researcher Emerson Puigh[4] once expressed the dilemma. This is evidence that what we have up here really is a colony, a branch of a higher intelligence. The only candidate for the post is the "Global Brain,"[5] the self-organized network of living cells, interconnected by trillions of links, stable for billions of years. The secret agreement of cooperation between different microbes is probably the only really existing world conspiracy at all, and its only aim is Life.

From the viewpoint of natural history, conspiracies are the evolutionary norm, the standard behavior of all social groups, and not only of con artists, secret services or state alliances. Perhaps that is why the theme of conspiracy has never really come under the lens of science, and even today, no general theory of conspiracy exists.

Mulder's Dilemma

THEY are behind it. When Agent Fox Mulder's eyes open wide and his partner, Agent Scully, gives a glance of despair which eloquently wrinkles her pretty forehead – then the viewers of the X-Files know: THEY have struck again. Just who THEY are remains a mystery after more than a hundred episodes of "unsolved cases of the FBI," but that somebody must be behind all these mysterious occurrences – and not just anybody, but a powerful structure or organization – that is clear. At least to Agent Mulder, because he finds piles of evidence, and where he finds none, there you have the proof that the evidence was destroyed. "A paranoiac," said William S. Burroughs, "always knows all the facts."

The tireless fact-digger Mulder would make a perfect paranoiac – in fact, without the skeptical, level-headed Dr. Scully at his side, he would have landed in the nuthouse by the third episode at the latest. Instead he was one of the most popular TV heroes, and *The X-Files* was one of the most successful TV series of the 1990's worldwide. A postmodern Don Quixote who fights the hopeless fight against the windmills of mysterious crimes and cover-ups, and also knows that the agency assigned to solve these cases, himself included, is part of the cover-up too. Mulder and Scully can never complete the picture from the puzzle pieces they put together – and if they do, then it doesn't show who THEY really are, because THEY manipulate the picture. Only one thing is clear, over and over: it must be a huge conspiracy that's behind it all.

Paranoia is not the worst alternative, when one cannot tell friend and foe apart at first glance.
Christoph Spehr, *The Aliens are among us!* Munich 1999.

Mulder has a double dilemma. On one hand, the whole world (including all the secret services, military and maybe even extraterrestrial civilizations) conspires against him and his investigations – and this conspiracy is so powerful and universal, that it can never be uncovered. On the other hand, nobody, not even his trusted Scully, can disprove his mad theories – because all the evidence against them also works *for* them at the same time. At least for Mulder. THEY are behind it again... Nothing is as it seems – against such a double blind, even superheroes struggle helplessly.

"If they can get you asking the wrong questions, they don't have to worry about the answers," Thomas Pynchon wrote in his great conspiracy novel, *Gravity's Rainbow.*[6] For our agent of an outgoing millennium, this fatal cognitive trap is his daily bread. Perhaps it is no coincidence that TV characters Mulder and Scully became superheroes, inextricably involved in a battle of mirrors between truth and lies, manipulation and reality. They mark the end of the classical Enlightenment: the belief in objective truth, in an unambiguous reality, clearly visible on its surface. The agency the two heroes work for is itself a part of the problem – and like the observer in quantum physics, Mulder can only track his prey by taking part in the experiment himself.

Conspiracies are something so common and unremarkable that it would seem they need no lengthy explanation. That A and B agree to gain an advantage over C is part of everyday life on all social and natural levels, and it is just as ordinary that A and B leave C in the dark about their little agreement. Such simple secrets have all the ingredients of a full-blown conspiracy – whether two parasites work together to rob a third one of a share of the booty, or two businessmen discreetly conspire to outwit the competition, or in politics, when intelligence agencies build empires in the shadows, or if gossip and intrigues rule in social circles. Even if we are stuck with masses of conspiracy theories with no general theory of conspiracy itself, the denizens of TV-Land at least are pretty well decided that conspiracies are a staple fact of life.

In September 1996 *George* Magazine published a poll showing that 74% of adult Americans – practically three out of four – believe that the US government is regularly involved in secret, conspiratorial operations. Have these deeply mistrustful US citizens somehow confused reality with TV? Although the results of such a poll might be less dramatic in Germany, where Authority is traditionally treated with naïveté rather than distrust, these three out of four average Americans are by no means all insane or paranoid. The same study showed that only 29% believe in magic; a full 10% are convinced that Elvis Presley is still alive.

Pretty ordinary folks, then – yet three-quarters of them harbor opinions about the State which a hundred years ago were only held by a handful of anarchists and professional cynics. They do know the difference between the news and *The X-Files* all right – yet they have an inkling that even the wildest scenarios of Mulder and Scully are not purely fictitious, while the official facts on the news are far from being the gospel truth. The trusting belief that the political parties and Uncle Sam, the federal government, are there to ensure democracy and justice, that the policeman is your friend and helper – this pious mindset learnt in school must seem hopelessly naïve from their viewpoint. Instead, the suspicion of being ruled by a corrupt, criminal clique spreads across the whole political spectrum and throughout all classes of society.

Of course, politicians and big corporations are not the only institutions that have suffered a massive loss of trust. There isn't a group in the entire human race that isn't the object of fearful suspicions and accusations by some other group. This goes from big groups like nations, races and religions, to professional groups like used car dealers, auto and TV repairmen or dentists, down to street gangs or the village clan across the road. Conspiratorial thinking is always in bloom – and there is no evil in the world, no local problem, that a group can't be found to peg the blame on. Historically the Jews were the first example, then heretics and finally witches were despised and feared as the root of all evil and "Antichrist."

After the French Revolution, the new targets were Freemasons, Capitalists and Communists, and the secret services too. Hitler combined two of the groups people most loved to hate into the "Judeo-Bolshevik World Conspiracy," and with this he incited his willing followers to world war, as the most horrifying conspiracy theorist of the past century. Since then, the choices and possible combinations of hated groups has grown apace. Because the human mind obviously tends to emphasize whatever fits into its own viewpoint, evil can be found anywhere. One only has to look for it long enough.

So conspiracy theories survive every critique. As a popular demonology, they share this elevated status with their classical twin, theology. That God is everywhere is just as impossible to prove or disprove by scientific experiments as to disprove that in the final analysis, Evil rules the world. Perhaps our numerous contemporaries who mistrust their government, their tax collectors, institutions, scientists, media, in short, who mistrust each and everyone, are believers in a kind of materialistic superstition; instead of seeing The Devil, evil spirits or the supernatural behind every misfortune, do they now assign this dark power to living individuals and groups? Even though no conspiracy theorist will admit to being influenced by faith or belief, and immediately begins to present facts, documents, and evidence, the structural parallels between the old belief in evil spirits and the new conspiratorial thinking is too striking to overlook. Both reduce the unmanageable complexity of Reality to a simple plan of cause-and-effect.

Appearances are Deceiving

Robert A. Wilson wrote the worldwide best-selling cult novel *Illuminatus*[7] in the 1970's with Robert Shea, and published a conspiracy encyclopedia under the title *Everything Is Under Control: Conspiracies, Cults and Cover-Ups.* [8] He says conspiracies are "innate" to our social order as a "completely normal continuation of our normal business and economic practices for completely normal purposes... In principle, every single individual behaves as a conspirator, like in a game of poker."

If every individual basically behaves like a conspirator, as a completely normal extension of completely normal business practices by completely normal means, so that conspiracies are something we take completely for granted – then why do most countries have laws against them? Because in practice, they aren't always so normal, or carried out by such normal methods.

The Chairman of the Senate Subcommittee on Narcotics, Terrorism and International Operations, John Kerry, was shocked during the investigations in the Iran-Contra Affair in 1992 by documents showing the CIA smuggled drugs into the country and used the profits from drug dealing to finance its operations.

> What we found at first frankly not believing it, at first saying: no this is too incredible, I don't believe that. And then someone in another part, place, somewhere, would corroborate it, detail for detail... Power of the narcodollar, that is buying countries, buying law enforcement agencies... on both sides of revolutions, altering geopolitics in ways that we really have never had to deal with. It's happening not just in Central America, it's happening in the Far East, it's happening in the Bekaa Valley. Is it true or isn't it true that almost every political group, revolutionary or otherwise, has used the profits of narcotics to buy weapons and fund their operations? [9]

A truthful answer from the head of the CIA to this stunned query – "That's right, sir. Because the Senate will never approve the budget we need to stabilize our geopolitical influence in all 150 countries in our portfolio, we are forced to seek out other sources of income. Narcotics are a prime candidate because of their high profitability, plus the arms trade, especially when we can supply both sides of a conflict" – don't count on getting an answer like this. Not because it would be untrue – since that hard and detailed evidence that rendered Committee Chairman Kerry speechless, many more carefully researched proofs have come to light – but because this truth would conflict with "National Security."

Here we come to a further important point for a theory of conspiracy theories: it's not the common people with their tendency to naïve scapegoat thinking who are the most fertile field for conspiracy theories to bloom, it is the chronically paranoid governments and power élites. In other words: three-quarters of the population nowadays may mistrust their government, but the government doesn't even trust its people to cross the street.

Wiretapping, video surveillance, urine tests, and "homeland security" are only a few current buzzwords. Beyond that, every state has laws against conspiracies, and has agencies and special staff to track and tail every kind of subversion from morning 'til night. If we are to believe the English historian R. J. Blackburn,[10] tribes, nations, states or intelligence agencies are actually not viable entities, since there is always another tribe from which they have to be separated and protected, and there is also the menace of potential enemies within, who are always sawing away at the throne of the ruler of the day.

Thus, the Conspiratorial is innate not only to commerce, but also to statecraft – which gives rise to a gruesome irony: the urge to fight conspiracies doesn't suppress conspiratorial behavior, it directly produces and promotes it. Mulder's Dilemma, that the agency for the uncovering of cover-ups itself is part of a cover-up, is not a fantasy, but reality, and his battle cry of "Trust No One" is no fiction, but has been far exceeded by history – not by some dreamer, but by one of the most powerful figures of the century: Josef Stalin.

Indeed, Stalin didn't trust even his most intimate collaborators, and after the murderous purges of the mid-30's in which he eliminated all opposition in the party and the army, his dear comrades didn't trust him either. Behind every criticism, every word "no," even behind every little joke, the dictator suspected a conspiracy – leaving his colleagues with no alternative but head-nodding sycophancy. No one demurred when he dismissed all reports of an impending German invasion as "questionable sources" or "British provocations," and ordered his army to take no action. Even after the German Army massed 3.2 million men on the Russian border, Stalin belittled reports of a coming attack as "unsubstantiated alarmism." His trust in the Non-Aggression Pact with Hitler was as unbounded as his distrust of disinformation and enemies within – and his fear of falling afoul of a British plot. "Few nations have been better warned of impending invasion than the Soviet Union in June 1941," wrote one historian of WWII.[11]

Even after the start of the invasion, on June 22, 1941 at a quarter past three in the morning, Stalin restrained any countermeasures for another eight hours. German spotter planes that made emergency landings were even repaired and sent back with a full tank. Up to this point, Stalin took the German attack for the actions of a few headstrong generals, perhaps instigated by the British against Hitler's wishes. Stalin's unfounded conspiracy theory led him to ignore the real conspiracy against his country. The German general staff noted in its log that the Red Army was completely unprepared to defend itself and was "tactically surprised on the entire front."

If Stalin had not talked himself into the wrong questions, and had let in the right ones instead, and raised his defenses on the western front, WWII would have followed a different course. His behavior exhibits another aspect of a theory of conspiracy: entanglement in conspiracy theories can influence the perception of reality so strongly that one loses sight of the present danger of a conspiracy. The isolated strongman in the Kremlin no longer believed anyone, neither his subordinates nor the intelligence reports from the corners of the earth which tallied with them.

He believed only one person, and the frightful irony of conspiracy – that the attempt to suppress it only helps it spread – reaches a ludicrous extreme here: the only person whom the paranoiac Stalin still believed in, to whom he had always kept his word, of all people, was Hitler.

"Appearances are deceiving." This axiom of conspiratorial thinking had become such a reflex with the Soviet dictator, that he took the steel skyscrapers of the German attack machine for Potemkin villages – and Hitler for a man of honor. While much has already been written about the parallels between the two Great Dictators, the conspiracy-theoretical approach brings out some further interesting points. One important reason why Stalin overlooked the threat of Hitler was his own personal devil incarnate and root of all evil, his erstwhile comrade-in-arms Leo Trotsky, whose henchmen Stalin saw at work everywhere after he had him murdered. For Stalin, danger came from within, and his obsession with such conspiracies made him deaf to all reports of real conspiracies from outside.

Hitler's conspiracy thinking worked exactly in reverse. He used an external conspiracy as an instrument – the supposed danger of a Judeo-Bolshevist World Conspiracy – to build a real conspiracy system internally, and unleashed a world war. And in one of those strange twists of paranoid thinking, it appears that he took for his scenario and guide-book the very conspiracy which he swore to destroy: the *Protocols of the Elders of Zion.*

"The Elders of Zion," Hitler and the Illuminati

In 1864 the lawyer Maurice Jolly wrote a pamphlet against the despotic rule of Napoleon III, and to fool the censors he disguised it as a dialog between Montesquieu and Machiavelli. The latter holds that mankind can only be saved by totalitarian rule, while Montesquieu presents the liberal views of the Author. For his wit Jolly paid 15 months imprisonment and a fine of 200 francs. He did not live to see his work become the basis for one of the most fateful forgeries in world history.

In 1898, Elie de Cyon, a Russian Jewish émigré in Paris, wrote a biting satire of the new Russian finance minister Witte, aided by long passages from Jolly's *Dialogue.* A copy fell into the hands of the *Ochrana,* the Russian Secret Police, who were on the lookout for conspiracies against the Czarist Empire in Paris, too, and they rewrote it as a textbook for gaining control of the world. Presented as a document of a secret Jewish government under the title *Protocols of the Elders of Zion,* Jolly's plea for democracy and tolerance was turned into anti-Semitic hate literature.

In 1903 the *Protocols* were printed for the first time in a St. Petersburg newspaper, and the Czar was so impressed that he had excerpts read out in 362 of Moscow's churches. But Nicholas II soon after prohibited its further usage when an investigative committee revealed it to be a fake. Since then, the World Conspiracy Theory of the *Protocols* has been proven as a fake dozens of times, and been so adjudged in court, but this is not enough to halt its circulation and spread. The automobile magnate Henry Ford feared the Bolshevization of America by liberal Jewry and reprinted the theses of the Protocol pamphlet in massive editions.

Yet the theory of the Jewish World Conspiracy had its most terrible triumph in Nazi Germany. Hitler first quoted the *Protocols* in 1921, and from then on they pop up in his speeches again and again. He was quite aware that it was a fake; the German edition pretends to be the protocol of a Zionist Congress that supposedly took place in Basel in 1897. For Hitler, as with any conspiracy theorist, evidence against his theory actually supported it, as he makes clear in the first volume of *Mein Kampf ("My Struggle"):*

> To what extent the whole existence of this people is based on a continuous lie is shown incomparably by the Protocols of the Wise Men of Zion, so infinitely hated by the Jews. They are based on a forgery, the *Frankfurter Zeitung* [Frankfurt News] moans and screams once every week: the best proof that they are authentic... once this book has become the common property of a people, the Jewish menace may be considered as broken. [12]

After taking power, Hitler saw to it that the contents of the *Protocols* became a common denominator in Germany. The claim that a Jewish World Conspiracy had unleashed the French and Russian Revolutions and was now undermining the rest of the world via democracy and liberalism was part of the curriculum in the schools. German aircraft even leafletted the just-conquered land of France with the tenets of the *Protocols* – an indication of the central role this fictitious conspiracy played in the propaganda of the Third Reich.

Even more interesting is the aforementioned circumstance: unlike Stalin, who overlooked a real conspiracy for a fictitious one, Hitler chose a fictitious conspiracy as arch-enemy, in order to imitate it in fashioning his own strategy of seizing world power. Thus Hitler was, as Hannah Arendt writes, a "student of the Elders of Zion":

> The totalitarian movements adopted the organizational model of secret societies while simultaneously emptying it of the only substance that could justify such methods or seem to give them a purpose, that is, secrecy and the need to protect it... the Nazis began with an ideological fiction of a World Conspiracy and organized themselves more or less consciously along the lines of the fictitious secret society of the Elders of Zion.[13]

Were the Nazi elite not only unconscious imitators of their fictitious organizational model of a secret Lodge of Zion, but actually directed by real secret cabals like the Thule Society? This question has become the subject of full-fledged conspiracy theories. Writing under a pseudonym, a young antique dealer from Southern Germany attempted a proof in several volumes[14] that all conspiracies come to light only to camouflage the Illuminati, behind whom stand the Rothschilds, who have incited all the nations to war and to indebtedness to their banks, including "their puppet Hitler." This crude opus, which was placed on the German Index of Dangerous Literature for Young Minds, thanks to passages reminiscent of the *Protocols* and *Mein Kampf,* portrays the Nazis as demented hate fanatics and low-level tools of a centuries-old Superconspiracy of Rothschild & Rockefeller plutocrats. In a somewhat more developed form, a similar thesis is presented in a current German conspiracy bestseller, *The Black Reich*:

> Neither the first nor the second World War, neither Communism nor Adolf Hitler's Third Reich were accidents of history... Occult esoteric power groups stood behind the experiment of a Third Reich built on a purely spiritual and magical basis, as well as the communist experiment in the Eastern Block, brought to an end with the help of the Vatican.[15]

On 900 extensively annotated pages, the author tries to prove that the Nazis not only adopted the organizational structure of a secret society, as Hannah Arendt believes, but that they more or less unconsciously carried forward the contents and goals of one: the Illuminati.

The Illuminati Order was founded on May 1, 1776 in the Bavarian city of Ingolstadt by Adam Weishaupt, a Freemason, professor of theology and ex-Jesuit. According to the *Encyclopedia Britannica,* the Illuminati were able to quickly bring many Masonic lodges under their influence and gain an important position in the republican free-thought movement. The new, cosmopolitan world order without states, princes or social classes which the Illuminati imagined, attracted many important men like Goethe and Herder. Yet the whole movement ended abruptly in 1784 under persecution by the government of Bavaria.

For many, the history of the Illuminati really starts after they were officially dissolved in 1785, since vanishing and working behind the scenes are counted among their tactics, as Weishaupt[16] and his lodge brother Adolph Freiherr von Knigge spelled out in their *Instructiones*:

> As long as the aim is reached, it makes no difference, under what cover it is done, and a cover is always needed. Concealment is a great part of our strength. This is why we should always hide behind the name of some other society. The Masonic lodges are a suitable cloak for our higher aims... [17]

This was grist for the mill of pious conspiracy hunters like the Abbot Barruel, who published a five-volume horror study in 1806 about a plot by Freemasons, Illuminati and Jews to unleash the French Revolution and secretly undermine the Catholic Church, already infiltrated by 800 Jewish priests and bishops. The Masonic historian Albert G. Mackey[18] wrote in 1869 that the Illuminati had at least 2,000 members in Masonic lodges throughout Europe. In his opinion the Baron von Knigge, one of the most influential members of the Order and a pious Christian, could hardly have given the Illuminati such support if the abolition of Christianity were one of their goals.

The Abbot Barruel linked the Illuminati with Islamic Sufi orders, heretical Knights Templar and a worldwide Jewish conspiracy – and thus laid the paranoid foundation for speculation that these "enlightened" lodge brothers, the Illuminati, first really got going after their official disappearance, and still continue with their sinister program after 200 years of conspiracy theorizing. The name of the distinguished Baron von Knigge is immortalized as a synonym for etiquette in Germany, thanks to his enduring handbook of good manners; that it should mask the demonic plotters of a conspiracy for world power, also still at work until the present day, is a typical twist in the twilight zone of conspiracy theory: nothing is what it seems.

If a layman asks a conspiracy expert, what is the story with these mysterious Illuminati? our expert may pull out a dollar bill to make the point. A picture says more than a thousand words, and the banknote shows a pyramid, tipped by a triangle, within it an eye, glowing magic-ally: the Great Seal of the United States. It is the seal of Weishaupt's Illuminati Order. The base of the pyramid is graced by the date MDCCLXXVI: the year of the American Declaration of Independence, 1776 – and also of the founding of the Illuminati. Beneath it stands *Ordo Novus Seculorum* – the New World Order, declared ultimate goal of the Illuminati.

This motto was brought into play again during the Gulf War by George Bush Sr. – a member, like his son, in the brotherhood of the Skull & Bones Club, about which more later – and Saddam Hussein, once raised up by the CIA, was cut down to size again in the name of this New World Order. But only enough, as conspiracy experts know, to keep Israel in line, and for the French, who stubbornly kept trading with Saddam, to finally lose their influence on the Near-East chessboard. Oil and the Illuminati Dollar are linked, of course... any more questions?

Well, yes. Isn't the eye in the triangle simply the old Egyptian and later Christian symbol for the eternal vigilance of the Lord? To meet this objection, a magnifying glass is needed, literally: the eye squints. Why? It is not God, but the all-seeing eye of Gnosis, the esoteric symbol of the Knowers, the Enlightened Ones – yes, the Illuminati, who have meanwhile nearly brought the World under the yoke of their currency and interest burdens.

As the relationships get more complex, ever simpler and more sweeping explanations must be brought into play. A really huge conspiracy, one that explains everything, finally explains nothing; and the Illuminati, supposedly operating in concealment for over 200 years, are such an example. For diabolical deceptiveness, the old demons of superstition don't hold a candle to them.

The Money Conspiracy

To a critically-minded conspirologist it is a familiar phenomenon that the wildest conspiracy theories rage where there is no sign of real conspiracies, and vice versa: that the biggest real conspiracies of them all are instigated and come to full bloom without ever even being suspected at all. Such is the money conspiracy, the interest racket, which makes a simple means of exchange multiply all by itself, or "money begetting money," to quote Karl the Red once at least.

From the time of Moses, the Greek city states and the Roman Empire, interest-free money was a religiously binding consumer protection measure. Usurious is as it sounds, like the luxurious growth of a jungle creeper. It's said that a pennyworth grain of gold, invested by Joseph the Carpenter on the birth of his son Jesus at 5% interest in the year zero, would have grown by the year 1749 to the value of a lump of gold the size of the whole Earth. By 2005, the interest on "Joseph's penny" would have ballooned into a quarter of a million golden globes this size. Sooner or later such growth bursts not only planetary limits, but all social ones, because it gives a moneyed few insurmountable advantages against the impoverished majority.

Notwithstanding, the ancient lawgivers knew that money must circulate in the economy, and that lending and credit are essential to business. So the law on interest which Moses brought from Mount Sinai contained further wrinkles: a year of release every "sabbath" or seventh year, when all debts were canceled, and a jubilee year, when land reverted to its original owner for the price of its unharvested crops. This was grounds for popular jubilation, and for the practice which continues even today, to celebrate jubilees, and also for a very far-seeing economic rule. From a global viewpoint, the ticking time-bomb of over-indebtedness is by far the greatest danger for the world economy – and on the local level, every big city would celebrate something like a "jubilee year" as a godsend, when real estate speculation drives prices in the city center so high that they cannot afford their own municipal property.

Because Christian and Muslim lawgivers continued the tradition of interest-free money, it remained the rule in East and West until the end of the Middle Ages. Money was purely a means of exchange, and that it later became a means of enrichment with magical, self-reproducing powers was the result of thoroughly successful conspiring, which blossomed first in hiding, in the taboo zones and fringes of society, and later became a tool of the powerful, which brought forth everything we now know as the world economy – and which we still scarcely understand.

What Max Weber remarked at the beginning of the 20th century is still true: "No normal consumer has any idea of the production methods of his items of daily consumption. The same applies to social institutions like money. How it actually gets its special qualities, the user of money does not know; indeed, the experts on the subject themselves are in dispute."[19]

To trace the secret of money, we need to shed a little light on the end of the dark ages: on the background, the actors and the struggle, that brought forth the monetary system of today.[20] Until the end of the first millennium the Jews, who unlike Christians and Muslims were allowed to take interest from other peoples, lent money for interest or usury as an underground racket in Christian Europe. They earned both contempt and respect for this "impure" but essential service. Whoever could get no credit from his Christian compatriots could get it half-legally for usury from Jewish lenders. Until the 11th century the lending took place mostly within a barter economy and did not involve large sums.

With the greater dynamism of the later Middle Ages, growing mobility, new tools and techniques of agriculture and manufacture, finance and credit all began to play an ever greater role. Thus the Jewish minority who traditionally operated on the taboo fringes of society were catapulted into a central position in economic life, to the unease of the better business minds among the Christians. In spite of all the sanctions against them, Catholic usurers soon appeared. As Jacques le Goff writes: "The truth is that in this era of St. Francis of Assisi and the sanctification of poverty, the poor were despised, and usury was a means of upward social mobility which could only be kept in check with the threat of hellfire."

Ecclesiastics and scholastics tirelessly pontificated on the shamefulness of usurers and vividly portrayed the pains of hell that awaited them. The usurer was lower on the moral scale than the common thief or robber; he was not only a criminal, but a sinner, who got rich from something intangible, from Time.

Thus St. Anselm writes: "The usurer lends the debtor nothing that belongs to him, but only time, which belongs to God. He may not profit from the lending of that which is not his." Moreover, the theft of time via interest was a spur to inequality and thus, according to St. Thomas of Aquinas following Aristotle, simply *contra naturam*, unnatural, because "money does not reproduce itself." It was only "invented as a means of exchange, and therefore it can not be permissible, to take a reward for the lending of money, called interest." Long before Karl Marx, St. Bonaventura sensed something of the secret of "surplus": "Money itself can bear no fruit, the fruit comes from elsewhere."[21]

Like many conspiracies, the money conspiracy is innovative and evolutionary. With growing mobility and economic development, the circulation of money is speeded up, as well as its availability when opportunities for investment are lucrative. Those expeditions of plunder and conquest adorned with the label "Crusades" required capital, and it is no accident that the Order of the Knights Templar, founded in 1117 by Hugo von Payens in the newly conquered city of Jerusalem, were the first to find a way around the dilemma of lending without interest or hellfire. The pious Knights not only invented checks and bills of exchange but "interest-free" mortgages which gave the lender a share of the rents and harvests on houses and land.

This shrewd circumvention of the prohibition on usury quickly turned the Templars into a multinational financial concern whose influence spread over all of Europe and the Near East. Soon no King, Prince or Abbot could carry on without financing from the *fratres militiae templi* who held the high and mighty in their control, as well as the entire commercial class by handling their international financial business. But affluence goeth before a fall: a papal council robbed the monopolistically dominant Templar Order of their financial bag of tricks, and set their fancy mortgage on the same footing with usury.

On Friday the 13th of October 1307, on the urging of the French king Philip IV, the Inquisition arrested the Grand Master of the Order on threadbare accusations. A mob of irate traders stormed their Temple in Paris, the Wall Street of the High Middle Ages. Thus the world's first internationally operating financial concern, the prototype of today's "global players," was brought to its knees.

Those who devour usury will not stand, except as one stands whom Satan has stricken with madness.
The Quran, Sura 2:275

Nonetheless, in barely one hundred years, the dynamics of interest released explosive social power. The fame of the Templars' success survived their official dispersal. In the Italian city states, which saw the Vatican as local competition rather than an authority in economic matters, the first Christian lenders set up to do to the business of the unlucky Knights, exploiting "time theft" as a resource for the creation of value. Though Luther the Reformer thundered with all his might against lenders as "bloodsucking werewolves," it was not long until in Germany, too, the trading house of Fugger in Augsburg grew into a giant concern by sponsoring an expert opinion from a theologian named Eck, who announced the good tidings that 5% interest was not too high to get into heaven. Only interest gouging would henceforth be branded as usury, and penitent usurers would no longer need to fear danger to the welfare of their souls from the Prophet Ezekiel's curse...

Who hath given forth upon usury, and hath taken increase: shall he then live? he shall not live: he hath done all these abominations; he shall surely die; his blood shall be upon him.
Ezekiel 18:13

It is no accident that the two groups that are the focus of many conspiracy theories until this day are the very ones which were involved at the center of the money conspiracy of the late middle ages: the Jews and the Knights Templar. So-called "religious" anti-Semitism, which stigmatized the Jews as "Christ-killers" and made them objects of hatred, appeared, significantly enough, at the same time as the Crusades, when the Knights Templar were trying to build up a professional financial business against the peripheral Jewish loan shops.

Like the German Nazis 800 years later, who aimed their slogan "Down with Interest Slavery" at Jewish capital, but not at the entire banking sector, the Templars and the armed hordes of crusading mobs raged against the Jews for much more basic motives than biblical or theological reasons. They were the only competition in a booming market which all turned on the alchemy of money, the high technology of growth capital.

The long bench – *banco,* or bank – of the money-changers, blithely lending in God's name without a look back at the furious Pope, became the word for the houses of the money trade, soon adorned with opulent facades like temples, reminiscent of the Templars and of the sacramental and sacrificial sites of the ancients. The money business, arising from the scum of the gutter to incalculable importance, celebrates itself and shows that in its temples a kind of ritual magic really does take place.

Is it no coincidence that today's World Central Bank, the US Federal Reserve Bank or Fed, is still nicknamed "the Temple," and its grand masters speak like delphic oracles, as in Alan Greenspan's famous dictum: "If you understood what I just said, you must not have heard me correctly." The bases of their magic remain the same since the rise of modern banking in the high middle ages, and even the motto of the American 20th century, "time is money," reflects the idea of "time theft" which the scholastics once made a taboo and a sin.

Nowadays, economic globalization has led to an ever greater concentration of capital in the hands of ever fewer actors. Never before in history have a few handfuls of people exercised such international power as today.

So has everything really been long since "under control" – the control of a dozen financial magnates and banking concerns, who command nations and governments to dance like puppets dependent on their drip-fed finance?

The Money Power

"I see in the near future a crisis approaching that unnerves me and causes me to tremble for the safety of my country... corporations have been enthroned and an era of corruption in high places will follow, and the money power of the country will endeavor to prolong its reign by working upon the prejudices of the people until all wealth is aggregated in a few hands and the Republic is destroyed."

US President Abraham Lincoln, Nov. 21, 1864 (letter to Col. William F. Elkins, in The Lincoln Encyclopedia, *Archer H. Shaw (Macmillan, 1950, NY)*

In Germany, nearly 50% of the entire government budget no longer goes on the needs of the population, but on interest on the national debt to the banks. Half of every tax dollar up the chimney. In some other countries it is even more drastic. No matter what you call the system behind it – it is headed for a fatal catastrophe. The gap between rich and poor gets wider and wider. The suspicion that before long everything really will be under the centralized control of a few financial moguls can no longer be simply pooh-poohed as a wild conspiracy theory.

Yet Robert A. Wilson for one does not believe that we are on the road to a system of total global control. The reason he gives is the very medium that has recently developed into a whole new breeding ground for the spread of conspiracy theories: the Internet.

> I think it's the most revolutionary development, the most dramatic step since living things first came out of the water onto the land. With the Internet, the lack of control over the entire system is the only way to maintain the system. No one little band of conspirators can ever get control over the Web. The only way to keep the Web going is by decentralized control... I think the Internet is forcing decentralization, and that's why I see the world in the 21st Century heading for an anarchistic rather than a fascist system. By that I don't mean total anarchy and chaos, but it's going more in this direction than to fascist control under strict hierarchies."[22]

The very Internet that has helped breed and spread a belief in conspiracies also gives us the means to draw our own picture of real conspiracies and false theories – and even to break up the one real conspiracy left, after deregulation of telephone, energy and other monopolies: the monopoly of money.

Already at the beginning of the 20th century, resourceful economists had discovered the weakness of both communist and capitalist economies. The communists hobbled the marketplace by barring the natural principle of free competition. And the capitalists hobbled it almost as badly; although they allowed competition, they burdened investments with expensive, interest-heavy money. This meant lasting permanent advantages not for free entrepreneurs, competition and innovation, but always and only for the wealthy owners of capital.

Silvio Gesell, the theoretician and economic minister of the short-lived Munich Council Republic of 1918-1919, held that the free market can only be achieved with free money – money without interest, used only as a means of exchange, not for accumulation of wealth, so that hoarded money would not gain, but lose in value. Practical experiments with this kind of money in communities and farm districts led to a great stimulation of the circulation of money and of the investment climate – to the delight of those economists. But Gesell's brilliant ideas disappeared as quickly the Munich Councils. In the 1940's they were taken up again by the renowned American professor of economics Irving Fisher, but this went no further than a minor Senate hearing on his "stamp money."

Since then, the money conspiracy continues unopposed and largely unnoticed – although everyone uses money for every purchase, and pays interest on bills, they have not heard of this conspiracy, and consider the link between money and interest to be as natural as water and moisture. The Internet could make banks superfluous that circulate high-cost money; users could settle on their own electronic money and circulate it without risk of counterfeiting via encryption software.

That will be bad news for the Illuminati, if they do exist, and for all who strive for centralized control. American intelligence agencies were unable to stop the worldwide spread of PGP, the "Pretty Good Privacy"[23] free encryption software, and no one will be able to prevent users from sending completely secret e-mails in uncrackable code, and someday their own means of payment, secure against counterfeiting and free of interest. This will make it possible to conduct covert operations on a scale that the most perfidious founder of secret lodges could only dream of, and will undermine the huge real conspiracy of Big Money. Who will be interested in the expensive credit line from the bank, when the Internet community offers money free of interest?

If the Illuminati really labored 200 years to establish the greenback, bearing their enlightened Seal since the days of Brother Roosevelt's New Deal as the currency of their secret world government, then the World Wide Web has tripped them up. During our new millennium they will just sadly sit on the mounds of murderous money which now burden billions of people, aching and sweating under the load of interest. The beauty of it is, that this liberation of the free market economy from capitalism does not even require a revolution, other than a prohibition on land speculation.

The dawn of the Internet Age, which makes centralized control more difficult and can undermine real bastions of conspiracy like the money monopoly, shows another general characteristic of conspiracies: that they are seldom so cunning and all-powerful as their theoreticians assume. But if a mega-conspiracy that swallows the earth in its tentacles exists only in the imagination of simple souls, this does not prove that all conspiracy theories are phantasmagoria. The contrary has been shown by the discovery of conspiracies like the radical right-wing lodge *Propaganda Due*, or P2. Exposed around 1980, its 950 agents occupied every key position in Italian society, including the government.

In the Name of the State

Like the historical Illuminati, supposedly most active after they were banned and went underground, many conspiracy experts believe that the activities of P2 did not end with the death of its architect Roberto Calvi, "God's Banker," who was found hanging under London's Blackfriar Bridge in a Mafia-style "suicide." They point to Silvio Berlusconi among others, who diversified from his construction business into media in 1978 – and also just happened to join the media affairs lodge Propaganda Two.

Berlusconi claims they sent him the membership card unsolicited, and he immediately threw it away – how believable that is, can be measured against the fact that his rise to monopolist of the Italian media was *due* to two high officials closely linked to P2: Bettino Craxi and Giulio Andreotti. The ex-leader of the Socialist Party and ex-prime minister were pawns brought to justice for involvement in Mafia racketeering, although they had only done "what the CIA, the great puppetmaster across the Atlantic, wanted from Italian politicians of every stripe."[24]

That is, to fight the communist world conspiracy using the links laid by the CIA to organized crime and the Mafia: that is the connection via "the honorable society" (the Cosa Nostra) and the Vatican or "ratlines" which American spooks used after the war to smuggle their top picks from the SS and Nazi officer corps into South America.

The structure that came to light with the P2 scandal, one of the best documented conspiracy cases of recent decades, is more scandalous than the individual crimes of money laundering, corruption and terrorism which members of P2 were brought to justice for. They were not merely actions of greedy criminals, but of initiatives taken with the participation and approval of official institutions: they were carried out *In the Name of the State.* That is the title of a book by Andreas von Bülow, who certainly can not be accused of a paranoid relationship to the power of the state – he was federal minister for science and research and state secretary of the defense ministry.

In the Investigative Committee hearings on Commercial Cooperation with East Germany, every time the dirty deals of western intelligence agencies came up, the topic was mercilessly squelched – because "national security" once again could only be secured by hushing up such conspiracies. So Member of Parliament von Bülow decided to do the research on his own, and the result was startling. He found "a frightening picture of a systematic, operational entwinement of intelligence operations – that is, the state – with organized crime, the drug trade and terrorism."[25]

When the US narco-police, the DEA, can't pursue 75% of cases because the sources are protected by the CIA; when those "nifty s.o.b.'s of Uncle Sam," as they have been known in spy slang – creatures like Saddam in Iraq or General Noriega in Panama – are kept in power for years with weapons and slush funds, to be paraded to the gallows when needed, as evil dope-dealers or the reincarnation of Hitler; and when in practically every civil war – whether in Nicaragua, Rwanda, Afghanistan or the Near East – western secret services are in there selling weapons; when even these few examples are accurate, out of the long list documented by von Bülow, then deep distrust of our democratic and even human-rights-respecting governments is hardly paranoia, but utterly appropriate.

What we have here are not conspiracy theories, but authentic reports of criminal intrigues which remain hidden only on the authority of paranoid states which fear for their "national security." No wonder that in their summit meetings, world leaders can never agree on anything sensible – like stopping the destruction of the earth's climate by the industrial nations, for example – yet practically every time, there is a joint communiqué declaring war on the international menaces of drugs and terrorism. Nothing could be easier, since the Devil that these exorcists rush so fervently to brand as a great evil upon the earth mostly comes from their own kitchens.

The intimate involvement of western intelligence agencies with organized crime and illegal arms and drug dealing may be proven and documented a hundred times over – yet this conspiracy will still not be publicly exposed. Fearing for their "national security," these states rein in their attorney generals and courts from prosecuting. They act like Stalin, ignoring the real danger of organized crime, and continuing to trust the Mafia, the drug cartels and the international networks of arms smuggling and corruption.

The conspiratorial sorcerer, that the trusting apprentices of "national security" first invoked to prevent conspiracies, has long since grown out of their control. The dilemma of our fictitious FBI agent Mulder, that his agency for the uncovering of conspiracies participates in them itself, is in the reality of our society a lot more than a curious conundrum – it has fatal consequences. The Iran-Contra deal alone was estimated at $80 billion; annual drug sales in the USA amount to about $100 billion. Such huge volumes of illegal dealings endanger not only the economy, but through corruption – the bureaucratic cousin of conspiracy – they threaten the rule of law throughout the world.

How can we be rid of these evil spirits? By letting dissonant perceptions in – and in whose ears wouldn't the claim sound off-key, for instance, that our own government works hand in glove with narcotics and weapons smugglers? "Nothing is what it seems" – this first principle of conspiratorial dynamics is always worth considering, even when a closer look shows that everything is completely normal. But a second look is important, it is a changed perspective. If the first question of all philosophy is, "Why does anything exist at all, rather than nothingness?" then conspirology immediately appends the key question: "And who is behind it?" and with it the beginning of critical perception.

What is true, what is false, what is information, what is disinformation, what is objective fact, what is subjective projection, how do observer and observed interact? The sphere of conspirological thought is a school for perception. "In the beginning of knowledge," says the psychoanalyst Jacques Lacan, "is hysteria." Fear of the world, of the incomprehensible, of the awful event out of a blue sky, this is the drive behind all curiosity and need for knowledge. Conspirological thinking retains something of this fear-driven fervor – and we have seen what paradoxical cases, what irrational folly unreflective conspiracy thinking can lead to. The no-man's land between critical thought and pathological paranoia is a mine field. Nevertheless, not only is it worthwhile to venture onto it, real conspiracies and their dangerous consequences for society force us to.

It is time to raise conspirology, this urchin of the theory of knowledge, to the status of a critical science of perception. Time to develop a general theory of conspiracy theories that can serve as a guide through the minefield. The new biology discovered a broader sense of the evolutionary struggle for existence with the principle of cooperation.

If our aforementioned hunch is right, that cooperation's dark side is the conspiracy principle, then we can establish something like a categorical imperative, a basic law for all conspiracies. If all living things from bacteria to the blue whale are obliged to act not only as consumers and profiteers of their living conditions, but also sponsors and supporters; if individuals must link themselves in cooperative and symbiotic ways to the overall network in order to attain their particular interests, then this basic law of evolution must also apply to conspiracies. To survive for very long, they must serve a purpose not only for the conspirators, but also for the whole. Parasites must become symbiotic.

Nine Theses on Conspiracies and Conspiracy Theories

1.

In the beginning there was conspiring. In order to win out over a hostile planet, various bacteria united and formed the first creature with a definite cell nucleus. Chance mutations and the competitive struggle for existence were not enough; conspiring and cooperation were needed to make evolution possible. The bacteriological conspiring is probably the only world conspiracy at all, has been going over 2.5 billion years, and its only aim is Life.

2.

Conspiracies are the most ordinary thing in the world: A and B agree behind the back of C for some gain. This happens in business just as in nature, is as common in politics as in the workplace – and above all, in love life. That the beloved secretly has another lover is probably the most commonly held conspiracy theory of all.

3.

Conspiracy theories include suppositions about real conspiracies, based on indications, suspicions, evidence. If the conspiracy theory is backed up by definitive proof – the partner is caught *in flagrante delicto*, the "Watergate" tapes on illegal political dirty tricks are given to the press – then the conspiracy is uncovered and ends. Often, however, such definite physical proof cannot be found. That is why real conspiracies are often as long-lived as unproven conspiracy theories.

4.

Conspiracy theories have a special quality that makes them so attractive: they reduce complexity. Many-layered, complex causes of events can be reduced to a single scapegoat. The blame game – or the tendency to ascribe an incomprehensible and painful reality to a specific guilty party – seems to be a basic characteristic of human behavior.

5.

In the course of internally processing incomprehensible external catastrophes, the oldest and most important conspiracy theory may have arisen, generally abbreviated under the name "God," the idea of an invisible, secret, all-powerful creator and string-puller, concealed behind the universe and our own existence. The supposition of a divine conspiracy also reduces complexity: it makes our catastrophic, chaotic, incomprehensible cosmos understandable and gives it and our existence meaning.

6.

The ability of conspiracy theories to reduce complex relationships to simple causes makes them an ideal instrument for propaganda and agitation. Without the specter of a sinister and bloodthirsty "Judeo-bolshevist world conspiracy," Hitler could not have roused his people to a world war, nor could Stalin have long maintained his dictatorship without the supposed threat of a "Judeo-imperialist world conspiracy."

7.

To conspire, to conjure, to capture and to control are related. The conjuring of invisible powers of good or evil has something of the conspiratorial spirit, as well as something captivating, since it makes complicated things simple. Conspiration comes from *conspirare*, breathing together, or *spiritus*, spirit. The spirit of conspiracies is always a group or social phenomenon. Nothing is more convivial, nor more dangerous, than a group conspiring together.

8.

The interaction of conspiracy, conjuration and captivation can be seen in the working of conspiracy theories: lacking definite proofs, the "truth" of the theory must be conjured again and again, and it can captivate only as long as skepticism and doubt of this "truth" are controlled and kept out.

9.

To immunize themselves against skepticism and doubt, conspiracy theories have a strange loop built in: every criticism is automatically turned into a further proof of the supposed conspiracy. This immune system of modern conspiracies is the same one as in their historical antecedent, the demonology of the Middle Ages: Whoever disputes the presence of the Devil must be possessed by him.

PART 2.
CONSPIRACY DIARY

In order to meet the need of your still hopeful Earth,
and finally now finalize the Final Victory –
plus consign any sign of resistance to history –
we successfully carpet-bombed her for all she was worth!

Und damit doch auf eurer noch hoffenden Erde
nun endlich der endliche Endsieg mal werde,
und damit sich dagegen kein Widerspruch regt,
haben wir sie erfolgreich mit Bomben belegt!

 – *Karl Kraus, 1926*

"They can rule by fraud, and by fraud eventually acquire access to the tools
they need to finish the job of killing off the Constitution."
"What sort of tools?"
"More stringent security measures. Universal electronic surveillance. No-
knock laws. Stop and frisk laws. Government inspection of first-class mail.
Automatic fingerprinting, photographing, blood tests and urinalysis of any
person arrested before he is charged with a crime. A law making it unlawful
to resist even unlawful arrest. Laws establishing detention camps for
potential subversives. Gun control laws. Restrictions on travel. The
assassinations, you see, establish the need for such laws in the public mind.
Instead of realizing that there is a conspiracy, controlled by a handful of
men, the people reason – or are manipulated into reasoning – that the entire
populace must have its freedom restricted in order to protect the leaders. The
people agree that they themselves can't be trusted."

The Illuminatus Trilogy *by Robert Anton Wilson and Robert Shea,*
1988, p. 197-8, cited in
http://kamita.com/misc/illuminatus/illuminatus.html

On September 11, a friend's phone call roused me from my work on a manuscript on conspiracy theories. In the following hours and days, I sat transfixed by images on television, as the very subject I was analyzing by historical and theoretical means sprang to life in full color.

Before the twin towers of the World Trade Center had time to collapse, the "bin Laden" theory was already born to the world. I had just jotted down that "conspiracy theories reduce complex events to a single scapegoat, and are therefore highly effective and successful tools for dumbing-down propaganda." And suddenly, I was observing the birth and growth in the wild of this very phenomenon.

In the next few hours, the buzzword "bin Laden," soon joined by "al-Qaeda," developed into a fully-fledged conspiracy theory. As there was still no evidence to corroborate that a real conspiracy masterminded by bin Laden was responsible for the attack, I wrote a commentary for *die tageszeitung* or *taz* (Germany's alternative daily paper) and the online magazine *telepolis,* raising a few "points on conspiracy theoretics."

At the time, I knew as much or as little of the background behind these attacks as most of the billions of people watching these incredible scenes. I hadn't recently concerned myself much with the situation in Afghanistan or the United States. The suspicion that something didn't quite add up was more of a gut feeling, and initially there were no tangible or rational reasons to explain it. But in the days and weeks that followed, such reasons were supplied on a scale I found hard to imagine on Sept. 12. Without benefit of evidence that would hold up in a court of law, the bin Laden conspiracy monster was created. Then the media mantra elevated it to the level of an unquestionable truth – and a possible pretext for a world war.

The articles that followed in *telepolis* are arranged by their date of publication. Except for a few cuts, they are presented and translated here largely unchanged,[1] and the original German version may still be read at http://www.heise.de/tp/r4/special/wtc.html.

Most of my research was done over the Internet, so I have given the website addresses for the most important sources. Links have been updated for this edition, and a live list of links in the footnotes is also available at www.zweitausendeins.de/broeckers.html. Readers who may want to follow them up should note, however, that Internet pages are fleeting, and that many of the sources cited in this book may no longer be available at the click of a mouse. In this case, a bit of "Googling" will usually help by entering the names sought along with keywords and dates. If no source is provided for a term or subject you are interested in, then enter the subject with one or more names in a search engine (for example, enter [Hitler Prescott Bush] to read more out about the support given to Hitler by the grandfather of the current US president).

For the publication of this journal in book form I haven't tried to alter either my miscalculations or the prognoses that proved to be correct. Any necessary corrections and additions – as of May 2002 – can be found in italics at the end of each article.

9/13/01
Conspiracy-theory Remarks on a Terrorist Attack

It happened on 9/11/2001: 9+11+2+0+0+1 = 23! An open-and-shut case for conspiracy theorists. Ever since *The Illuminatus Trilogy* by Robert A. Wilson and Robert Shea in the 1970's made the absurd connection between the number 23 and conspiratorial phenomena, 23 has become the sign, as it were, of the Illuminati, the secret world conspirators.

Current conspiracy theories – seamlessly contradicting one another – tell us exactly who these people are. For example, one line stretches from Egyptian mystics to the Solomonic Temple in Jerusalem, to the Knights of the Templar Order and their multinational banking group in the 12th Century, various Freemasonic lodges during the Renaissance, up to today's "Rothschild Clan." Another line stretches from the Assassin death squads of Sheikh Sinan, the "old man of the mountain," to the grail-seeking Cathars, the occult Thule Society as forerunners of the Nazis, up to the present day "Rockefeller mob," the influential grouping around the family of the Standard Oil founder – including its CIA and Mafia units.

For conspiracy theorists it is significant, of course, that not a single news report mentions whom the World Trade Center belonged to – Rockefeller – and that Britain immediately imposed a no-fly zone over the City of London – the Rothschild financial center. It also fits this picture that a former CIA asset and cousin of Bush's Saudi business partner Sheikh Salem bin Laden is now being touted as the main villain responsible for the attacks, namely Osama bin Laden, who got his start in the CIA's campaign against the Soviets in Afghanistan.

Didn't the Bushes first build up Hitler with Standard Oil and DuPont money, then finish him off and re-arrange the face of Europe? Wasn't it the current president's grandfather, international banker Prescott Bush, of all people, who in 1942 was indicted for his business dealings with Hitler's Germany? (see "9/26/01: Skulls, Bones & Bush")[2] Wasn't it the same old story during the Gulf War against Saddam, the "re-awakened ghost of Hitler," and what Poppy Bush (President Bush Sr.) dubbed the "New World Order?"

First, Saddam was built up against Iran, then forcefully disarmed, to remain in place as a geopolitical pawn to secure the influence of the "mob" on the Middle East (and on the price of oil). Was Khomeini calmly allowed to install the first Islamic theocracy from Paris because nobody understood his ideology, or was it all about the Iranian oil output which the Shah would not cut voluntarily? Aren't these militant Islamic "villains" all of the same homemade variety? Didn't the Pentagon and Wall Street watch unperturbed for years as Israel broke international and human rights law in Palestine?

More than 2,000 years ago, didn't the first military theoretician Sun Tze[3] already know that one must never drive the enemy so far into a corner that suicide attacks, against which there is no defense, are the only option left to him? While the fuse to the Middle East powder keg has been alight for the past year and rockets destroy one Local Trade Center after another in Palestine, Rockefeller-man Bush calmly takes a four-week vacation. And now he wonders why desperate kamikaze warriors are hitting back and unleashing a catastrophe?

Back at Pearl Harbor, when a massive assault by the Japanese had already been forewarned three weeks before, the "sneak attack" was allowed to happen in order to rally the country to war. The conspiracy theorist now asks how it is possible, three months after Egypt warned of a large-scale attack, that the logistical *tour de force* of simultaneously hijacking four airplanes and flying them undetected to their targets could succeed?

Passengers were able to telephone their relatives from aboard the aircraft, but air traffic control and the military – whose snooping systems usually detect if anyone breaks wind as far away as China – were caught completely unawares? And this right over their own headquarters, the Pentagon? Strangely enough, this scandal is not mentioned even in a single word, while a dozen cheering Palestinian kids become "worldwide news."

When news of the attacks is whispered in Bush's ear during a school visit, he remains remarkably unperturbed, and in his first statement, there are no worry wrinkles marking his face, no sign of being truly appalled. Maybe because the villains were right on schedule – before 9 a.m. there are no important bankers and no visitor crowds in the WTC, only the "rank and file" are present. They fall under the inevitable "collateral damage," the term used to describe civilian casualties ever since the bombing of Baghdad. The next steps the powers of world order take will show whether a motive really exists for this unimaginable, this staged catastrophe, like Pearl Harbor.[4]

Requiem for the Twin Towers

The collapse of the towers is a symbolic event of major proportions. Imagine the towers hadn't collapsed or only one had collapsed, the effect wouldn't have been the same. The striking display of the global power's fragility wouldn't have been the same. By missing the White House, they unwittingly showed that it wasn't the decisive target, that political power doesn't really carry much weight anymore, that the main focus lies elsewhere. It is impossible to decide what to erect in place of the towers, simply because it is impossible to imagine anything that would be worth destroying – that is worthy of destruction.

Jean Baudrillard, European Graduate School Faculty, http://www.egs.edu/ faculty/baudrillard/baudrillard-requiem-fuer-die-twin-towers.html

When I calculated the cross total of the date of the attacks I had to cheat a little in order to arrive at the magical number 23. Actually, the cross-total equals 14 if 11 is correctly added as 1+1, but I noticed that too late. A correction would have ruined my lovely introduction, so I left it at 23, even if the credibility of my article suffered greatly in the eyes of some readers who take their numerological magic more seriously than I do.

Another inaccuracy was to say that the WTC still belonged to the family who originally built it, the Rockefellers. They sold it to the Port Authority of New York City, which sold it shortly before the attack to Larry Silverstein. This inaccuracy arose when the article was shortened to newspaper format. Originally, I wrote that the very foundations of the Twin Towers rested on highly conspiratorial, some even say criminal real-estate speculation by the builders, the Rockefeller brothers.

Bush's lack of a reaction when he heard the news has been "explained" in the meantime. Before arriving at the school he had already been informed by his chief of staff about the first crash. Later, Bush claimed to have seen the first plane crash into the WTC before entering the classroom,[5] but it had not yet been broadcast by any TV station.

Quick Thinking under Fire

I was in Florida. And my Chief of Staff, Andy Card – actually, I was in a classroom talking about a reading program that works. I was sitting outside the classroom waiting to go in, and I saw an airplane hit the tower – the TV was obviously on. And I used to fly, myself, and I said, well, there's one terrible pilot. I said, it must have been a horrible accident.

But I was whisked off there, I didn't have much time to think about it. And I was sitting in the classroom, and Andy Card, my Chief of Staff, who is sitting over here, walked in and said, "A second plane has hit the tower, America is under attack."

And, Jordan, I wasn't sure what to think at first. You know, I grew up in a period of time where the idea of America being under attack never entered my mind – just like your Daddy's and Mother's mind probably. And I started thinking hard in that very brief period of time about what it meant to be under attack. I knew that when I got all of the facts that we were under attack, there would be hell to pay for attacking America.

http://www.whitehouse.gov/news/releases/2001/12/20011204-17.html

My uneasiness over the official version which led to this first article was a gut feeling, yet the questions asked here already hint at the motives and background whose uncovering (or rather, their covering up) in the following months led me to continue this commentary as a series.
My suspicion that the perpetrators were possibly desperate Palestinians proved to be false. Palestine is clearly one of the big losers in the wake of 9/11, and the cheering Palestinian kids turned out to be a trick photo-op produced by handing out candies.

9/14/01
Osama bin Laden

The suspicion that Osama bin Laden is behind the attacks is "hardening," at least according to news agency reports. Of course, no one has yet produced a single shred of tangible evidence. NBC reported on Sept. 12 that the "secret service" purportedly listened in on a telephone conversation between two of his followers, who spoke about the successful operation. Imagine that – there's proof for you!

Yesterday, we already pointed out that the mysterious bin Laden is an old comrade of the CIA. As for the business dealings of the bin Laden clan, who run one of the biggest construction companies in the Middle East, you need go no further than George W. Bush himself. In 1979, he got the start-up capital for his first oil exploration company from James R. Bath, his neighbor and flying buddy at the National Air Unit, who had made a fortune as the representative of two Saudi billionaires, Khalid bin Mahfouz and Salem bin Laden. Mahfouz, who during the last few decades often resided at his sumptuous second home in Houston, Texas,[6] settled out of court by paying $225 million in 1991 for his key role in the BCCI scandal.

The bank had operated a money laundering system for the drug trade, as well as for channeling secret service funds during the Iran-Contra affair, in which the US government ran an illicit arms and drug trade to fund the Nicaraguan Contra terrorists. Sheikh Salem bin Laden had been of great service as a go-between in the controversial operation "October Surprise,"[7] the secret agreement between Republican party operatives and Iranian fundamentalists to keep the US hostages in the Teheran embassy captive until after the elections, which cost Carter his reelection and brought Reagan to power.

As a result, the secret service also hired his young cousin Osama in 1980. His mission was to arm the Saudi Mujahideen in Afghanistan and turn it into an effective fighting force against the Soviets. From then on Osama, armed with suitcases full of BCCI dollars and Jihad slogans, recruited mercenaries for the holy war to drive the Soviets from Kabul. After this succeeded in 1988, Sheikh Salem was killed when his plane crashed in mysterious circumstances in Texas, the same plane he is said to have provided for the secret hostage talks with the Iranians.

And Osama? According to the conspiracy theory of Lyndon La Rouche,[8] bin Laden is being directed by the British secret service as paymaster for various Islamic terror groups operating in North Africa and the Middle East to further Britain's geopolitical goals. According to this "Osama-bin-London logic," perfidious Albion, the London-based Rothschild clan, got the better of its rival for world domination, the Rockefeller mob. Nevertheless, both stand to gain yet again in the coming war of the Christian on the Islamic world...

Scarcely had the bin Laden conspiracy theory been born right after the attacks when I started my research with a Google search on Osama bin Laden. Twenty years ago, an information ferret like Google, made possible by the Internet, would have been heavily guarded in top-security areas reserved exclusively for the military and the secret services. Nowadays, Google allows everyone and his brother to gather news and information on a scale that "the services" could only dream of until very recently. All the information I used for this article is available to the public, and the spring from which it flows is www.google.com.

That Osama bin Laden wasn't just a ("former?") CIA associate, but that longstanding business contacts existed between the bin Laden and Bush families, was hinted at in this article (the first time, as far as I know, in the German media), but none of this was echoed by other media in the weeks that followed. If at all, only "former" contacts between the Saudi terrorist and the CIA were mentioned. Likewise, hardly anything appeared in the media about the longstanding relationship between the Bushes and the BCCI banker Khalid bin Mahfouz, also a Houston resident and patriarch of one of Saudi Arabia's richest families.

9/15/01
Surprised by Homemade Villains

On Nov. 25, 1941, following a conversation with President Roosevelt about the Japanese, US War Secretary Henry Stimson wrote in his diary: "The question was how we should maneuver them into the position of firing the first shot without allowing too much danger to ourselves."

Only two weeks later, the time had arrived. As early as 1932 and 1938, practice attacks on the naval base were staged during navy maneuvers, once by 152 airplanes, and on each occasion the naval base's defenses proved to be completely inadequate. As a result, Pearl Harbor was considered particularly vulnerable. When Roosevelt ordered the fleet to be re-deployed from the West Coast to Pearl Harbor, Admiral Richardson protested and eventually even refused to carry out the order. He was replaced by Admiral Kimmel, who was accused of dereliction of duty after the Japanese attack and brought before an inquiry.

But Kimmel had to be acquitted once it emerged that all information gleaned from deciphered Japanese messages had been withheld from him. The Dutch, British and Russian intelligence services had also warned the United States of an impending Japanese attack, but these communications had also been blocked in Washington. A 1946 navy report cited 188 deciphered messages that clearly indicated the impending attack, including the exact date and time. When two of America's most renowned historians of the 1920s and '30s, Professors Charles Beard and Harry Elmer Barnes, rejected the official government version of events, they were denounced as cranks and wackos and fired from their teaching posts. Since then, "surprise attack" is writ in every encyclopedia.[9]

Stimson apparently talked too much – not only to his diary, but later to a Congressional Committee of Inquiry on Pearl Harbor in 1946. There he said:

"One problem troubled us very much. If you know that your enemy is going to strike you, it is not usually wise to wait until he gets the jump on you by taking the initiative. In spite of the risk involved, however, in letting the Japanese fire the first shot, we realized that in order to have the full support of the American people it was desirable to make sure that the Japanese be the ones to do this so that there should remain no doubt in anyone's mind as to who were the aggressors."[10]

On July 25, 1990, the US ambassador to Iraq, April Glaspie, delivered a message from the White House to Saddam Hussein: "We have no opinion on your Arab-Arab conflicts, such as your dispute with Kuwait. Secretary [of State James] Baker has directed me to emphasize the instruction, first given to Iraq in the 1960's, that the Kuwait issue is not associated with America. [Saddam smiles].[11]

Of course, Saddam's troop concentrations in the previous weeks had been noticed. It was obvious that an invasion of Kuwait was imminent, as indeed it took place a week later, on Aug. 2. Evidently, this was yet again a case of inviting the enemy to fire the first shot. Otherwise, the subsequent bombing of Baghdad would have appeared to be an act of aggression – just as Hiroshima and Nagasaki couldn't have been passed off as acts in defense of civilization without Pearl Harbor, but would have been seen for what they were, a genocidal weapons experiment and terrorist attack. Is it any wonder then that any mention of a "surprise attack" is met with great mistrust? Following in the footsteps of the Japanese and Saddam Hussein, the latest homemade villain is evidently bin Laden...

It took more than half a century until it was possible to uncover the facts behind the Pearl Harbor "surprise" on the basis of publicly released files. Since then, there is no longer any doubt that intelligence about the Japanese attack was withheld to allow it to take place – but it will probably take another 50 years until encyclopedias are revised accordingly. The fact that a democratically elected president sacrificed 2,000 of his compatriots to rally the country to war still appears to be unpalatable for public consumption. Only in retrospect of the glorious ascendancy of the United States to the rank of sole superpower of the

21st Century – which would have been seriously hampered by a victorious Hitler in Europe – will it be possible to celebrate Roosevelt's "dirty trick" as a deed of strategic brilliance.

9/16/01
Question authority! Think for Yourself!

The journalist and lawyer Barbara Olson, a conservative commentator for CNN, was one of the victims of the airplane that crashed into the Pentagon. She was able to speak by cell phone to her husband Ted, a top-level Justice Department official in the Bush Administration, twice before the crash, telling him among other things that the plane was flying towards the Pentagon. But there was no mention of the hijackers' nationality or skin color. Strange?

In an emergency phone call, what would be the natural reaction of a white, blonde woman, a schooled observer and journalist from a conservative background, if Arabs, people of different skin color or speaking a foreign language hijacked her airplane? Wouldn't she at least briefly mention this important fact? Or the other way around: can we deduce from this omission of "color" that it must have been "normal" white people who spoke without any accent? Retrospectively, the AP report that first mentioned the various phone calls made from aboard the hijacked aircraft[12] poses some new questions.

The homegrown fascist militias in the United States clearly demonstrated with the 1995 Oklahoma bombing that they won't even shy away from mass murder in their fight against the hated ZOG (Zionist Occupied Government). They share their radical anti-Semitism with bin Laden's terror squads. It appears, however, that from the very first moment after the 9/11 attacks it was a done deal that the perpetrators were to be found in the Islamic arena – just as 20 years ago it would have automatically been "the Russians." Now, the NSA, CIA and FBI, fast asleep up to this point, find one suspicious Arab after the other, among them the alleged "terror pilot." The "typical" image that is publicized of him only reinforces the suspicion that Mrs. Olson should have found it worth mentioning…

Questions regarding the motive should always start with the basics. Who benefits from the enduring conflict between Muslims, Jews and Christians in the Middle East? Who built up the "radical Islamic" evildoers like bin Laden or Saddam Hussein with billions in aid, weapons and terrorist know-how? Who has permanently promoted the Islamic world's militant resistance by supporting feudal regimes with no respect for human rights like Saudi Arabia while subsidizing illegal Israeli land grabs? Who must make themselves indispensable as the guarantors of security by inciting Jews and Muslims against each other? Who refuses to surrender control of the world's largest oil reserves?

In 50 years time, when oil has lost its power-political significance, the Middle East will be a peaceful paradise, guaranteed! But now bandits have shot off the sheriff's star and set his pistol holster on fire, and "the civilized world" has been summoned to wage a global war. Actually, the sheriff should be fired for his irresponsible foreign policy and ordered back to his ranch along with his troops – and a Jewish-Christian-Muslim roundtable under UN auspices should be convened in Jerusalem. Only this would put an end to terror.

For investigative Internet reporter Joe Vialls, the case of Barbara Olson and her telephone conversation with her husband Ted, then US Solicitor General, is the "mother of all lies about 9/11." The first CNN report on Sept. 12 said:

> *Barbara Olson, a conservative commentator and attorney, alerted her husband, Solicitor General Ted Olson, that the plane she was on was being hijacked Tuesday morning, Ted Olson told CNN.*
>
> *A short time later the plane crashed into the Pentagon. Barbara Olson is presumed to have died in the crash.*
>
> *Her husband said she called him twice on a cell phone from American Airlines Flight 77, which was en route from Washington Dulles International Airport to Los Angeles. Ted Olson told CNN that his wife said all passengers and flight personnel, including the pilots, were herded to the back of the plane by armed hijackers. The only weapons she mentioned were knives and cardboard cutters.*
>
> *She felt nobody was in charge and asked her husband to tell the pilot what to do.*[13]

This story, according to Vialls,

> *was the solitary foundation on which the spurious "Hijacker" story was built. Without the "eminent" Barbara Olson and her alleged emotional telephone calls, there would never be any proof that humans played a role in the hijack and destruction of the four aircraft that day. Lookalike claims surfaced several days later on September 16 about passenger Todd Beamer and others, but it is critically important to remember here that the Barbara Olson story was the only one on September 11 and 12. It was beyond*

question the artificial "seed" that started the media snowball rolling down
the hill.

*Ted Olson, who was only paraphrased in the CNN report, didn't speak
up on the matter until six months later – and the details he revealed
about the phone conversations made them all the more dubious.
According to him, his wife didn't call from her cell phone but from a
phone at her seat, and because she had no credit card handy (itself
incredible enough for a well-to-do American traveling) she placed a
collect call.*

*But Vialls says that without a credit card one can not activate the
airphones on the Boeing 757s of American Airlines. And if she had
borrowed a credit card she could have phoned as long as she wanted.
Vialls concludes: "Sadly perhaps, the Olson telephone call claim is
proved untrue. Any American official wishing to challenge this has only
to subpoena the telephone company and Justice Department records.
There will be no charge originating from American Airlines 77 to the US
Solicitor General."*[14]

*A bold statement, considering that the various cell phone calls from the
hijacked planes are as firmly embedded in the mass mind as the "19
hijackers." More in-depth research shows that the clues about the "box
cutters," so important for the reconstruction of events, actually came
from Olson. Apart from the reported phone calls by the "heroes" aboard
flight 93*[15] *that crashed in Pennsylvania in dubious circumstances, the
Olson story forms the basis of the box-cutter legend. A flight attendant,
who called from one of the WTC planes and spoke with ground control,
mentioned a hijacker with a bomb.*

9/17/01
Nifty SOB's, Courtesy of the USA

In response to my call in the last article for a Jewish-Christian-Muslim
roundtable in Jerusalem and for the withdrawal of US troops from the
Middle East, my friend S. says: "This is geopolitical naïveté, another
typical example of anarcho-hippie-do-gooder romanticism. It's Babylon
all over again and you the fool still believe in progress. It's quite clear:
as long as our technology depends on oil we can't surrender control to
the camel jockeys, as Kissinger used to say. So, think long and hard
about how far you want to take your anti-Americanism."

I immediately rejected the label vehemently, praising a few highlights of American culture – Bob Dylan, Frank Zappa, *Some Like It Hot* – but S. said they don't count. "The first two are counter-culture and Billy Wilder is German." Who cares! If the methods and consequences of US foreign policy drive the world to war, then sharp criticism must be allowed, and above all a skeptical look at what really lurks behind all this. Terror doesn't come out of the blue. The bin Ladens, Saddams and Hitlers are not natural phenomena.

General Motors, controlled by the chemical magnate and fervent Nazi Irénée DuPont[16] in the 1930's, not only provided the German Wehrmacht with the most important vehicle for its "Blitzkrieg," the Opel Blitz, but together with Rockefeller's Standard Oil it also provided the fuel, as well as patents and capital for IG Farben. George W. Bush's great-grandfather and grandfather made a fortune in 1942 with investments in the Third Reich.[17] Coca-Cola was, of course, a major sponsor of the 1936 Olympics and increased its turnover in Germany twentyfold during the Third Reich.

In his book *Facts & Fascism* (1943), the author George Seldes,[18] a sort of 1930's and '40's Ralph Nader, listed a whole phalanx of high-ranking US investors who were massively involved in business with the Nazis. So Hitler was also one of these "nifty sons of bitches" courtesy of the USA. This doesn't diminish the culpability of his ardent followers in any way, but it does put the gratitude to the liberators in a new perspective. Without their prior immense investments in fascism, there presumably wouldn't have been anything to liberate from – and without mobile forces, the "nation without enough room" would have had to stay at home.

Our Strength Won't Help Us

The disconnect between last Tuesday's monstrous dose of reality and the self-righteous drivel and outright deceptions being peddled by public figures and TV commentators is startling, depressing. The voices licensed to follow the event seem to have joined together in a campaign to infantilize the public. Where is the acknowledgment that this was not a "cowardly" attack on "civilization" or "liberty" or "humanity" or "the free world" but an attack on the world's self-proclaimed superpower, undertaken as a consequence of specific American alliances and actions? How many citizens are aware of the ongoing American bombing of Iraq? And if the word "cowardly" is to be used, it might be more aptly applied to those who kill from beyond the range of retaliation, high in the sky, than to those willing to die themselves in order to kill others. In the matter of

courage (a morally neutral virtue): whatever may be said of the perpetrators of Tuesday's slaughter, they were not cowards.

Our leaders are bent on convincing us that everything is O.K. America is not afraid. Our spirit is unbroken, although this was a day that will live in infamy and America is now at war. But everything is not O.K. And this was not Pearl Harbor. We have a robotic President who assures us that America still stands tall. A wide spectrum of public figures, in and out of office, who are strongly opposed to the policies being pursued abroad by this Administration apparently feel free to say nothing more than that they stand united behind President Bush.

A lot of thinking needs to be done, and perhaps is being done in Washington and elsewhere, about the ineptitude of American intelligence and counter-intelligence, about options available to American foreign policy, particularly in the Middle East, and about what constitutes a smart program of military defense. But the public is not being asked to bear much of the burden of reality. The unanimously applauded, self-congratulatory bromides of a Soviet Party Congress seemed contemptible. The unanimity of the sanctimonious, reality-concealing rhetoric spouted by American officials and media commentators in recent days seems, well, unworthy of a mature democracy.

Those in public office have let us know that they consider their task to be a manipulative one: confidence-building and grief management. Politics, the politics of a democracy—which entails disagreement, which promotes candor—has been replaced by psychotherapy. Let's by all means grieve together. But let's not be stupid together. A few shreds of historical awareness might help us understand what has just happened, and what may continue to happen. "Our country is strong," we are told again and again. I for one don't find this entirely consoling. Who doubts that America is strong? But that's not all America has to be.

Susan Sontag in "Talk of the Town," The New Yorker, September 17, 2001
http://www.wworld.org/archive/archive.asp?ID=120

The situation seems to be much the same with the impending liberation of the world from terrorism. According to CNN, the US and the Saudis invested $6 billion in bin Laden's mercenary troops; in the 1980's, the first Jihad world conference was held in New York, of all places, under the auspices of the CIA; its Office of Services to Holy Warriors recruited them for battle through 38 US branches.[19]

It is no conspiracy theory that conspiracy, force and terror are concealed and yet self-evident devices of US foreign policy – fanatical Jews and Muslims are equally used as instruments. But the spirits the US has always been wont to conjure up when "defending American interests" have now hit back to haunt it in a gruesome manner. It's high time for America to rethink its notorious "son-of-a-bitch" policy.

Asides like those from CNN and Der Spiegel *(a German newsweekly) that Jihad was promoted and built up as an unofficial extension of US foreign policy didn't feature much in news reports in the following weeks. It comes as no surprise that the "brown past" of the Bush family and of other top US industrialists and their financial engagements in Germany are not widely known. More than half a century after Hitler, the historical truth slowly comes to light.*[20] *The role of grandfather Bush as banker and financial administrator of the early Hitler financier Fritz Thyssen has been dealt with in detail by Webster G. Tarpley and Anton Chaitkin in 1992 in* George Bush: The Unauthorized Biography.[21]

9/19/01
Primate Politics and Thought Control

We now know that the "killer" paraded the day after the surprise attack on John F. Kennedy and the backdrop to the events were fake. The same goes for the above-mentioned Pearl Harbor surprise, as confirmed once more by the BBC documentary *Pearl Harbor: The Bait for War* which was broadcast by Phoenix, a German cable and satellite TV channel, on Sept. 16. Equally, it is no idle fantasy that the "New World Order" introduced by Bush Sr. with the Gulf War involves more than the ostensible aim of disarming nifty son of a bitch Saddam because of a staged "surprise attack." Here too, the world public was deceived.

All this could still be irrelevant to 9/11. It is perfectly possible that events unfolded exactly the way Bush Jr. and the media have been declaring *unisono*: a commando of Arab suicide attackers directed by Osama bin Laden committed this heinous act. As long as there is no solid evidence for this, however, questions must not only be permitted, they are the foremost duty of any journalist.

The German journalist Henryk Broder sees this differently. On his website[22] and in an angry radio commentary he accuses me of having a "sick mind" that is only surpassed by the *Protocols of the Elders of Zion* and Holocaust denier David Irving. Already during the Gulf War, as a journalist, Broder joined the team of Teutonic cheerleaders who hushed up all doubts about "Operation Desert Storm" as anti-Semitic and anti-civilization. Just too bad that it was the guys from the CIA, and not somebody like Arafat, who sponsored the first Jihad world conference in

New York and pumped billions into bin Laden's outfit. That complicates his argument and explains why everyone investigating along these lines has to be disqualified as "sick." I have assured Broder of my understanding for his pathological zeal and recommended that he make the case for a revenge bombing of Mecca and Medina. The subsequent world war would surely eliminate at least half the terrorists along with half of humanity…

So, why do these super-terrorists leave behind Arabic-language flight manuals in rental cars? Why do they book flights under their real names? Why are bags containing goodbye letters left behind at the airport? Who was supposed to read these letters if the bag had been taken on board? If they were genuine goodbye letters to relatives, why weren't they posted before the flight? Why has no one claimed responsibility? Who plots this kind of mega-operation without claiming responsibility afterwards? Unlike other large-scale terrorist attacks, why are there no political demands, no statement – nothing at all? Why does the mysterious Dr. No lurking behind this James Bond-like terror not threaten further attacks, set ultimatums, exert pressure?

There are many, many unanswered questions – starting with "Operation Soporific" that had the secret services and flight control fast asleep at the wheel until things went bang – and it's much too early to expect all of them to be answered immediately. But these questions must be asked, and they must be asked now. Not to reduce the confusing complexity of the situation to a simplistic conspiracy theory – which is what the mainstream media are doing – but quite the opposite: for the sake of truth, to prevent these mind-dulling simplifications and their dangerous consequences. Wishful thinking, I admit. Decades ago, Carl Schmitt, the "crown jurist" and power theorist of the Third Reich, knew that in times of crisis only a clear-cut friend-foe dichotomy guarantees supremacy.

If the questionable telephone conversations by the Olsons represent the "mother of all lies about 9/11," then the "19 hijackers" are looking like additions to the family. Strangely, none of the names released by the FBI as early as the evening of Sept. 12 appear on the passenger lists published by the airlines. Meanwhile it has emerged that five of the alleged hijackers are still alive and that one of them already died some time earlier. Following the FBI's release of the list of the alleged suicide attackers, five of the accused contacted their embassies, or rather the police in Saudi Arabia, Morocco and the United States. Nevertheless, the lists have not been corrected to this day.

Likewise, it became known that some of the "terror pilots" behaved in conspicuous ways and celebrated in strip bars the night before – not exactly the typical preparation for Islamic suicide terrorists. Furthermore, it emerged that several of the alleged attackers had been under observation as terrorism suspects for some time. Nevertheless, in March 2002 (!), two of them received residency visas from the US immigration service pursuant to their applications in the summer of 2001.

Yet again, it is astounding how published opinion – that is our media – shuts itself off from all the sources freely floating around the Internet. The web gives access to the passenger lists, none of which reveal an Arabic sounding name.[23] It allows you to study the FBI list of the 19 alleged hijackers[24] and to learn about the "identities" of this evil bunch, at least five of whom are still alive and one of whom has been dead since the year 2000.[25]

9/22/01
Scapegoats, Human Casualties and the New "Pax Americana"

Thunder and lightning will drive male chimpanzees up hillsides, clubs in hand to rage against the heavenly foe. So the cry for revenge is under-standable – two thirds of Americans favor war, according to opinion polls, even though they're not sure against whom. It's a kind of genetic scapegoat reflex, so to speak.

In the early history of mankind, which was marked by global cata-strophes like deluges and colliding comets, this reflex generated a culture of victimhood. Those who survived the traumatic aggression of an invisible enemy re-enacted the catastrophe – like children who have suffered a traumatic event overcome it by re-enacting it and thereby putting themselves in control. Up to now, however, the theory of recent catastrophes – the fairly well backed-up hypothesis that in the last 12,000 years or so the history of civilization has been decisively shaped by the impact of celestial bodies[26] – is still only a peripheral academic topic.

The same is true for the theory of victimhood, the re-enactment of traumatic catastrophes as a healing process.[27] According to German academic Gunnar Heinsohn, the actual root of anti-Semitism can be found in the revolutionary innovation of the Jewish religion that dispensed with blood offerings to the comet gods. This religion without rites of blood sacrifice was a provocation, and as long ago as the 2nd century, the Greco-Roman writer Philostratus, whom Heinsohn cites, interpreted this as a kind of conspiracy against the rest of the world.

> The Jews rose have long been in revolt not only against the Romans but against all mankind. They live in impenetrable seclusion and deny the rest of the world their presence at the table. They exclude themselves from the burnt offerings, the prayers and offerings of thanks. They appear to us more alien than Susa and Bactra [two exotic Persian cities with which Rome was at war] or even the distant India.

Precisely because they rejected burnt offerings, unlike all other peoples and religions, the Jews themselves become the scapegoat of choice and the "burnt offering" of the Holocaust, according to Heinsohn. I recalled these thoughts when I was reading the German writer Hans Magnus Enzensberger's latest essay in which he writes of the "return of the human sacrifice" in its globalized form. (Unlike the Gulf War, when Enzensberger spontaneously railed against the monster Saddam as the "re-awakened soul of Hitler," he approaches the 9/11 atrocities from a more critical angle, although in the end he rejects any doubts about the CNN version of reality.)

> It is no coincidence that doubts were immediately voiced about the authorship of the attacks. On the Internet, the neo-conservatives in the United States were held responsible, others spoke of Japanese terror groups or of a Zionist secret service plot. As always in these cases, all types of conspiracy theories blossomed. Such interpretations show to what degree the delusions of the perpetrators are contagious. They do, however, contain a kernel of truth because they show how interchangeable the motives are…In the case of the New York mass murder, the credibility of the Islamic motive will also have to be questioned; any other motive would have done just as well.[28]

Yet, from the very start, no serious doubts of any kind have been raised about the authorship of the attacks. And ever since the 19 Arabic-sounding names of the suicide pilots were released, only the Islamic motive will do as an explanation. In the news, any efforts to unravel the case have taken a back seat to the events that were its result.

All that is available after one week of large-scale, global inquiries is a handful of biographies of Arab model students and hobby pilots. Constantly waving this skeletal "body of evidence" around is all it takes to elevate the conspiracy theory code-named "bin Laden" to its global status of factual truth, making it a pseudo-reality. The function of this conspiracy reflex to confer identity, to stabilize and turn trauma and paralysis around is obvious.

It was Osama!

Americans are asking: Who attacked our country? The evidence we have gathered all points to a collection of loosely affiliated terrorist organizations known as al Qaeda. They are the same murderers indicted for bombing American embassies in Tanzania and Kenya, and responsible for bombing the USS Cole.

Al Qaeda is to terror what the mafia is to crime. But its goal is not making money; its goal is remaking the world – and imposing its radical beliefs on people everywhere.

The terrorists practice a fringe form of Islamic extremism that has been rejected by Muslim scholars and the vast majority of Muslim clerics – a fringe movement that perverts the peaceful teachings of Islam. The terrorists' directive commands them to kill Christians and Jews, to kill all Americans, and make no distinction among military and civilians, including women and children.

This group and its leader – a person named Osama bin Laden – are linked to many other organizations in different countries, including the Egyptian Islamic Jihad and the Islamic Movement of Uzbekistan. There are thousands of these terrorists in more than 60 countries. They are recruited from their own nations and neighborhoods and brought to camps in places like Afghanistan, where they are trained in the tactics of terror. They are sent back to their homes or sent to hide in countries around the world to plot evil and destruction. (...)

Our war on terror begins with al Qaeda, but it does not end there. It will not end until every terrorist group of global reach has been found, stopped and defeated. (Applause.)

Americans are asking, why do they hate us? They hate what we see right here in this chamber – a democratically elected government. Their leaders are self-appointed. They hate our freedoms – our freedom of religion, our freedom of speech, our freedom to vote and assemble and disagree with each other.

They want to overthrow existing governments in many Muslim countries, such as Egypt, Saudi Arabia, and Jordan. They want to drive Israel out of the Middle East. They want to drive Christians and Jews out of vast regions of Asia and Africa.

These terrorists kill not merely to end lives, but to disrupt and end a way of life.

http://www.whitehouse.gov/news/releases/2001/09/20010920-8.html

And on the wings of the new "Pax Americana," not the "old" but the "ancient economy" – the military-industrial complex – rises Phoenix-like from the billion-dollar ashes of the dot.com bust. If the WTC events were no conspiracy, no sanctioned surprise attack like Pearl Harbor, no "neo-fascist" coup like the Kennedy assassination, but indeed a wholly unexpected declaration of war by Islamic extremists, the emperors in Washington couldn't have wished for anything more propitious to secure their global empire. For the sake of pipelines in Eastern Europe and the Near East (in other words against the rising influence of the European Union) and of oil reserves in the Middle East (and against the rising influence of the "camel jockeys") the whole world will be blessed with "Infinite Justice" from now on.

The forecast comeback of the "ancient economy" could be observed in the following months on the basis of the rapidly rising share prices of defense companies. One of the main beneficiaries is the privately-held Carlyle Group, which happens to have Bush Sr. on its payroll. With the momentum generated by the hugely inflated defense budget, the company is now heading full-throttle towards a stock-exchange listing. News of the largest corporate debacle in US history – the Enron bankruptcy – had not yet become public at this point, but the Dow Jones Industrial Average fell 900 points between Aug. 20 and Sept. 10 alone.

After the dot.com bubble had burst, a further stock market crash was looming. Vice-President Cheney held talks with Enron CEO Kenneth Lay behind closed doors to discuss ways to save the company. If there had been the option of saving the economy with new government debt instead of war, then Bush's biggest political campaign funder would have stood a chance. But with the declared war against terrorism, the worst economic debacle in US history became palatable for public consumption, and it was possible to sacrifice Enron. The executives had taken care to cover their own rears, so that *only* a few ten thousand employees were affected, losing their pensions and retirement savings.

9/24/01
Zero Evidence at Ground Zero

Fakes have been a strategic device since long before the "Ems dispatch," a telegram from the German Kaiser staying in the spa town Bad Ems. Bismarck manipulated and edited the message to goad the French into a war. Germany won and the "Iron Chancellor" was able to forge the longed-for empire, so Bismarck's dirty trick was never held against him. The same goes for Henry Kissinger, whom Norwegian sociologist and peace researcher Johan Galtung described as "Chile's bin Laden."[29] Today, few begrudge his use of every type of terrorist tactics sanctified by the crusade against communism. After all, capitalism was victorious. If an orchestrated fake is now invoked as a justification for war 12 days after 9/11, despite no tangible proof that Osama bin Laden is to blame, nobody should later be offended by it either, provided the war is won in the end.

Now imagine the 9/11 attackers had staged a large bank robbery, had all died during their escape and the police tried to arrest the boss of a gang on the basis of "the guy just hates banks and probably was also involved in two robberies in Africa." It's a fair assumption that the police probably wouldn't even get a warrant for his arrest from a local judge, let alone secure his extradition from another country on the basis of this kind of "zero evidence." Meanwhile, following Bush's martial but hollow declaration "you are either with us or against us," a critical observation like this is likely to tarnish you as a Taliban accomplice and bin Laden camp follower. Anyone not instantly clicking heels to attention and cheering for "infinite justice," anyone whose nose says it smells fishy, can only be a terrorist. And yet, according to any standard of justice, the circumstantial evidence presented in the case of 9/11 is not enough to charge bin Laden. Even with cold-blooded mass murderers, the presumption of innocence must be upheld until proven otherwise.

If more proof is needed that conspiracy theories are a powerful instrument of propaganda and manipulation, the unproven bin Laden conspiracy that is about to spark a world war should do just fine. Meanwhile, even the FBI has noticed that the attacks apparently neither required large amounts of money – $200,000 at most – nor the support of a rogue state; in other words, any conspiratorial, fanatical terror cell could have committed the attacks, but this is no longer of any importance. The public *knows* – after 12 days of CNN penetration – that bin Laden is to blame, and if not him then some other Islamic "terror network." That such may exist is not in question, and that it has chosen the United States and Israel as its archenemies is also certain. Yet whether it can be dealt with by a grandiose war against Iraq and Afghanistan is more than questionable. Before we try that, there is Mossad's recommended method of targeted assassination of leaders, or the suggestion by the Israeli Defense Ministry, only a few days ago, to kill the families of suicide bombers as a deterrent. Only, they usually don't do us the remarkable favor of booking tickets in their real names…

Blood-feud as deterrent?

Israel has considered many options in dealing with the threat. In August, Israeli deputy public security minister, Gidon Ezra, called for eliminating the relatives of suicide bombers as a deterrent. Radio Monte Carlo on 22 August aired the possible Hamas response to such an Israeli policy in an interview with Sheikh Yassin who said: "This means that he would give the Palestinian resistance men the justification to kill all Israelis who have relatives working in the ranks of the Israeli army." Ezra also suggested burying suicide bombers with pig skin or blood, defiling the corpse and thereby making the shaheed ineligible for holy martyr status with a promised place in heaven.

Jane's Security, Sept. 17, 2001

But let's turn the tables around, suppose they did just that on purpose, so they wouldn't be wholly anonymous as "heroes?" Perhaps, they really were directed and financed by mastermind bin Laden, who also eliminated the leader of the Northern Alliance in Afghanistan and potential US ally, Sheikh Massoud, bang on time. And maybe more "sleepers" are waiting to commit similar or worse attacks in all Western cities, once the West makes its next move. The US secret services know only too well whom they are dealing with, as bin Laden was a star pupil of the CIA – precisely for this reason they have been "prudent" about blindly bombing back. Tanks and missiles are no defense against the psychological power of the enemy's kamikaze weapon – yet they are being deployed.

I wouldn't be surprised if "evidence" of Iraq's involvement emerges very soon, allowing America to exploit worldwide support for its campaign of punishment to secure a foothold for the next half century in strategically indispensable oil regions of the Gulf and the Middle East. Most likely, the Saudi regime (perhaps the most backward-looking Muslim state in the world after the Taliban) will soon be replaced by a more moderate puppet, and the holy sites will remain within firing range of the US Army. Likewise, it can be expected that the Balkans will also be "pacified"[30] in line with the interests of the Anglo-American pipeline consortia and against the European interests of Elf-Fina. That's also why there probably won't be a solidly united campaign, but only acquiescence in a British presence, just as in the Gulf War. A strong, enlarged EU, encompassing the Balkans and Eastern Europe with its epicenters in Paris and Berlin, is not in the interests of the United States. If events should indeed unfold in this way, then history books should record now that yet again a fake, an orchestrated catastrophe exploited for propaganda purposes, was employed to set in motion a world-historical event.

This gloomy forecast has largely materialized. After Afghanistan, it is now Saddam Hussein who is on the firing line – and then it's the remainder of the "axis of evil" – of a military campaign that could last "for more than a generation," according to Defense Secretary Rumsfeld.

Half a year later, nothing has changed in terms of the "zero evidence" collected after 10 days of large-scale inquiries. On May 1, 2002, the BBC reported:

> *US intelligence officials have admitted they failed to unearth any sort of paper trail leading to the 11 September attacks. In the most detailed account so far of the investigation, the head of the Federal Bureau of Investigation (FBI) said that after seven months of relentless work America had found no hard evidence mentioning any aspect to the attacks on New York and Washington.*

It is a sobering thought that better evidence is required to prosecute a shoplifter than is needed to commence a world war.

Anthony Scrivener, QC (Queen's Counsel), Times, *Oct. 5, p. 7.*[31]

9/26/01
Skulls, Bones & Bush

One of the classics of modern conspirology, the British historian Antony Sutton's work on the secret "Skull & Bones" order of Yale University,[32] deserves another look in light of the current world situation. Not only the first but also the current President Bush is a "Bonesman," just like their grandfathers and great uncles, as are so many other members of the East Coast WASP (white Anglo-Saxon Protestant) elite found in influential positions of US foreign and economic policy. Sutton concluded that the Skull & Bones people had financially built up the Nazis in Germany, as well as the Communists in Eastern Europe, in order to demolish them again in the "great synthesis" of the Second World War and the subsequent Cold War…

Sutton's revelations about "The Order," as he calls the elitist "Skull & Bones" lodge, have partly been taken up in right-wing theories of a "Jewish world conspiracy" in continuation of the *Protocols of the Elders of Zion*, even though this was never Sutton's intention. His work documents the opposite: the racially elitist character – "blue-blood," anti-Jewish, anti-people of color – of this brotherhood founded in 1832, whose core has always consisted of the wealthy families of the New England aristocracy. The token membership from other nations and religions serves only as an alibi. The annals of the order vaunt grand-father Prescott Bush, initiated in 1917, for stealing and "bringing home" to the order's temple one of the club's most important trophies – the skull of Geronimo, the Apache chieftain. You may dismiss these kinds of pranks as reactionary gothic hocus-pocus – and the traditional rituals of the brotherhood are more reminiscent of Harry Potter than sinister occultism – yet, in his position as chief executive of Union Banking Corp. and the Hamburg-Amerika Line, Bonesman Bush became one of the most important financiers and supporters of the Nazi regime.

That the German SS adopted the skull and cross bones of Skull & Bones as their symbol must have pleased grandfather Bush and his partner William A. Harriman, initiated in 1913. Like many other US investors, they supported the Nazis not covertly but so overtly that the US ambassador to Berlin, William E. Dodd, told a *New York Times* reporter in 1937:

> A clique of U.S. industrialists is hell-bent to bring a fascist state to supplant our democratic government and is working closely with the fascist regime in Germany and Italy. I have had plenty of opportunity in my post in Berlin to witness how close some of our American ruling families are to the Nazi regime... Certain American industrialists had a great deal to do with bringing fascist regimes into being in both Germany and Italy. They extended aid to help Fascism occupy the seat of power, and they are helping to keep it there. [33]

The Bonesmen bred a "nifty son of a bitch" in the shape of Hitler. In the early 1930's, even before his rise to power, the US embassy cabled Washington to inquire about the financial background of Hitler's extravagant election campaign and the arming of his 300,000 Brown Shirts. Employees had noticed that the SA was equipped with American-made weapons. German steel tycoon Fritz Thyssen later admitted that he invested in the Hitler project from around 1930 – his bankers and financial administrators at the time were Bush and Harriman. [34]

One member of the Skull & Bones roll of presidents, secretaries of state, big bankers and industrialists who stands out is Col. Henry L. Stimson, initiated in 1888, who served as Secretary of State under seven presidents until his death in 1950. He was admitted to the brotherhood not because of his ancestry but because of his accomplishments, and later described this as an experience that marked his life. As Roosevelt's Secretary of State for War, "The Colonel" was an architect of the Second World War and the subsequent Cold War. We already made his acquaintance in connection with the Pearl Harbor fake, which was instigated to make the war palatable to the US public. Stimson wrote in his diary:

> When the news first came that Japan had attacked us, my first feeling was of relief that the indecision was over and that crisis had come in a way which would unite all our people. This continued to be my dominant feeling in spite of the news of catastrophes which quickly developed. For I feel that this country united has practically nothing to fear... [35]

Surely, a few thousand sailors don't matter if there is "nothing to fear" afterwards because great unity ensues. According to his biographers, Stimson was of the opinion that America should go to war once every generation; this would strengthen the nation's bond and cleanse it morally, as well as economically. Before George Bush decided to strike against Saddam Hussein in 1991, the *Washington Post* reported that he spent the holidays with a copy of the just-published biography of one of his true heroes, *The Colonel: Life and Wars of Henry Stimson*.[36]

The Skull & Bones brothers are not only convinced of the superiority of the white race, but also of their self-bestowed right as elite knights of this race to control the fortunes of mankind. According to Sutton, their philosophy is Hegelian – to construct the thesis, as well as the antithesis, and to emerge from the synthesis of this "constructive chaos" as masters of the situation. Sutton illustrates this with the example of William A. Harriman, Prescott Bush's partner at Union Banking who financed the Nazis while also supporting the Soviet war machine through his Guaranty Trust Company. Just as his Bones brother Stimson advised presidents in matters of war, Harriman advised a total of six presidents in matters of finance.

The way George H. W. Bush engineered and executed the 1991 Gulf War, true to the spirit of Stimson, was wholly in accordance with "constructive chaos." As a state Iraq remained intact as a threat and potential antithesis, yet the sheikdoms of the Gulf, the OPEC states and oil-dependent allies Japan and Germany have since been wholly reliant on the United States when it comes to oil. Bush Sr. then billed Japan and Germany for $16 billion to help pay for his nice little colonial war in defense of his Kuwaiti business partners – Bush's first oil company, financed by father Prescott and various Bones brothers, built Kuwait's first off-shore pumping station.[37] The future "anti-terror coalition" can expect the "loot" will stay under Anglo-American control, while the costs are defrayed by fellow comrades in the "fight against international terrorism."

George W. Bush, a Texan by choice – for generations the Bush family belongs to the East Coast WASP establishment – has always been keen to play down his membership of Skull & Bones and tried to portray himself as a true cowboy standing up to the elitist East Coast snobs. Yet when push came to shove, he always fell back on the connections and money of the elite mafia.[38]

Now, in times of war, he will listen all the more to his father and to the old S&B war horses of the Trilateral Commission, the Council of Foreign Relations and the Manhattan Institute. Among other things, these right-wing-heavy institutions and "think tanks" first provided him with his election campaign slogan of "compassionate conservatism" and now with the formulation "axis of evil."[39] They will also have advised him to let the simmering chaos in Palestine seethe a bit longer, to first take a nice long vacation and to calmly await the big bang heralded for so long by bin Laden and other fanatics…

The fact that Israeli Prime Minister Sharon constantly resists US pressure to enter into talks with Arafat speaks volumes. He doesn't trust those Knights of the Skull in the White House for a minute, that "Rockefeller mob" with its racist, Nazi-friendly, anti-Semitic, pro-Arab, oil and power-interested background. In my opinion, this also invalidates all speculation that Israel's Mossad was the secret instigator of 9/11. Such an enhancement of power for Bush and for the powerful men behind the scenes can be as little in Israel's interest as it is in the interests of an average New York Jew that Rudolph "Gestapo" Giuliani gains in popularity. His Zero Tolerance policy rightfully earned him this sobriquet in the last few years.[40]

The Axis Powers

The phrase "Axis of Evil" is misleading from the start: what connection is there between Iraq, Iran and North Korea? And what connection is there between these countries and the 9/11 attacks? When we really want to go after the countries that harbored the terrorists, then we would have to bomb Germany, parts of Spain or Saudi Arabia.

Barbara Ehrenreich, Frankfurter Rundschau, 4/5/02,
http://www.weltwoche.ch/artikel/?AssetID=1895&CategoryID=60

These indications are not meant to identify the WTC attack as a Skull & Bones conspiracy. But, for an appraisal of the actors on the world stage, it is of some importance to know their family and ideological background, especially if it is traditionally rooted in the membership of the United States' most influential secret society. Antony Sutton's revelations about the activities of the brotherhood cost him his career as a professor at Stanford University.

Following the publication of a three-volume study in which he detailed the arming of the Soviet Union with US technology and money, and asked "Why?"[41] an anonymous Bonesman passed him two volumes of documents about the order. Only since then have the illustrious S&B members and their supremacist ideology become known. Of course, from then on, Professor Sutton could only find small publishers for his work. Now the Bonesmen are going to war again, and Poppy Bush's old guard is at the controls. It is unlikely that matters will rest with the punitive action against the Taliban and the hunt for bin Laden – their tradition speaks against it.

If someone had filmed "The 9/11 Files" after The X-Files, *the Skull & Bones background of the presidential family would have had to be invented – but unfortunately it is real. And our Sept. 24 forecast that things won't end with the hunt for Osama bin Laden has unfortunately been confirmed; and so too has the suspicion that Israel's Sharon doesn't trust the Bush faction. An added bit of spice is that the Israeli secret service Mossad was probably able to tap nearly all phones in the United States, including those of the White House, for years. So far, the arrests of dozens of Israeli spies in the United States after 9/11 haven't featured much in the mainstream media, but they have been recorded by the watchful eyes of several websites[42] (see also "3/03/02: The Kosher Conspiracy").*

In 1991, Paul Goldstein and Jeffrey Steinberg wrote about the philosophy of the secret Skull & Bones order:

> To the Bonesmen, the use of military power is a natural and essential corollary to political power. The Bonesmen are taught that, although ideas have their place, to truly transform history, military force is almost always required. Critics of the Order have pointed out that this philosophy of power and the imperial use of military force comes straight from the chronicles of the Roman Empire – especially the Roman Empire during its phase of decline and collapse.

> The criticism may prove to be most prophetically true of the current generation of Bonesmen who are leading the United States under the presidency of George Bush. During the final phase of the Roman Empire, legions were deployed out around the world to conquer and subjugate vast territories, while back in Rome, there was a breakdown, a crisis in which the entire social and cultural fabric of the early Roman republic was eroding and giving way to something akin to the drug, rock, sex counterculture of today.

The Roman imperial policy of attempting to gloss over the decadence at home by engaging in constant wars of expansion led ultimately to the total collapse of Rome.

In this regard, the Spartan-Roman imperial outlook of the American WASP warrior caste, exemplified by Skull & Bones, cannot be precisely compared to the Japanese samurai code of Bushido. The Japanese Bushido code emphasized honor among the warriors and presumed a fundamentally moral or ethical vision of the world. No such emphasis on morality and honor exists in the code of Skull & Bones.[43]

9/29/01
If they can get you asking the wrong questions, they don't have to worry about the answers

As noted, conspiracy theories are a good example for the discovery in quantum physics that a description of reality is impossible without including the observer. Burroughs says "The paranoid is the guy with the real facts": he doesn't admit inaccuracies, obfuscation or fuzziness, there is a reason for even the most obvious coincidence. For him, theory and practice are one and the same – he perceives a real conspiracy where others see at most vague clues pointing to a connection, and yet others see nothing at all. Conspiracy theories reduce complexity, disentangle what is confusing, explain the inexplicable. This is true for the paranoid schizophrenic, who projects his inner despair onto external persecution, as well as for the rational conspiracy theorist, who satisfies the need for explanation by connecting vague links into logical causal chains.

If George W. Bush, his father G. H. W. Bush and other important US decision makers and bankers are members of a secret elitist society, and this brotherhood built up Hitler and Stalin back in their time, thereby provoking the Second World War, then it becomes logical that they are also involved in the making of the impending third world war. Or: since the dollar's gold backing was abandoned in 1971 and the oil price was linked to the dollar at the same time, oil was directly linked to the US currency, and that is why since then, hot and cold oil wars have been fought over output levels; that is why the Islamic opposition poses an internal threat to the US-controlled oil regions; and that is why the terror attack is now being used to eliminate this opposition.

Or: a network of Islamic extremists has declared war against the entire Western world, their aim is to establish theocracies à la Taliban; this attack was only the first declaration of war; more will follow; soon our women will have to wear veils!!!

Not one of these three scenarios is devoid of logic, and within each one the observer can hit upon so many more pieces of the puzzle that a complete picture – the truth about secret plutocratic masterminds, politico-economical geostrategic chess moves or a religio-cultural clash of civilizations – seems to emerge. But in reality all three of these scenarios and causal chains exist simultaneously – and a few others more – and all play a part in the socio-chemical reaction that led to the 9/11 catastrophe.

Normally, the brain is capable, at least in principle, of verifying and weighing up the alternatives, but in times of crisis this validation mechanism is apparently switched off. Five minutes later, "Osama bin Laden" became the tunnel of reality the world public willingly succumbed to in its quest for order, structure and sense as it faced this senseless, gruesome atrocity. And Nostradamus, who once again predicted it all in one of his little verses, according to a Web canard[44] – it doesn't come any simpler than that – was the number-one bestseller on Amazon in the days following the attacks.

"If they can get you asking the wrong questions, they don't have to worry about the answers," according to Thomas Pynchon's labyrinthine conspiracy novel, *Gravity's Rainbow*. It goes on:

> We are obsessed with building labyrinths, where before there was the open plain and sky. To draw ever more complex patterns on the blank sheet. We cannot abide the openness: it is terror to us... If there is something comforting — religious, if you want — about paranoia, there is still also anti-paranoia, where nothing is connected to anything, a condition not many of us can bear for long.[45]

These are two important clues to the observer-created, conspiratorial character of reality – and the difficulty of enduring open, undecided questions or disturbing, inappropriate answers.

In times of crisis, simple solutions are in demand, and nothing works better than a good conspiracy theory, a clear image of the enemy. The vague biographies of the terror pilots are currently a bit disappointing in this respect. The only truly promising lead to the real masterminds would seem to lie on the trail of the stock market speculation before the attacks. And this leads straight into the cesspit, the brown conspiracy quagmire, at least according to one of the experts interviewed by German television ARD.

Stock market watchdogs in several countries are currently investigating the extremely high trading volumes in put options on shares in American and United Airlines in the days before and after the attacks. Put options are a way of placing a bet on falling share prices – the steeper the fall until a certain date, the higher the betting win, which can easily be 10 or 20 times more than the amount invested. The ARD TV business program Plus Minus interviewed Luxembourg financial expert Ernest Backes on this matter:

> *On the Thursday before the attacks, the turnover in so-called put options on United Airlines experienced an explosive increase. 200,000 were traded, normally it was often not even 1,000. And the same happened in the case of American Airlines, as with the insurance companies. Terrorists may have earned billions with this on the stock markets."*
>
> *According to Backes, the clues lead to Switzerland, to the accounts of an organization that was founded years ago by the late lawyer François Genoud and apparently still exists.*
>
> *"One of the connections is that the Swiss lawyer had strong links with the bin Laden family, that he was one of the family's advisors, one of their bankers. It is known that he supported terrorism and that he was the administrator of the Hitler fortune...* [46]

This is not an esoteric conspiracy theory, but the opinion of an ARD-tested expert. How strong this lead is, this suspicion, isn't clear from the report. Of course, the keyword "François Genoud" immediately rings a bell with conspirologists. Genoud had already gained the trust of Hitler and of other important NS party figures in his days as a fervent Swiss Nazi youth. He then played a key role as banker and pusher for the so-called "Rat Line," which channeled hundreds of top Nazis and large amounts of money for them to South America at the war's end, under the aegis of the Vatican and the US secret services.

After the war, Genoud is said to have set up a neo-fascist "black international" in the Middle East and to have supported all anti-Jewish terrorists in recent times "from Hitler to Carlos." [47] To this day, the Nazi money moved by Genoud purportedly serves as a financing pot for nationalist, extreme right-wing movements in Europe. If the stock market transactions can really be traced back to Genoud's financial empire, then the headline "the trail leads to Germany" would take on a whole new dimension.

As with all the inquiries, attempts to track down the financial speculators have still come to nothing half a year later, although this is by far the hottest lead to finding the masterminds and accessories. But to pursue it would have meant draining by force the widespread off-shore and gray-market swamp of the current financial and banking system. In this case, of course, it is felt that the lesser evil is to immediately lose sight of the apparent lead to Genoud's brown network.

10/01/01
Banks, Bourses, Berlusconi

If one of the leads from the insider stock market transactions before and after 9/11 really points to the brown financial empire of the Swiss François Genoud, who died in 1996, then the background can be traced not only to the historical Nazi-Vatican-US secret services connection but also to Silvio Berlusconi, a present-day convicted conspiracy expert, who opened his mouth too wide on a recent state visit to Berlin. In other words, he spoke in plain fascistoid language.

> We must be fully aware of the superiority of our civilization which consists of principles and values that have brought widespread well-being to the general public.

> The West will continue to conquer nations, just like it conquered the Communist world and parts of the Islamic world, but another part still remains backward by 1400 years.

> Western society espouses values like love of freedom, the freedom of nations and the individual, that do not form part of the heritage of other civilizations, like the Islamic one…[48]

As noted, when Berlusconi moved from the construction trade into the media business in the 1970's, he joined the secret society *Propaganda Due* (P2); which he later denied, of course, but on the basis of available evidence, he was found guilty of perjury for that. Thanks to a general amnesty, however, he managed to avoid sentencing. The P2 case is one of the best documented conspiracy cases of recent times. In view of the meteoric re-ascendancy of the new Duce Berlusconi, some observers say that it is still in power.

The top Nazis who used the rat lines and Genoud's network to ensconce themselves in safe havens after the war included figures like Adolf Eichmann, Klaus Barbie and Oberst Rudel, but also the Italian fascist and SS man Licio Gelli (born in 1919), who then ran arms deals from his South American hideout. German terror experts of the same stamp as the "beast" Barbie proved very useful in building, or rather in destabilizing several South American countries. Many of the "freedom fighters," death squads and "Contras" armed and equipped under the patronage of the CIA were trained by German "pros."

Gelli returned to Italy at the start of the 1970's and is said to have founded P2 there to take power in Italy in a "white coup." In 1981, when the plot failed, a list of P2 members was found in his house. It listed the names of 43 members of the government and parliament, over 900 top civil servants, leading officers of the military and the secret services, as well as business leaders from the media, industry and banking, including Berlusconi.[49] Shortly thereafter, as noted, one of the top P2 members, banker Roberto Calvi, was found hanged under a London bridge. Later, it was discovered that "God's banker" ran a big money-laundering operation for Mafia and drug money through his Banco Ambrosiano and the Vatican Bank (IOR).

Among the numerous banks and fake banks that Calvi had founded across the world was Cisalpine Bank on the Bahamas, whose second largest registered shareholder was Archbishop Paul Marcinkus of the Vatican Bank. In 1981, Cisalpine fell into disrepute when it became embroiled in the court case against World Finance Corporation (WFC), a Miami bank whose chief executive, a "former" CIA agent, stood accused of laundering money from the cocaine trade of South American dictators through the "black hole" of the Calvi-Marcinkus-P2 consortium. Journalist Penny Lernoux[50] researched the case, and she reckons P2 was the main financial channel for fascist regimes in Latin America. This strong nexus with the "nifty sons of bitches" of US foreign policy explains why Michele Sindona – partner of Calvi and Gelli in the money-laundering business – was invited to President Nixon's inaugural ball, and why Gelli attended the ball for the inauguration of President Reagan.[51]

The reason why the Mafia is also known as "the honorable society" is that New York Mafiosi who collaborated with the US secret services in the 1944 US invasion of Italy gave them a list of members of Italy's "honorable society" who were to be protected. Once those out-of-control "SOB's" Hitler and Mussolini were stopped, the CIA built up a new anti-Communist channel of influence based on the Mafia and the Vatican. In the terror-rife 1970's it became active with several bomb attacks, among other acts, that were blamed on the "Red Brigades" by setting false leads.

The best-known case was the Aug. 2, 1980, bomb attack on Bologna's central train station, which marked the peak of the terror wave and left

85 people dead and 200 wounded. Two years before, the biographer of the Bush-Nazi links Webster Tarpley had exposed the *Brigate Rossi* as patsies of a P2 false-flag op, but the warning was ignored. The real masterminds behind the attack were only sentenced in November 1995. Two of the bombers were given life sentences, while their ringleaders, P2 grand master Licio Gelli and his right-hand man, CIA agent Francesco Pazienza, got off with ten years each.

Even if there is as yet no proof, the recent bomb attacks in Genoa and Venice, which were used as a pretext for brutally clamping down on anti-globalization protesters, seem to bear all the hallmarks of these typical Italo-American counter-intelligence operations – especially with Gelli's apprentice Berlusconi now at the helm of power and the media.

I am skeptical whether the investigations into the short-term specu-lative deals and financial transactions before and after 9/11 will really bear fruit. Finding out who was responsible for the 20 times-higher-than-normal turnover in put options on airline shares would constitute far better evidence than anything that has been brought against bin Laden so far. But pursuing this type of financial crime – and above all its future prevention through oversight, which is technically possible – would be seen by some anti-terror comrades as hitting them where it hurts: bank secrecy. Of course, it would be possible to bring transparency to off-shore banks in the Caribbean or to discreet deposits in Liechtenstein, Luxembourg and elsewhere as part of the global anti-terror measures. This radical cure in matters of money laundering would have practically no effect on around 97% of the world population, but the remaining 3% or so who are crucial would quickly lose interest in domestic security and transparency as soon as money is involved.

So from now on, Huey, Dewey and Louie will have to get used to increased oversight mechanisms of the Orwellian kind, but the money in Uncle Scrooge's vault can still be moved largely uncontrolled – to the joy of all safe crackers no matter whether they work for Jihad Terror Inc., for McDope in the drug business (global annual turnover: $300 billion, top heroin producer: Pakistan) or in the counter-intelligence business.

Berlusconi's crude hereditarian theory of civilization corresponds with Samuel Huntington's thesis that in order to survive, the West must transform its demographic inferiority into military control in a "Clash of Civilizations."

10/03/01
The Assassins are Back!

The spiritual and practical instructions, allegedly found in the travel bag of one of the terror pilots left behind at the airport, have now been made public.[52] They can be traced back in style and wording to the roots of militant Islam and to the forefather of terrorism – Hassan i Sabbah. In the year 1090, he set up the first terror hideout in history in the fortress of Alamut in northern Iran. Hassan invented the suicide attack and bestowed an infamous as well as enduring world reputation upon his secret society, the Assassins. To this day, the word *assassin* stands for "murderer" in many languages with the special connotation of "sly," "treacherous," "terrorist."

For centuries, European notions about the Assassins derived from Marco Polo's travel tales from Persia. These told of an "old man of the mountain" who intoxicated his followers with hashish and opium, and pampered them in heavenly gardens to then goad them into murderous attacks in order to return to this paradise. It is still popularly believed that the name *Assassin* comes from hashish; the real etymology is "the Founders." Scientific Orientalism later debunked these legends – the rather ascetic Assassins had as little to do with hashish, which was well known in the Orient of the Middle Ages, as with heavenly luxury resorts. But they – or at least Hassan's faction – were clearly accountable for the innovation of religiously motivated suicide attackers blinded by the promise of redemption.[53]

In the 7th Century, the fight over the Prophet Mohammed's legitimate successor caused a schism within Islam into the Sunni and Shia traditions. In the 9th Century, the latter gave rise to yet another splinter group, the Ismailis. Hassan i Sabbah adhered to this small minority which opposed the caliphate for its decadence and worldliness, and he set out to restore the pure and true Islam to power by radical means. In Persia, Syria and Arabia, the Ismailis' mission was successful, but the suicide attack on the Seljuk grand vizier in 1092 caused them to split yet again, with the moderates headquartered in Cairo and the radicals in the Assassin fortress of Alamut. Sinan, one of Hassan's successors in Syria, later became known as "the old man of the mountain." His suicide attackers in many disguises were feared by the Islamic establishment and by European crusaders as dangerous "sleepers." "Like the devil they transform themselves into angels of light by adopting the gestures, apparel, language, customs and behavior of other peoples. These wolves in sheep's clothing choose death as soon as they are discovered."

During the crusade of Richard the Lion Heart no fewer than 40 suspected Assassins were unmasked in his camps. By this time, the radical Ismailis were not alone, and other insurgents had adopted their self-sacrificing kamikaze techniques. In 1332, an expert on internal security, the German cleric Brocardus, said true to the spirit of German Interior Minister Otto Schily: "I know of only one remedy to ensure the safety of the king. No one should be admitted to court, not even for small, temporary services, unless their home country, place of residence, family, status and person can be reliably, definitively and fully ascertained."

It is frightening and fascinating at the same time to study these old tales against the background of 9/11. Frightening because of the fatal recurrence of events that rob you of any hope that the human unconscious can evolve at all. Somehow this must also dawn on that simple soul of a businessman President Bush when he realizes that it's nonsense to fire a $1 million missile at a $1 tent. When unfinished business from the psycho-historical drama of humanity resurfaces, all the technological progress isn't worth a single shot of gunpowder.

Fascinating from a conspirological point of view because in essence these stories are nothing other than a conspiracy theory, the oldest, most influential and controversial of all. It is usually abbreviated by the code name God. The catastrophes that triggered the invention of gods have already been briefly mentioned in connection with the emergence of human sacrifice. The traumatized survivors of the impact catastrophes make sense of this senseless, gruesome and deadly destruction of their surroundings by inventing secret, almighty masterminds of the catastrophe – gods – who want to punish mankind with this heavenly terror attack. In order to rid themselves from the horror and psychologically master the situation, the survivors re-enact the catastrophe like children by staging sanguinary animal and human sacrifices. But no celestial body can be influenced by the offerings of virgins and muttons.

Together with the abolition of the "childish" sacrifice, whose once helpful ritual character propagated a parasitic kingdom of priests with a multitude of conspiracy theories embodied as gods, the Egyptians Akhenaten and his pupil Moses implemented possibly the most decisive rationalization measure in all of history – monotheism. With the reduction to one central god, the confusion over the conspiracy of the gods and the fight over the masterminds and instigators ended. From then on the main conspirator was nameless and invisible, and the cult of sacrifice had served its time as a way of doing business with the Almighty. But soon renewed fighting ensued over the correct interpretation and implementation of the laws said to come directly from God, and with the prophets Jesus and Mohammed two great sects split away, modifying and developing the original Egypto-Hebrew theory. Whether this was beneficial or detrimental has since been the subject of fierce disputes among the followers of God, fiercer than with unbelievers. "To spill the blood of a heretic is of greater merit than the killing of 70 Greek unbelievers," remarked a devout Sunni in a text against the Assassins.

According to his supposed testament, the alleged terror pilot Atta belonged to the Sunni strain of Islam. At least in theological terms he cannot be traced back to the lineage of terror pioneer Hassan i Sabbah. In practical terms, however, the Assassins are back. Without their 900-year-old human-disdaining version of the God conspiracy theory – the teaching that death in the battle against the enemies of God gives direct access to the eternal VIP lounge of paradise – the bin Laden theory of 9/11 would not be possible. Accordingly material means are only of limited help when it comes to successfully combating suicide terrorists. Even the smartest missiles are futile against a brainwashed, death-defying spirit lusting for paradise.

In the end, the only thing to be of any help will be a policy of embrace. So, let's send the Taliban our sex bombs; let's pamper them with the gentlest, coziest, most delightful pleasures, sensations, sounds and smells; let's seduce them into using the wonderfully relaxing Afghan hashish. In short, every warrior of God who hands in his shooting iron to Uncle Sam will get a six-week holiday for starters in the paradisiacal all-inclusive "Club de l'Assassin!" If further re-education should be necessary, it's only a matter of making clear that God is just a conspiracy theory for which there is no collectively accessible evidence. It can only be found individually, and due to the observer principle it is bound to vary so much that it makes no sense to beat each other about over the true God. "Truth is the invention of a liar!"

Of course, the "Club de l'Assassin" was never opened. Instead of sex bombs and a policy of embrace the response came in the shape of cluster bombs and missiles, the policy of terror, which cost the lives of thousands of people. Of course, the treacherous Assassins, the "sleepers" of the diabolical bin Laden network, had no alarm clock and slept right through further murderous provocations. But the widely fanned hysteria over treacherous killers who live "in our midst" created the ideal climate for introducing new security, surveillance and control laws (Patriot Act, Homeland Security) to curtail constitutional rights of freedom and civil liberties practically unopposed.

10/06/01
Jihad Inc. – Made in USA

It's hardly surprising that with all the current "emotional correctness," drawing even the slightest attention to the United States' catastrophic foreign policy is seen to be "anti-American." Dubya Bush, until recently rated an intellectual cripple, has attained the status of a wise, prudent and almost holy grand emperor. Not so long ago, hardly anyone thought him capable of spelling Afghanistan correctly, but now all non-terrorists are supposed to think he's the coolest thing around because he is liberating the world from terror. Meanwhile bin Laden, whose family clan has been in business with the Bush family for more than 20 years, and who was trained and financed by the US as the leader of the Saudi Mujahideen contingent in the war in Afghanistan, has mutated into the global Satan of the 21st Century. And the Taliban, installed in the mid-1990's under the patronage of the CIA by the Pakistani secret service Inter Services Intelligence (ISI), have become an archaic sub-human species earmarked for extermination. The most fitting title for this drama is one that conspirologist Antony Sutton once coined for Wall Street's financing of Hitler and the Soviets – *The Best Enemy Money Can Buy.*[54]

Bin Laden's cooperation with the CIA in the 1980's does get a cursory mention when his life is described in the CNN version of reality – it was so open and so well-documented that it could hardly be left without mention at all – but the biographies of the Saudi heir turned global terror monster usually start with the 1990's. Given the media conformity, hardly anyone in the West notices anymore, but the "loss of memory" affecting the super Mecca of information technology, of all places, when it comes to its former employee is noticed, not without irony, in other parts of the world – as noted by the Indian newspaper *The Hindu* in a Sept. 27 article on "The Creation of Osama":

> The Revolutionary Association of the Women of Afghanistan (RAWA), which has a long tradition of opposing the Taliban regime and paying for it with blood, raised this issue in its September 14 press statement. While condemning the terrorist attack, the statement went on to underline the fact

that "the people of Afghanistan have nothing to do with Osama and his accomplices. But unfortunately we must say that it was the Government of the United States who supported Pakistani dictator Gen. Zia-ul-Haq in creating thousands of religious schools from which the germs of the Taliban emerged. In a similar way, as is clear to all, Osama has been the blue-eyed boy of the CIA."[55]

Of course, a feminist and presumably left-wing cell may not be seen as adequate proof of the United States' active role in breeding new Assassins. But it's another matter altogether when it comes to the source of the article, which is frequently mentioned and quoted, the spring 2000 Yale University Press publication *Taliban, Militant Islam, Oil and Fundamentalism in Central Asia*. The trustworthiness of its author Ahmed Rashid is beyond question: senior correspondent for the *Far Eastern Economic Review* and the (conservative) *Daily Telegraph* in London, and a well-known expert on the region. Yet he leaves no doubt that it was the Americans who promoted and massively supported the breeding grounds of Islamic terror in Pakistan and Afghanistan.

In 1986, says Rashid, CIA director William Casey intensified the war against the Soviet Union in three ways. He persuaded Congress to arm the Afghan Mujahideen with Stinger missiles and to provide them with training and support in the guerrilla war. Furthermore, it was planned in conjunction with the Pakistani ISI and Britain's MI6 to destabilize the neighboring Soviet republics of Uzbekistan and Tajikistan with "Islamic" terror attacks. Thirdly, the CIA backed the ISI's efforts to recruit fighters for the Holy War in other Islamic countries and to train them ideologically and militarily in a network of camps and "religious schools."

Between 1982 and 1992 some 35,000 Muslim radicals from 43 Islamic countries in the Middle East, North and East Africa, Central Asia and the Far East would pass their baptism under fire with the Afghan Mujaheddin. Tens of thousands more foreign Muslim radicals came to study in the hundreds of new madrassas that Zia's military government began to fund in Pakistan and along the Afghan border. Eventually more than 100,000 Muslim radicals were to have direct contact with Pakistan and Afghanistan and be influenced by the Jihad.

In camps near Peshawar and in Afghanistan, these radicals met each other for the first time and studied, trained and fought together. It was the first opportunity for most of them to learn about Islamic movements in other countries and they forged tactical and ideological links that would serve them well in the future. The camps became virtual universities for future Islamic radicalism.[56]

It was not in Hamburg-Harburg but at these terror universities that the new Assassins were bred and the new species of brainwashed Islamic warriors for God were programmed. And now their fellow students turned on their erstwhile sponsors with the outrageous attack of 9/11. "Friends one minute, foes the next" cynically springs to mind. Just as the holy war against the "empire of evil" justified all means in the eyes of the Americans – even the immorality of setting religious fanatics to drill innocent young Muslims to become suicide bombers and then hand them a stick of dynamite – neither do the holy warriors recognize any moral boundaries in their battle against their mentor.

All this needs to be recorded not for the sake of saying "serves you right" or "it's your own fault," but to make progress on the question of how we can combat terrorism successfully in future. A start must be made in the dirty backyard of unofficial US foreign policy, that geostrategic gene lab that has released such monstrous products as bin Laden and his Assassins – and which sponsored a regime like the Taliban as recently as May 2001 with $43 million, as well as the death squads in Colombia, the "liberation army" in Kosovo, etc.[57]

In his book, Ahmed Rashid notes another interesting detail in connection with Osama. The ISI complained to the Saudi secret service director Prince Turki bin Faisal that the only Saudis to volunteer for Jihad were taxi drivers, simple students and Bedouins, but that no members of the royal family had stepped forward. In 1982, however, a leader for the Saudi contingent in the Holy War was finally found in the shape of bin Laden – although he is not a true "royal," he is still the offspring of one of the country's most powerful clans. Bin Laden's family, as well as the royal household, are said to have welcomed the decision enthusiastically.

That the Saudi-American involvement with the Mujahideen and bin Laden ended in 1990, as the mantra of the CNN version of reality has claimed repeatedly, has not been confirmed by Ahmed Rashid's study. As recently as July 1998, Prince Turki visited Kandahar. Only a few weeks later, 400 pick-up trucks were delivered to the Taliban, still with Arabic number plates. Shortly thereafter, bombs went off at the US embassies in Africa; likely organizer: bin Laden; his likely location: Kandahar – the place where the first bombardments of the Taliban "terror camps" are expected. Finding them shouldn't pose any problems for NATO – after all, they built them themselves.

Ahmed Rashid's books about the Taliban and Central Asia have since
been published in German, and when he visited Germany in the spring of
2002, even Foreign Minister Fischer listened to what he had to say.
So he knows the facts about the game played by the CIA, the ISI and the
Saudis in Afghanistan, but as Germany's top diplomat and Uncle Sam's
vassal, he has no choice but to grin and bear it.

10/10/01
Uncle Sam's Junk: Heroin, Taliban, Pakistan

"Germans to the front!" The last time this command by an allied general
rang out was in the summer of 1900 when a German contingent
supported British troops against the "Boxer Rebellion," in which the
Chinese rose up against the occupation by the colonial powers. Kaiser
Wilhelm gave his infamous "Hun speech" to the soldiers as they
departed.

> When you meet the enemy, crush them, show no mercy, take no prisoners.
> Just as the Huns under King Etzel created for themselves a thousand years
> ago a name which is handed down even today as a mighty legend, you
> should give the name of Germany cause to be remembered in China for a
> thousand years, such that no Chinese will ever so much as dare look askance
> at a German.[58]

A hundred years later, we are not very far off from this type of martial
rhetoric. A misleading report from the secret services – like the false
report to the Kaiser at the time that all German embassy staff in China
had been murdered the day before – should be all it takes, and the
"Huns" would be back on the scene. Of course, in the background of the
"clash of civilizations" other rather uncivilized, conspiratorial business is
at stake, now as then. And in Afghanistan, just as in China, a very special
product is at the secret center of it all – opium.

"Nature demands that man sometimes be drugged without falling
asleep." Even though Goethe's insight can be interpreted as an early plea
for the natural right to intoxication, the Germans played no important
role in the drug business of the colonial powers. In China, all they left
behind is their "Tsingtao Beer," which is famous to this day, and despite
Kaiser Wilhelm's spontaneous Hun tirade, they didn't earn themselves
any reputation as brutal emperors. Quite a different story with the
English, who started trading with China towards the end of the 17th
Century. Their trade goods like wool and iron were hardly in demand in
China, so to avoid paying in silver for the desired Chinese silk fabrics,

teas and spices, the British East India Company started to export opium
to China from the recently conquered province of Bengal. Not even a
1729 Chinese imperial ban on importing and smoking opium could deter
them, when 200 crates (13 tons) were delivered. By 1767, it was already
five times as much, in 1820, 670 tons, and in 1838 as much as 2,680 tons
of opium were delivered to China. This made opium the product with the
highest turnover in the world economy. So, when the upright Chinese
civil servant Lin Tse-Hsu ordered 950 tons of the lucrative substance to
be destroyed, Britain launched the first Opium War, at the end of which
it had conquered Hong Kong and five other Chinese ports – and cranked
up the business still further. In 1880, a colossal 7,000 tons were shipped
from India to China, and at least 10 million Chinese were addicted to
opium. In comparison: one hundred years later, in the 1980's, around
1,700 tons of opium were produced for world medicinal demand. In
1999, Afghan farmers produced a CIA-estimated 1,670 tons, around 80%
of illegal global demand.

The wealth that raised the fish-and-sheep island of England to the
heights of world power as the British Empire came largely from this
dirty backyard business of the "Honourable East India company." And
when the Chinese finally grew weary of these "imports of civilizing
services," the "alliance agreement" came into effect for the Germans,
and they were called to the front, even if only for a small skirmish.[59]

Any more questions?

**We are facing a murderous and totalitarian challenge. Those who watched
yesterday on television how new mass murders were being announced and
who know that this is not merely rhetoric anymore, no longer ask for
evidence, which is there, which exists. Everything points towards this.
There is no alternative viewpoint, neither for us, nor for the whole alliance
or for other agencies.**

*German Foreign Minister Joseph Fischer speaking before the German Lower
House of Parliament on 10/11/2001.*
http://www.documentarchiv.de/brd/2001/rede_fischer_1011.html

That Tony Blair, of all people, now singles out the Taliban as "the
world's biggest heroin producers" while another alliance agreement
takes effect for the Germans does create a sense of déjà vu, especially if
you look at how the opium and heroin trade is organized in the Pakistani-
Afghan region. When the pioneers of psychedelic wholesaling, the
"Brotherhood of Eternal Love" in California, created initial international
demand for the local hemp and poppy products in the 1960's, they paid

$5-$10 per kilogram of hashish and $50-$100 for a kilo of opium. The rediscovery of these substances in Western culture and tougher prohibition and control measures assured more than a hundredfold price increase for these agricultural products over the next two decades. Heroin still played no role in the region, but this changed abruptly with the 1979 invasion by the Soviet Union. The Pakistani military intelligence service ISI set up heroin labs along the border. Professor Alfred McCoy, author of the standard work, *The Politics of Heroin: CIA Complicity in the Global Drug Trade* (Chicago 1991) wrote on this in 1997:

> CIA assets again controlled this heroin trade. As the Mujaheddin guerrillas seized territory inside Afghanistan, they ordered peasants to plant opium as a revolutionary tax. Across the border in Pakistan, Afghan leaders and local syndicates under the protection of Pakistan Intelligence operated hundreds of heroin laboratories. During this decade of wide-open drug-dealing, the US Drug Enforcement Agency in Islamabad failed to instigate major seizures or arrests.

> In May 1990, as the CIA operation was winding down, The *Washington Post* published a front-page exposé charging that Gulbudin Hekmatyar, the CIA's favored Afghan leader, was a major heroin manufacturer. The Post argued, in a manner similar to the San Jose Mercury News' later report about the contras, that US officials had refused to investigate charges of heroin dealing by its Afghan allies "because U.S. narcotics policy in Afghanistan has been subordinated to the war against Soviet influence there."

> In 1995, the former CIA director of the Afghan operation, Charles Cogan, admitted the CIA had indeed sacrificed the drug war to fight the Cold War. "Our main mission was to do as much damage as possible to the Soviets. We didn't really have the resources or the time to devote to an investigation of the drug trade," he told an Australian television reporter. "I don't think that we need to apologize for this. Every situation has its fallout... There was fallout in terms of drugs, yes. But the main objective was accomplished. The Soviets left Afghanistan.[60]

The "fallout" included a surge in the population of Pakistani heroin addicts from zero to around 1.5 million, a worldwide heroin glut in the 1980's, and the "heroinization" of the Pakistani economy, which persists to this day. According to recent Indian government estimates,[61] the Pakistani heroin industry's $11 billion turnover in 1999 was 30% greater than the entire state budget, which would have long since collapsed after ten years of recession if it were not for this clandestine financing.

When the Cold War ended, the "collateral damage" of heroin in Pakistan did not, nor did the training of Assassins in terror camps, because they still had their uses. The Holy Warriors were still needed for the destabilization of the CIS (Commonwealth of Independent States) in Chechnya and elsewhere, and the heroin dollars were needed to pay for Pakistani weapons purchases (over $30 billion in the 1990's). Only in 1998, when the CIA brass really started to feel uncomfortable about their creation Osama bin Laden, did they seriously urge the Pakistanis to reduce heroin production – which they obediently did, moving production onto Taliban territory but maintaining Pakistani control. Since then, poppy cultivation in Afghanistan has surged, constituting the sole source of income for the Taliban, until they agreed to stop production in response to US pressure. In May 2001, the Taliban ambassador negotiated compensation payments for the farmers with the Americans in Islamabad, demanding "for the Afghan people" almost exactly the $12 billion that the heroin business generates every year. At first, he was offered only $1.5 million, but then $43 million were promised and transferred. That is how much the Taliban are thought to have earned with the raw opium trade the previous year, according to Pakistani estimates.

In his very last interview with two regular reporters from *Le Figaro* and *Rolling Stone*, Sheikh Massoud, the leader of the Northern Alliance who was murdered a few days later by two suicide reporters, commented on this issue.

> The Taliban have sufficient stocks to continue exporting for another two or three years. By the way, it was the large drug traffickers who stopped production, not Mullah Omar. They want prices to rise…The Taliban collect 10% agricultural tax on the opium fields. Then they take a production tax of $180 per kilogram package, which gets an official stamp. Then there is sales tax and transport tax, when the goods are first flown to Kabul and then to Kunduz. Without a stamp and a declaration from the Taliban no package crosses the border.[62]

The real money is then made in the CIA- and ISI-controlled labs along the border and in distribution. Here we have together in a nutshell the two monsters of modern times – "terrorism" and "drugs" – and we can see that we are dealing with two interconnected and homemade phenomena. The junkies of this world – mostly Americans, given that the US with its 5% of world population consumes around 50% of all illegal drugs – have financed the corrupt clique of a military intelligence service for the past 20 years, the creation of Islamic schools (Taliban means "students") and the breeding of thousands of brainwashed terror fighters.

All this for their government's higher purpose "to inflict as much damage as possible" on the Soviets. As no democratic parliament in the world would publicly authorize such a geopolitical guerrilla strategy, let alone fund it, other clandestine sources of income were needed. That is why in 75% of big cases, investigators from the Drug Enforcement Agency are blocked by the "protective hand" of the secret services, as the already quoted Andreas Bülow once said.[63]

To date, illegal drugs and their enormous profit margins were indispensable to the secret services as a "lubricant of terror," and it will be curious to see how the situation now develops. Since the 1999 military coup, Pakistan has been excluded from any new IMF loans, and has only been able to service its existing loans thanks to huge "private" contributions from the heroin business. If this arrangement were now seriously threatened, Pakistan's bankruptcy would be imminent. The US is hardly likely to inflict this upon its currently most important ally. As the largest global debtor the US is broke itself and is in no position to willy-nilly hand out $12 billion a year in a Marshall Plan gesture, so those "nifty sons of bitches" from the Pakistani ISI can probably continue producing their heroin for the time being.

In April 2002, news agencies report one of the largest opium harvests in Afghanistan for a long time. Everywhere on its advance, the Northern Alliance has encouraged farmers to take up poppy cultivation again. According to the BBC, the harvest should cover heroin-lab demand for the next two to three years.[64]

10/15/01
Controlled Demolition

The renowned British journalist Robert Fisk raised doubts in the British newspaper *The Independent* about the authenticity of the instructions allegedly found in the luggage of Mohammed Atta, on the basis that they included formulations and turns of phrase that no Muslim "however ill-taught" would have used. The invocation at the beginning of the text "in the name of God, of myself and of my family" is ludicrously atypical (not to say blasphemous) as no Muslim would include himself or his family after invoking God in a prayer, but would next mention "God the Merciful" or perhaps the Prophet Mohammed. The translation issued by the FBI suggests "an almost Christian view of what the hijackers might have felt," according to Fisk.[65]

I know too little about the Islamic rules for prayer and speech to be the judge, but the article refers to other peculiarities that give much food for thought. And also the *Washington Post's* "Watergate" expert Bob Woodward discovered a number of inconsistencies in this text.[66] They add up to a whole chain of increasing and strange coincidences.

Four weeks have passed since the most gruesome murder in the history of mankind, and the world public is still groping in the dark as to who the masterminds are. Nineteen Arabic sounding names, some of whom were supposedly trained as hobby pilots in Florida and had briefly studied in Hamburg – that's all we get, and this was already given out a few hours after the attack. Since then, apart from the documents belonging to the alleged 9/11 pilot Atta, only a few alleged Saudi bank transfers to his account have emerged. As for the definitive lead to the world-spanning al-Qaeda of the mysterious bin Gaddafi, bin Saddam, bin Laden: Zero Evidence. But plenty enough to start a war – and no one in the Western world any longer even asks for any evidence anyway...

"Atta was so soft" – that is how one of his perplexed fellow students described a perfectly normal, shy, sensitive university colleague, who is supposed to have been the leader of the suicide pilots.[67] If this was him, he was also soft in the head, or he simply wasn't what the CNN version of reality makes him out to be.

He leaves behind Arabic flight documents in a rental car, coincidence number one, as well as a Koran, coincidence number two, and is seen by a witness as he gets out, coincidence number three. Every Muslim, especially one on his final "holy" mission, would take the Koran with him; and no cold-blooded top agent who has been trained for years would leave behind flight documents in an empty rental car, unless he wants to plant evidence. Big coincidence number four, the suicide pilot with a one-way ticket has luggage, not just hand luggage, but a bag that is checked in, and which, super-coincidence number five, is somehow left behind at the airport! This bag then contains the released prayer and instruction script, mega-coincidence number six.

If the suicide pilot as presented by the FBI and CNN intended to leave behind evidence of his "heroic deed," why didn't he simply leave the bag in the airport hall instead of checking it in? If this script contained instructions for the final minutes, why wasn't it in the hand luggage? If it was really penned by the ringleader of al-Qaeda, why does it contain, on the one hand, wholly "un-Arabic" expressions like "100 percent" or "optimistic," while, on the other hand, it also includes the morning prayer, which every Muslim child knows by heart and which has needlessly been cited in full? Could this have something to do with the Islamically uninformed Arabic translators of the CIA, as Robert Fisk suspects? Until now only the translation has been released but not the "original text." It could then perhaps be resolved whether it's a case of mistaken translation or whether we are dealing with a fake, which means the mistakes were already made in the first translation from English into the Arabic "original"…

In connection with the question asked here four weeks ago, why top terrorists booked domestic flights in their real names – giga-coincidence number seven! – these clues with their "manipulated" wording made-up to look Muslim make no real sense – unless the intention is to paint a clear-cut and unquestionable profile of the attackers with circumstantial evidence that convinces even the most simple-minded viewer of early-evening cop shows.

Moreover, the 19 Arabic attacker-names do not appear at all on the passenger lists published by CNN. But this is hardly surprising for the professional paranoids at PsyOpNews. According to the theory on their website, the jets were steered to their destinations by remote-controlled auto-pilots, and the WTC towers were brought down with the help of additional remote-controlled explosions.[68]

Similarly, as in the Oklahoma bombing, whose magnitude cannot be explained on the basis of the explosives deployed by the "lone bomber" McVeigh, according to many experts,[69] a little extra help was also forthcoming in the case of the WTC. At least that's what the PsyOp specialists for psychological warfare think, pointing out that coincidentally it is the same demolition company that has now won the billion-dollar contract for the WTC clean-up (or rather, destruction of evidence) – "Controlled Demolition Inc."

Meanwhile, the controlled demolition of Afghanistan has begun and the public is being mentally prepared for a long-lasting war. What the CIA theoreticians Brzezinski[70] and Huntington[71] prepared as a map exercise is being put into practice on the ground. The new arch-enemy "Islamic terror" has finally raised its ugly snout and provides all the reason needed to seize the geostrategic hot-spot between Europe and Asia – to initiate a "controlled demolition" of a strong Paris-Berlin-Moscow-Beijing axis, forestalling the rise of a rival which in a few decades' time could threaten the sole world power economically and militarily; as well as to delay the collapse of the over-valued dollar, of the over-indebted US economy and thereby the global financial system.

Who cares about a few thousand dead on the home front when it's a question of long-term survival for the empire, of energy reserves for another "American century," a new world order and global currency? The 1941 decision by Henry Stimson and his secret service chiefs to sacrifice 2,000 souls and a few ships in Pearl Harbor to rally the country to war against Hitler – wasn't it justified by the end? Haven't the United States and particularly the Bush family benefited hugely from the arming and financing of Hitler and IG Farben between 1929 and 1941, as well as from the subsequent "controlled demolition" of Europe? Didn't the United States emerge as the sole world power from the Second World War, which really ended only in 1989? Looking back on the 20th Century, is there anything wrong with the covert foreign policy involving those nifty sons of bitches bin Hitler, bin Pinochet, bin Noriega, bin Laden? From the ethical perspective of morality and human rights a whole lot, but from Washington and Wall Street's power perspective – absolutely nothing! That is also why it is possible to imagine that "9/11" was a provoked, observed and permitted kamikaze attack à la Pearl Harbor – more so with every day that the "investigation" becomes more nebulous.

The entire list of suspected individuals is more than questionable after it was discovered that seven of the alleged 19 hijackers were still alive – yet it still hasn't been officially corrected. The fixation on Atta as the "leader of the terror pilots," the astounding speed with which the authorities, who were unsuspecting until 9/11, compiled a list of attackers with dates and backgrounds within 48 hours, the obviously purposely planted evidence like that dubious testament – all this points to a body of evidence fabricated to indict a single crazed perpetrator as the mastermind, like the Kennedy assassination and Oswald or the Oklahoma bombing and McVeigh.

10/20/01
The Money Trail

When seven "poor knights" founded the Templar Order in Jerusalem in the 12th Century, the ostensible motive was to protect the pilgrims making their way to the Holy Land in the wake of the successful crusade. In reality, the pious knights had something more profane in mind.

Thanks to a number of financial innovations, like checks, promissory notes and "interest free" pawnbroking, they were able to circumvent the ban on charging interest espoused by all religions since Moses, Jesus and Mohammed. Within the shortest time, these money-multiplying tricks turned the Templar Order into a multinational financial group, whose influence stretched across all of Europe and the Near East. The Wall Street of the high Middle Ages was in Paris, and the World Trade Center was the castle of the Order of the Templar Knights – until the Holy Inquisition finished them off in 1307 on the orders of the deeply indebted French King. Similarly, as with the return of the Assassins – with whom the Templars always got on well, by the way, just as Wall Street does with Jihad via the CIA – something seems to be repeating itself with the attack on the twin temple of modern high finance and with bin Laden, who is as medieval as it gets, in the role of grand inquisitor. The question is only on whose orders he is acting this time. And, as in the case of the Templars, who later had a multitude of occult myths ascribed to them, the best way to solve the puzzle is to follow the money trail.

We already did suspect that the only truly hard lead to the masterminds of 9/11 – the conspicuously high stock market turnover in put options on airlines and insurers before the attacks, in other words bets on falling share prices – would somehow vanish into thin air. No bank and no business tycoon wants to miss out on the $300 billion pie that is generated by the global annual turnover of the drug trade alone. That's why uncontrolled off-shore banks, tax havens and large-scale money laundering will continue.

Nor will "enduring freedom" seriously rattle this network of financial terror, these redoubts of our modern-day rogue knights. That's why the lockstep conformist media also show little interest in pursuing and investigating strong clues to the money trail; otherwise an informative article in the Sept. 29 *San Francisco Chronicle*[72] would have long since generated worldwide headlines and special bulletins. Above all German headlines, because it identifies one of the banks that ordered large quantities of put options on United Airlines before 9/11 as Alex Brown, which belongs to none other than the honorable Frankfurt financial institution with the two mirrored towers – Deutsche Bank.

The news that Deutsche Bank became the largest bank in Europe with its acquisition of Bankers Trust Alex Brown in 1999 pushed into the background the fact that Alex Brown itself was ranked as one of the top 20 US banks suspected of money laundering. That one of its clients ordered 20 times as many put options as traded on average at the beginning of September could be a "coincidence," of course. The stock market source that provided the *Chronicle* reporters with this information remains unnamed.

Another piece in the jigsaw puzzle makes it clear why investigations along these lines would be worthwhile but are also likely to come to nothing. The chief executive of Alex Brown – and also vice chairman responsible for "private client relations" after the takeover by Bankers Trust in 1997 – was "Buzzy" Krongard: since March 2001 executive director and No. 3 at the CIA.[73] How indiscreet!

The transactions cited in the *Chronicle* report only refer to options contracts executed on the Chicago exchange which generated "betting wins" of $12 to $15 million in the space of a few days. What happened in New York, London, Frankfurt and on other large options markets remains off the screen, now as ever, apart from a few short meaningless news reports in the CNN-CIA version of reality. The same is true for the insider speculator who, according to the Chicago exchange watchdog, has so far failed to cash in United Airlines options with a profit of $2.5 million. Could it be that one of "Buzzy's" colleagues, perhaps busy watching over the terror pilots, quickly placed a private bet with the house bank – and found it too risky to cash in after four days of stock market closures? Or was it bin Laden after all, who smoke-signaled buy orders to his brokers from his Hindu Kush cave, and the messenger on horseback is still on his way to cash in? Whatever – the crucial question is why something like this can be printed in San Francisco's biggest newspaper on Sept. 29, and on Sept. 30 the authorities still haven't found out which banks bought these betting slips for which clients at the beginning of September.

Or, should we imagine it went like this: an upright FBI agent in Chicago or somewhere and his colleagues have already investigated all these financial transactions and handed a thick bundle of papers with the outcome to their boss – and now like a real-life Fox Mulder, our man must look on as further investigation of the clues is suppressed from above? And we hear no more about the only hard lead to the master-minds and accessories of the attack, because these clues would currently threaten the "national security" of the United States? That's probably also why all eight flight recorders of the four airplanes have allegedly been damaged so badly – although they can withstand twice the heat of a kerosene conflagration – that not a shred of data can be retrieved. Sorry.

Just as it is obvious that the money trail won't be pursued any further, so the 19 suspected attackers with Arabic names conjured from a hat, the puzzle of the passenger lists[74] and the other mountains of inconsistencies[75] remain shrouded in mystery.

It was enough to start World War III – and also for money operations on a much wider scope. Since 9/11, the Federal Reserve Bank, also known as "The Temple"– whether *in memoriam* of the holy Templar Knights or because of the oracular sayings of its top priest Alan Greenspan ("If you think you understood what I said, then I obviously did not make myself clear") – is printing around $1 billion a day, devaluing the already overvalued greenback at the turbo speed of a sliding banana currency. A gigantic inflationary wave, "the inflation tsunami,"[76] is rolling towards the United States. When even dramatic scandals like these from the main hall of the temple are not adequately publicized, then it's hardly surprising that the 9/11 financial transactions on the dirty billion-dollar backyard of the banking and financial system are swept under the carpet.

When a bank executive like "Buzzy" Krongard of Alex Brown transfers into a top position with the CIA, it's only natural to ask what qualifies him for this new job. The only answer that really comes to mind is that in his old job he was already handling his new employer's financial affairs. With regard to the United States' gigantic debt load and financial crisis, the public was not yet aware of Enron's imminent bankruptcy, the biggest bust in US economic history so far – but the White House knew very well. Vice President Cheney negotiated with Enron management behind closed doors, but to this day he refuses to publicly release the minutes of the meetings (and thereby his prior knowledge of the impending bankruptcy).

10/26/01
Manus Manum Lavat –
Money Money Laundromat

It's a question of cleaning out two Aegean stables at once – the secret services, and the money and banking system. That's why a chief investigator of 9/11 endowed with real powers would probably end up with a bullet in the head very soon. The things he would discover just on second glance would compromise "national security," be barred from public consumption and kept under lock and key for the next 50 years.

The $500 billion illegally channeled into the US financial system every year, according to a US Senate committee investigation,[77] have to be laundered somehow and somewhere. This is such big business that any attempt to impose comprehensive legislative controls on "private banking" in the fight against terror would be tantamount to revolution. That's why the desperate FBI agent who is trying to find out who exactly placed bets with Alex Brown on falling airline share prices won't find any names or real-life account holders, but instead an almost impenetrable web of conspiracy. Like Russian dolls within dolls, this interconnected system of off-shore banks, correspondent accounts, pooled contingents and discreet numbered deposits is the most sacred aspect of high finance, sovereign and immune. Unwanted side effects like terror or drug problems simply have to be accepted as collateral damage, just like the billions extorted from their countries by corrupt dictators and privately stashed away in the safe haven of Citibank or some other prominent laundry named in the Senate report. Not only the investigations into the pre-9/11 insider speculation with airline shares, but most other investigations into really big criminal fish also get bogged down in this quagmire.

The virtual rogue-knight castles of modern times – regardless of whether they harbor terrorist Assassins, Mafia drugs and arms pushers or corrupt white-collar fraudsters – would be cut off from the outside world if it weren't for the intersection at the point of money laundering. It would be possible to raise the drawbridges, that is to establish internal financial security, by watching all account movements, fingerprinting or recording biometric characteristics of all account holders.It would be perfectly possible to prevent the rogue knights from using their dirty money. Why isn't this happening? It seems there is only one answer to this question: we are not ruled by our elected governments but by these rogue knights. Just now, the *New York Times* reported[78] that a whole group of them, bankers and big industrialists, lobbied President Bush against including planned anti-money laundering laws in the new "anti-terror bill." This would damage "international competitiveness." With clean money bankers generally have to content themselves with a modest profit margin of 5%-10%, but "dirty money" pays 25% per year. Nobody gives up such a cash cow voluntarily.

It is no speculative body of circumstantial evidence, no paranoid conspiratorial thinking, no dubious conspiracy theory but a definite fact that our financial system conceals, facilitates and defends by every means a very real conspiracy code-named "banking secrecy." It is this conspiratorial web of discreet financial transactions that makes large-scale organized crime, corruption and terrorism possible in the first place. To apply real control and discipline to this network for the sake of internal and global security constitutes the big opportunity presented by the 9/11 tragedy. But this requires not so much air supremacy over Afghanistan as supremacy overseeing banks in the Bahamas, Cayman Islands etc., and their honorable correspondent banks in the US and Europe. As this supremacy is not forthcoming, investigators are not making any progress along the money trail.

That leaves only the trails that lead to the alleged perpetrators. From the very start there was the strong suspicion that such a large-scale operation couldn't be prepared and executed without the secret services getting some wind of it. And the available evidence to date, like the Koran that was left behind, the questionable wording of the instruction document and so forth, have only reinforced this suspicion.

And if the *Times of India* report[79] about last week's dismissal of Pakistan's secret service director – on whose orders $100,000 were transferred to none other than the "terror pilot" Atta – is correct, well then we find ourselves right in the middle of a secret service plot that would make even a doyen like John le Carré's hair stand on end.

Money laundering and the off-shore, rogue-knight castles of our financial system are examples of a perfectly open and legal, yet nonetheless criminal, conspiracy. The fact that this insider trading was not pursued makes it clear that this won't change in future either. The Times of India *report, based on FBI sources and telephone conversations tapped by the Indian secret service, seems to be one of the most important puzzle pieces in finding the ringleaders of the attacks – and probably contributed to Bush stopping "in depth investigations" of 9/11 in January.[80]*

According to this report, $100,000 was transferred from two Pakistani banks to accounts in Florida set up by Mohammed Atta. The payments were made on behalf of Ahmad Umar Sheikh, a British national and top agent of the Pakistani secret service director General Ahmed. Although both these figures are prominently involved in this case, they are hardly known to the public. Ahmed, who happened to be in Washington at the time of the attacks, had to resign "very unexpectedly" in mid-October – and Umar Sheikh vanished from the media limelight with lightning speed after being arrested in Pakistan for the abduction and murder of Wall

Street Journal *reporter Daniel Pearl. Why didn't it make headlines in the "war on terrorism" news that the arrested Umar Sheikh was a key figure who was very probably responsible for paying Atta, as well as for murdering a US journalist? Why was this not only no top news but practically no news at all? Could this have anything to do with the* Wall Street Journal *reporter overstepping his official agenda and having shown a little too much interest in the connection between CIA, ISI, heroin, Taliban and terror? That is, precisely those operators and networks that directed the 9/11 attackers and who are supposed to remain concealed under all circumstances – especially through the media's large-scale deployment of the propaganda villain "Osama?"*

What makes a Pakistani agent and terrorist leader like Umar Sheikh and a fired Gestapo honcho like General Ahmed so sacrosanct that hardly a line is written about their machinations? Just a cautious question – might this enforced silence about the terror masterminds mean that the long leash that guides them would become visible – and that it reaches all the way to Langley, Virginia, into the CIA headquarters? If the reports about the payments to Atta, which were also disseminated by AFP and ABC News, were "red herrings," false leads, then why weren't they formally denied? Did Bush and Cheney try to prevent all deeper investigations[81] because there was nothing to deny, or because a sliver of "truth" was threatening to come to light?

Meanwhile, the "Terrorism Information and Prevention System" (TIPS) has been launched in the US, under which millions of citizens are now being recruited as informers. I would volunteer without further ado to draw attention to the suspicious activities of the US government in connection with the top ISI agent Umar Sheikh, who has now been sentenced to death for the murder of Wall Street Journal *reporter Daniel Pearl. He's that shady character who is said to have transferred $100,000 to Mohammed Atta in Florida on behalf of the ISI – something the German newspaper* Frankfurter Allgemeine Zeitung *gave only a cursory mention of in its July 16, 2002, article about his conviction.*

Yet looking at this in the right light, it's clear, that this is the hardest, most direct lead to the masterminds and ringleaders of 9/11. The British press, usually praiseworthy in comparison with Germany and the US, reported extensively on the 13-day secret trial against British subject Umar Sheikh, yet fails to mention this more-than-spicy detail altogether. Even the usually so reliable Robert Fisk surmises in The Independent *that Pakistan is afraid to extradite Sheikh to the United States out of fear that he will talk about the link between the ISI and al-Qaeda. Of course, the FBI already knows all about this from Atta's bank statements. Turn it around, however, and things start to fit like a glove. It's better to have Sheikh executed after a secret trial in Pakistan so the connection between ISI, al-Qaeda and the CIA doesn't becomes public in the US.*

10/31/01
Beyond Bush and Evil

"The opposite of a great truth may well be another great truth," Nils Bohr, the quantum physicist, once said about the observation paradox of particles and waves. This art of finding non-dualistic truth should also be applied in the case of 9/11. Civilization vs. barbarism, "freedom" vs. "terror," crusade vs. Jihad, new World Order vs. theocracy, oil business vs. Kyoto Protocol, CIA vs. al-Qaeda, pampered millionaire oil heir vs. pampered millionaire oil heir – not just one but all these bipolar areas of influence play a part in the current upheavals. Their exact contribution is difficult to assess in the fog of war and in times of news blackouts and psychological warfare, but patterns, structures and parallels are at least discernible.

Around 70 BC, an ambitious Roman senator, Marcus Licinius Crassus, decided to take over the government. Crassus is credited with inventing the fire brigade, and owed his fortune as Rome's largest private land-owner to his particular interpretation of this profession. He would rush to the scene of a burning building with his brigades and offer to buy the building on the spot for a fraction of its value. If the owner agreed, the fire was put out, but if he refused to sell, the fire-fighting slaves were withdrawn. In a similarly gallant fashion Crassus proceeded to soften up the highly restricted powers of the republican senate, but to this end he needed a suitable arsonist.

The slave revolts had just been put down and their leader Spartacus and his men had hired a mercenary fleet to sail away into freedom. Crassus bribed the fleet so it would sail away without Spartacus. He then positioned two Roman legions in such a way that Spartacus was forced to retreat towards Rome. When news broke that the much-feared gladiators were marching on Rome again and terror threatened, Crassus was immediately appointed praetor, had Spartacus and his troops annihilated, and nothing stood in the way of his election as consul. This marked the end of the Roman republic. After a transitional triumvirate, Rome was henceforth governed by god-like emperors endowed with dictatorial powers. By the grace of the real-estate king Crassus, Julius Caesar was the first to be installed.

It's one of the oldest tricks in the book, dating back to Roman times: creating the enemies you need.

Michael Rivero, "Dictatorship through Deception,"
http://www.eionews.addr.com/psyops/news/dictatorship_thru_deception.htm

Both the film *Wag the Dog* and this ancient history seem to fit the modern American empire. There is the end of the Communist "slave revolts," an enemy on the verge of disappearing. The ambitious senator has cheated his way into the presidential office with the help of his wealthy family, and now urgently needs to shake off the perception that he bought his election. There are the father's business ties with Islamic billionaires – according to the *Wall Street Journal*, Bush Sr. and other former members of his cabinet have close business ties via the Carlyle Group with the bin Laden clan and their "gladiators," who once fought under the empire's banner but now hate it because the "Romans" have occupied Saudi Arabia. If these fighters could now be persuaded to attack "Rome" and instill terror and fear in its citizens, if the inexperienced son could then defeat them once and for all in a major battle, then this would not only strengthen his profile as president, but above all it would mean an immense increase of domestic political control and power. And business. And the end of the republic?

Business Partners

The *Wall Street Journal* reported in September that the former president, the father of President Bush, worked for the bin Laden family business in Saudi Arabia through the Carlyle Group. The senior Bush had met with the bin Laden family at least twice. (Other top Republicans are also associated with the Carlyle group, such as former Secretary of State James A. Baker.) The terrorist leader Osama bin Laden had supposedly been "disowned" by his family, which runs a multi-billion dollar business in Saudi Arabia and was a major investor in the senior Bush's firm. Other reports have questioned whether members of his Saudi family have truly cut off Osama bin Laden. Osama's sister-in-law, in a recent interview with ABC News, said that she believed that members of her family still supported bin Laden.

Judicial Watch, 11/27/01, www.judicialwatch.org/archive/2001/1082.shtml

Until last year, Vice President Cheney was chief executive and main shareholder of the Halliburton group (oil wells, pipeline construction), which worked on the billion-dollar contract to build the planned pipeline through Afghanistan.[82] Brown & Root is a unit of Halliburton – if a novel were written about the brown roots of the Bush clan any editor would criticize the name for laying it on too thick! – and is the biggest supplier of construction and troop support services to the US military (Motto: "Where cannons shoot, call Brown & Root"). When drug investigator Michael Ruppert stumbled across a covert CIA operation in the late 1970's – cocaine was being transported onto oil rigs and thence onto freighters – the ships that caught his attention belonged to Brown & Root. When he insisted on investigating the case further he lost his job. Since then, the incorruptible, patriotic sheriff has remained hot on the trail of the secret services' drug deals.[83] If only 10% of his carefully documented evidence about the CIA's machinations (and also the Bush clan's drug connections) is accurate,[84] then Bush Jr. had good reasons indeed to deflect attention from the scandals brewing around him with "Wag the Dog 2."

Does George W. Bush think (or rather his father for him) along the same lines as Marcus L. Crassus? If we put on the "imperial" glasses, the pattern seems to be pretty much identical, especially when looking at the crucial question of who in the world actually benefited from the attack. Apart from Dubya, who has mutated overnight from electoral thief into global statesman, and the secret services, which have been rewarded with an increased budget, I see absolutely nobody on the winning side so far.

But a strong motive doesn't necessarily show guilt. Even though this basic presumption of innocence was repealed in the case of Osama bin Laden, as a counter move it would be wrong to demonize the sinister Bush clan as the source of all evil. The mistake made in most conspiracy theories is to overestimate the linear influence exerted by the actors and to underestimate the dynamic complexity of the processes (as well as the power of Murphy's Law and the ubiquity of stupidity).

Even if Crassus was a scheming politico-businessman who unscrupulously expanded his power on the basis of "prepare the solution, then create the problem," and even if the Bush clan's oil men sometimes emulate Crassus by deploying their Gulf War fire brigade with their business partners in Iraq and Kuwait, they are not the only factors influencing these developments. Hitler financier Fritz Thyssen and his US financial administrator, grandfather Bush, are not the only ones to blame for the terror created by Hitler and his 300,000-strong private army from 1930 onward, which then allowed Hitler to play the role of savior and take power after the highly symbolic, 9/11-like shock of the

Reichstag Fire. Nevertheless, such lines of power, wheels discreetly turned by crucial people at crucial moments, are of great importance for the evaluation of historical processes. NOT to think of conspiracies is just as naïve as ascribing EVERYTHING to a conspiracy.

A few links in the strange chain of coincidences compiled after the attack have been explained since – for some years now you have to identify yourself even on US domestic flights, which is why Atta & Co. reserved flights under their real names; one flight recorder from the Pennsylvania crash has been found, so not all eight recorders are missing or blank. But then so many more odd things have emerged, like the latest news about the financing of Atta by the Pakistani secret service, which makes it practically irresponsible to accept the mainstream version of reality when after six weeks and the biggest manhunt of all times, there is little more evidence or clues on the attackers than six hours after the attack. Yet in geopolitical terms there have been greater shifts in these six weeks than in the entire preceding decade. Miraculous wonders of transformation – in a 70-minute conversation on Sept. 23 Bush and Putin simply rearranged the world coordinates, says a report on the Israeli intelligence website Debka files.[85] Overnight on CNN the Chechen "freedom fighters" transmuted into "terrorists with clear links to Osama bin Laden." On Sept. 28, President Bush called on the Chechen rebels to "break their links with bin Laden."[86]

I do believe apparitions of the Virgin Mary are possible (at least on good-weather days), and occasionally sudden enlightenment may transform a person from Saul into Paul – but a whole army?

Those who ask themselves, dazed by such great miracles, whether something isn't quite right in their head or with reality can rest assured – the head is alright! Beyond Bush and evil an abyss beckons.

The Axis of Good

Bush and Putin in Nuclear Tit-for-Tat Accord

Perhaps the most earthshaking outcome of the epic 70-minute conversation between Presidents George W. Bush and Vladimir Putin last week was the nuclear understanding they reached in a flash, as part of a new US-Russian political and military pact to fight international terrorism together.

Their conversation also covered a possibly over-optimistic shared vision of a post-war Afghanistan and a post-Saddam Iraq. Afghanistan under a restored monarchy was assigned a special geopolitical role in the regions of Southwest and Central Asia.

Russian and American officials have made no disclosures on the nuclear accord, but DEBKA-Net-Weekly's military and intelligence sources report that Putin gave the nod to Bush to arm the US forces now arriving in Central Asia with tactical nuclear weapons, such as small neutron bombs, which emit strong radiation, nuclear mines, shells, and other nuclear ammunition suited to commando warfare in mountainous terrain.

Debka-Net-Weekly, *5.10.2001, http://www.debka.com/article.php?aid=111*

Six months after the attack, no further evidence has emerged. Meanwhile, for me there can be hardly any doubt that the Bush Administration used the attacks on the World Trade Center and the Pentagon as a beacon, in the same way the newly elected NSDAP government used the Reichstag Fire. The United States' global politics of force, euphemistically described as "unilateralism," the refusal to accept international courts, the ignorance regarding environmental destruction (Kyoto Protocol) and the "double standard" applied to justice (military tribunals for foreigners), all have little to do with the old American values – freedom, tolerance and "pursuit of happiness," but they have everything to do with a new American imperialism in foreign policy and a police state in domestic policy.

11/02/01
A Long-planned War

Conspiracy theories are always "spaghetti theories," according to Robert A. Wilson. No matter which strand you pull out you get your fingers dirty. But McMedia's menu on the background to 9/11 always offers the same bare bones. So we'll have to continue reaching into the spaghetti pot – today *al'olio.*

US oil companies want to build a pipeline from the Caspian Sea to Pakistan. The route through Afghanistan is made uncertain by the government in power, so the Taliban are removed in a war that is supposedly waged against terror but is actually being fought in the interests of oil. So far, so logical. If we continue to look through the oil glasses, we discover very quickly that the last boss of Halliburton, which wants the multi-billion-dollar job of building and maintaining the pipeline and has put out a project assessment, happened to become vice president and is called Dick Cheney.

The oil barons' Caspian "pipedreams"[87] weren't dreamt up just the other night. When the Taliban regime was installed by Pakistan and the

CIA, the "students of Islam" had already been chosen as the guardians of the pipeline, and negotiated the matter with the Americans at the highest levels. It was only after human rights organizations and American environmentalists massively warned the Clinton Administration about Afghanistan's terror politics of repressing women's rights that the oil cronies of United Oil of California – Unocal is actually based in Texas – felt compelled to break off their negotiations with the Taliban. In 1998, the pipeline plans were officially shelved. Unofficially, however, it had already been decided that this situation wasn't acceptable and that an alliance with India and Russia would be sought to exert military pressure on the Taliban, according to the specialist defense publication *Jane's Security*.[88] In other words, the invasion launched at the end of September 2001 was planned for years!

But then, would the US citizenry agree to a war for no other purpose than promoting the president and vice president's private oil businesses? Of course, a "war on terror" is a completely different matter. Those who don't support it and point to those ignoble business interests are almost automatically labeled as unpatriotic scum.

We already suspected a few weeks ago that the investigations into 9/11 would soon throw up "clues" leading to Iraq, because for many decades the imperative of US foreign policy has been cheap oil. And what do you know – terror pilot Atta supposedly met several times with an Iraqi embassy official in Prague, and it's possible, according to the Czech secret service, that anthrax was passed on during these meetings.[89] Is it a coincidence that this "lead" emerges now and that it's widely reported, while the really sensational discovery by the *Times of India* that Atta received money from the Pakistani secret service – which means he acted on the orders of the closest of US allies – finds no echo at all?

Will it be established "beyond any doubt" that a letter was laced with anthrax from the strain once sold by the USA to that nifty "son of a bitch" Saddam? By the way, he should well remember poisoned letters. In the early 1960's, then Colonel Saddam Hussein was involved in an American plot to eliminate the "Soviet-friendly" leader General Kassem. While the CIA supplied Saddam's Baath Party with the addresses of "Communists," who were then eliminated by death squads, the leading CIA chemist Sydney Gottlieb – the infamous director of the "mind control program" or drug and brainwashing project MK ULTRA[90] – had a spore-contaminated handkerchief sent to the general's home. It didn't work, and Kassem had to be shot dead during the coup that followed.[91]

In the days after 9/11, I wondered why there was so much chatter in the media about possible follow-up attacks with biological agents like anthrax. The panic that was being created struck me as a self-fulfilling prophecy once the first cases emerged two weeks later. Was it meant to encourage a few loony sympathizers and members of extreme right-wing militias, who had carried out similar attacks with anthrax in the past?

Or was the anthrax hysteria a psychological operation to divert attention from the authorities' abject failure to prevent or explain the 9/11 attacks, and to create a climate of fear to push through surveillance and "Homeland Security" laws, while also preparing the ground for the next enemy in the great geopolitical game? If in the near future Baghdad comes into the firing line over anthrax,[92] we can safely assume that the mysterious anthrax letters were not sent by al-Qaeda but are greetings from the CIA's poison labs.

Blessed are the Peacemakers

When he announced the air strikes, President George Bush said: "We're a peaceful nation." America's favorite ambassador, Tony Blair (who also holds the portfolio of prime minister of the UK), echoed him: "We're a peaceful people."

So now we know. Pigs are horses. Girls are boys. War is peace.

Speaking at the FBI headquarters a few days later, President Bush said: "This is our calling. This is the calling of the United States of America. The most free nation in the world. A nation built on fundamental values that reject hate, reject violence, rejects murderers and rejects evil. We will not tire."

Here is a list of the countries that America has been at war with – and bombed – since the second world war: China (1945-46, 1950-53), Korea (1950-53), Guatemala (1954, 1967-69), Indonesia (1958), Cuba (1959-60), the Belgian Congo (1964), Peru (1965), Laos (1964-73), Vietnam (1961-73), Cambodia (1969-70), Grenada (1983), Libya (1986), El Salvador (1980s), Nicaragua (1980s), Panama (1989), Iraq (1991-99), Bosnia (1995), Sudan (1998), Yugoslavia (1999). And now Afghanistan.

Certainly it does not tire – this, the most free nation in the world.

http://www.guardian.co.uk/Archive/Article/0,4273,4283081,00.html

It becomes clearer by the day that the bombardment of Afghanistan is not a police operation aimed at seizing terrorists. To extend the war to Iraq in the present circumstances would, however, lead to an immediate break-up of the already fragile "anti-terror alliance." Only after a further atrocity or attack on a high-level statesman would the mood change. This needs to happen soon. The US public isn't going to spend another three weeks watching the mindless bombing of Afghan huts without complaint, and the "alliance" may need to be welded together, not in the US but in Europe. Should a further atrocity throw up "evidence" of Iraqi involvement, then it would be high time to take aim at a certain "terrorist haven" or at least put it under the strictest observation – namely the Central Intelligence Agency headquarters in Langley, just outside Washington.

In the following brilliant comment in the British newspaper *The Guardian*, Indian writer Arundhati Roy spares no criticism of the CIA and its inglorious Pakistani partner, the ISI. Giving her a friendly mention nearly cost German TV news presenter and writer Ulrich Wickert his job. She also doesn't forget to mention the Carlyle Group, one of the largest US investment groups in the defense industry, which incorporates the Bush and bin Laden families and a number of other leading lights in the US administration, who can all expect a special windfall from the war in Afghanistan. Roy suspects this is also the reason why Bush has reneged the last few weeks on his promise, "When I take action, I'm not going to fire a $2m missile at a $10 empty tent and hit a camel in the butt."[93]

President Bush should know that there are no targets in Afghanistan that will give his missiles their money's worth.

Perhaps, if only to balance his books, he should develop some cheaper missiles to use on cheaper targets and cheaper lives in the poor countries of the world. But then, that may not make good business sense to the coalition's weapons manufacturers. It wouldn't make any sense at all, for example, to the Carlyle Group – described by the Industry Standard as "the world's largest private equity firm," with $13bn under management.

Carlyle invests in the defense sector and makes its money from military conflicts and weapons spending.

Carlyle is run by men with impeccable credentials. Former US defense secretary Frank Carlucci is Carlyle's chairman and managing director (he was a college roommate of Donald Rumsfeld's). Carlyle's other partners include former US secretary of state James A Baker III, George Soros and Fred Malek (George Bush Sr.'s campaign manager). An American paper – the Baltimore Chronicle and Sentinel – says that former president George Bush Sr. is reported to be seeking investments for the Carlyle Group from Asian markets.

He is reportedly paid not inconsiderable sums of money to make "presentations" to potential government-clients.

Ho hum. As the tired saying goes, it's all in the family
– Arundhati Roy,
http://www.guardian.co.uk/Archive/Article/0,4273,4283081,00.html

It is remarkable how *SpiegelOnline*, which has taken up Roy's *Guardian* article, has cleansed the above section for German readers.

> "President Bush should know that there are no targets in Afghanistan that will give his missiles their money's worth. Perhaps, if only to balance his books, he should develop some cheaper missiles to use on cheaper targets and cheaper lives in the poor countries of the world. But then, that may not make good business sense to the coalition's weapons manufacturers."[94]

That's it. The crucial passage about who rakes in the business – Bush Sr. and his old clique, precisely what the overpaid *Spiegel* journalists should be investigating further and in greater detail – has simply been excised. Why? It couldn't have been a problem of space, nor a coincidence. It must have to do with the fact that the full story could demoralize German troops' solidarity with Bush's colonial war. And in this case, *Der Spiegel's* narrow-minded people's guardians prefer to err on the side of preventative censure…

Until now, on the important question of "cui bono?" we have only listed Bush Jr. and the American secret services on the winning side. They benefited from the tragedy with an enormously improved image and budget. The arms industry and friendly family businesses like Carlyle can now also be named as direct beneficiaries. Aside from them, the insane bombardments are of no use to anyone in the world.

Orient expert: Doubts about the course of events on 9/11
The director of the German Orient Institute, Udo Steinbach, gave an interesting interview to *Spiegel Online* (02/26/02). For the first time, a renowned expert on the Orient outlined the massive doubts that 9/11 was really carried out by Muslims. Steinbach said: "The more the US unilaterally singles out new enemies in the region – Iran, Iraq, Somalia, Yemen – the greater the impression that America isn't out to fight terror, but instead is pursuing a policy that serves its oil interests. That convinces people in the region even more that the Afghanistan campaign was part of a policy to defend American interests. There is deep mistrust in the region with regard to everything connected to 9/11. Those who doubt that 9/11 was instigated by Muslims aren't few in number." So far, so interesting. Much more interesting, however, is how *Spiegel Online* immediately slams on the brakes until the tires screech. *Spiegel Online*: "These conspiracy theories are absurd." Steinbach: "Of course." But yes. Why so scared of your own thoughts…
"Zweifel am Tathergang vom 11. September," http://www.gerhard-wisnewski.de

Meanwhile even the conservative British *Mirror*[95] runs the headline "This War is a Fraud" for an incendiary report by its chief correspondent John Pilger. Among other things, he draws attention to the fact that Saudi Arabia, the biggest supporter of Jihad, is also the biggest buyer of British-made weapons, and that it's not about capturing terrorists, none of whom were from Afghanistan, it's about conquering another "oil colony."

The mood on the ideological home front is souring. To keep the people in fear and their hearts in the "war against terror," a new psychological stimulus will be needed soon. If this war has been planned for so long, surely it cannot fail now because of a lack of terrorist attacks.

Our speculation that the anthrax letters were a psychological operation with a CIA background rather than an Islamist attack was confirmed shortly thereafter.[96] *The authorities' continuous warnings about further attacks (on bridges, power stations, etc.) created a climate which allowed the Bush Administration to implement an unparalleled domestic and foreign political "security" program.*

That Der Spiegel *preferred to ignore the financial background to the "war on terrorism" and the Bush clan's business dealings with Carlyle and other companies is hardly surprising. Otherwise attention could be drawn to the past of this frightfully nice family – and to the fact that grandfather, father and grandson Bush have always nurtured close ties with "nifty sons of bitches" and other dictators when it suited their business interests.*

11/04/01
Osama meets the CIA!

One argument often cited by critics of conspiratorial thinking is that in major conspiracies involving many actors, as for example the Kennedy assassination, it would be impossible to keep the lid on all the witnesses and evidence over years and decades, so that simply because of this implausibility, conspiracies of this sort rarely hold water. At first glance, this seems to make sense, but on second glance it's also quite naïve, because only the dumbest conspirators would let all those involved in on the whole plan. Generally, even the most minor sub-department of the Mafia operates according to the "need-to-know" principle – the little individual, cell or cog only knows what it needs to know and little or nothing about the scheme as a whole. If one or the other hireling gets busted, the heads of the conspiracy remain unshorn.

In terms of 9/11, a conspiracy on such a large scale could not remain completely under wraps in the long run, regardless of whether it was carried out by a secret organization like al-Qaeda, or by one like the CIA, by both of them together or by some completely different group. One or the other of these small cogs will emerge, will be unmasked, will come to the light of day – but that's still a far cry from uncovering the overall structure, especially because efforts will be made to cover up, disguise and deceive.

A potential small cog in this strange case is currently in jail in Canada. And his story, reported in the daily *Toronto Star*,[97] is so crazy that it could hardly be invented. The 35-year-old American Delmart E. Vreeland was arrested in Toronto a few months ago on charges of credit card fraud. He had committed similar crimes previously in California and Florida, so the US asked for his extradition. After his arrest, Vreeland claimed to be working for US Navy intelligence and to have been involved in covert operations. He demanded to speak to members of the Canadian secret service to make a statement, claiming he had information about a big impending terrorist attack. No one believed him, especially because inquiries with the Navy showed he had been "dishonorably" dismissed in 1986 after two years of service.

Vreeland claimed to the contrary that since 1986 he had organized drug smuggling and then other covert activities on behalf of the Navy. Given that he was classed as a common criminal and was no longer listened to, he compiled a written statement four weeks before 9/11 containing his information and handed it to the prison wardens in a sealed envelope to be added to his file. On Sept. 14, the prison administration opened the statement and immediately passed it on to government authorities in Ottawa. So far, the contents of the statement have not been disclosed at Vreeland's trial. His lawyers are fighting his extradition on the basis that their client would supposedly face the death penalty in the United States. The case remains interesting because not even George W. Bush would have somebody executed for credit card fraud.

It's possible to imagine that a small cog involved somewhere on the margins of events digs around a little bit, adds up the numbers, fills in the gaps with a pinch of imagination and informs the authorities of a large-scale conspiracy in an attempt to save his skin. It's also not atypical that a wannabe James Bond and ex-colleague who has strayed into a demi-monde existence – Vreeland allegedly used uncovered checks to buy a yacht and van-loads of the best champagne – still carries out the occasional shady job for the "firm." The question is, what will happen if Vreeland's ominous statement really does contain information about the attacks?

But while I'm still pondering the supporting role played by minor shady agents, the Parisian daily *Le Figaro* has dropped a real bombshell which goes far beyond the dubious roles of marginal actors. The regional CIA representative in Dubai made a special "field hospital visit" to the local American Hospital to see the current No. 1 world enemy Osama bin Laden, who is said to have been admitted there July 4-14, 2001.

> While he was hospitalised, bin Laden received visits from many members of his family as well as prominent Saudis and Emiratis. During the hospital stay, the local CIA agent, known to many in Dubai, was seen taking the main elevator of the hospital to go to bin Laden's hospital room. A few days later, the CIA man bragged to a few friends about having visited bin Laden. Authorised sources say that on July 15th, the day after bin Laden returned to Quetta, the CIA agent was called back to headquarters.[98]

Surely, from a journalist's point of view it would be tempting to give this guy from the branch office of the "firm" in Dubai a good grilling on the exact details of his friendly chat with the top terrorist urology patient eight weeks before 9/11. So what do you bring along on a hospital visit to such a prominent millionaire evildoer who already has everything? Surely not a handful of box cutters, a little vial of anthrax maybe – with friendly greetings from the chemical lab – a kilo of coke to freshen up worn-out holy warriors, the Carlyle Group's latest annual report – with greetings from the entire Bush family to the whole bin Laden family?

Or the codes the hijackers will need to outsmart air traffic control and lead direct telephone conversations with "Air Force One"[99] (Bush supposedly received a "threatening phone call" on the plane shortly after the attack)?[100] What a pity such an interview can not be, for reasons of "national security." The question why Osama could wing his way over the water from Dubai to Pakistan on July 14 in his private jet, unchecked by the US Air Force and vanish into his cave must remain unanswered for the same reason. This all provides one more reason why Langley, the sleeper hideout of the CIA headquarters, should not only be receiving more attention, but also draw some real investigative fire.

Based on such links and on historical parallels, the conspiratorial axis of influence "CIA-ISI-Osama-Taliban" that we have been airing for the past four weeks now leaves the realm of conjecture and suspicion and enters that of plain facts. A detailed Web article by Michel Chossudovsky provided a well documented account[101] on Nov. 2: "Cover-up or Complicity of the Bush Administration? The Role of Pakistan's Military Intelligence Agency (ISI) in the September 11 attacks." Where was Lieutenant-General Mahmud Ahmed on 9/11, the ISI director who has resigned after his money transfer to Atta became public? In the US. And what was he doing there? Holding talks with top officials from the Pentagon and the Foreign Relations Committee. And about what? About the post-war order.

Of course, the Figaro *report was immediately denied by the CIA. Bin Laden later also denied his stay in Dubai in an interview with a Pakistani newspaper. But George Bush's reaction to the report that was making the rounds worldwide was telling. In an address to the UN on Nov. 15 he proclaimed his ban on "outrageous conspiracy theories," as quoted on the first page of this book.*

The suspicion that ex-comrade-in-arms Osama bin Laden continued to be a current geopolitical tool of US foreign policy could not be dispelled in the following weeks and months.

The aforementioned Web article by Michel Chossudovsky can now be read as a chapter in his America's War on Terrorism.[102]

11/13/01
If the CIA wasn't Involved,
What in the World *was* it Doing?

One of the dangers of conspiratorial thinking is to overestimate the causality of the conspirators' direct and all-encompassing influence and of the linear process of cause-and-effect chains. We know from quantum physics and chaos research that effects without cause exist and that a tiny "disturbance" from the seemingly insignificant flapping of a butterfly's wings can ultimately lead to a dramatic effect. In open systems – in reality, in life and also in the undercover world – things are not so linear, but much more chaotic and fuzzy than criminalistic logic would like.

When I saw the second plane crash into the tower my first thought was: "Whoever did this must have been terribly hurt." This act of violence went far beyond the usual escalation of aggression as found on the playground, in working-world rivalries, on the battlefield and in war zones. This wasn't just an unloved, frightened and angry child that trampled another child's pretty sandcastle. The aggression vented here blew the entire sandbox to smithereens. At some point, the investigation into the background to the attack should turn up this deeply hurt and immensely disappointed "child." It's difficult, however, to imagine this bundle of emotions as an activist planning a callous, cold-blooded conspiracy.

When we ask ourselves which of the children reared by "Uncle Sam" has been disappointed so much that it would want to inflict such an atrocity on its superdad, we recall the roughly 100,000 men who have been channeled through the brainwash and guerrilla camps in Pakistan since the start of the 1980's to fight in the holy war against Communism (see "10/06/01: Jihad Inc. – Made in the USA").

A revealing interview that General Hameed Gul, former director general of the Pakistani secret service ISI, gave to the news agency UPI at the end of September shows just how shamefully let down they felt once the Soviets had withdrawn from Afghanistan. Gul, for decades a close ally of the CIA and also a secret leader of the Mujahideen and Osama bin Laden, is well acquainted with both sides of the current divide. "As ISI director, I held the whole Mujahideen movement in the palm of my hands. We were all pro-American. But then America left us in the lurch and everything went to pieces, including Afghanistan." For the general, only Israel's Mossad could have been the culprit of 9/11.

Jews never agreed to Bush 41 (George H.W. Bush, the 41st president) or 43 (his son George W. Bush, the 43rd president). They made sure Bush senior didn't get a second term. His land-for-peace pressure in Palestine didn't suit Israel. They were also against the young Bush because he was considered too close to oil interests and the Gulf countries. Bush senior and Jim Baker had raised $150 million for Bush junior, much of it from Mideast sources or their American go-betweens. Bush 41 and Baker, as private citizens, had also facilitated the new strategic relationship between Saudi Arabia and Iran. I have this from sources in both countries. So clearly the prospect of a Bush 43 was a potential danger to Israel.

Jews were stunned by the way Bush stole the election in Florida. They had put big money on Al Gore.

Israel has now handed the Bush family the opportunity it has been waiting for to consolidate America's imperial grip on the Gulf and acquire control of the Caspian basin by extending its military presence in Central Asia.

The destabilization of Pakistan is part of the US plan because it is a Muslim nuclear state. The US wants to isolate Pakistan from China as part of its containment policy. President Nixon's book *The Real War* said China would be the superpower of the 21st Century. The US is also creating hostility between Pakistan and Afghanistan, two Muslim states, to reverse the perception that the Islamic world now has its own nuclear weapons. Bush 43 doesn't realize he is being manipulated by people who understand geopolitics. He is not leading but being led. All he can do is think in terms of the wanted-dead-or-alive culture, which is how Hollywood conditions the masses to think and act.

Bush 43 follows Bush 41. Iraq was baited into the Kuwaiti trap when the US told Saddam it was not interested in his inter-Arab squabbles. Two days later, he moved into Kuwait, which was an Iraqi province anyway before the British Empire decreed otherwise. Roosevelt baited the Pearl Harbor trap for the Japanese empire, which provided the pretext for entering World War II. And now the Israelis have given the US the pretext for further expansion into an area that will be critical in the next 25 years – the Caspian basin.[103]

That is the conspiracy theory according to General Gul, whose reputation as an anti-democrat, a Jihad hardliner and an ex-director of a heroin-peddling, Gestapo-like secret service wouldn't really qualify him as an objective source. On the other hand, as a top insider and expert on the filthy business he is basically no less credible than let's say an ex-CIA director. Gul doesn't produce any more tangible evidence for his Mossad speculation than the West can for its al-Qaeda conspiracy.

He finds the idea that his old acquaintance bin Laden is supposed to have directed this operation by remote control from his cave totally absurd. Of course, he deliberately leaves us in the dark as to how Mossad is supposed to have organized this rogue act – let's recall that Gul's ISI successor Ahmed supposedly transferred Atta the funds for his operation. Just as the CIA and FBI diverted attention from their apparent inaction by yelling "bin Laden!" 10 minutes after the attack, Gul is deflecting from the sloppiness and roguery of his own secret service by pointing the finger at "Mossad!" Yet the geopolitical motives and strategies he puts forward cannot be simply dismissed out of hand, either.

On the other hand, as Seymour Hersh, one of the best-informed US foreign-affairs journalists, wrote in the *New Yorker* magazine,[104] that the Pentagon, the CIA, Israel and India are currently planning the destruction of Pakistan's nuclear arsenal. Of course, Pakistan can't possibly have any interest in such a destabilization – and yet, the CIA-ISI-Osama-Taliban axis of influence is obvious. How does this all fit together?

As long as we use terms like "axis of influence" and linear cause-and-effect chains like "CIA-ISI-Osama-Taliban" without quotation marks, the causality trap mentioned at the beginning is a danger, because within the CIA, the ISI, and the Taliban factions could form which pursue different strategies. And perhaps there are even further axes of influence that become active themselves or instrumentalize one or the other of these factions for their own purposes. In terms of General Gul's Mossad theory, this means the Israeli secret service had to infiltrate the ISI and instrumentalize Atta & Co. for the operation. This theory may be perfectly plausible in the Islamic world where Mossad is already the No. 1 scapegoat, but in the West it sounds highly improbable.

Unlike CNN, which spouts pure propaganda, BBC-World still practices what in times of peace is called "journalism," and in recent weeks it has repeatedly pointed out the potential for conspiracy in Afghanistan. For a hundred bucks or even just one goat, fighters there are prepared to fight for the Taliban today, for the Northern Alliance tomorrow and the day after tomorrow for an autonomous Pashtun clan.

"They change sides so often that it becomes difficult to distinguish any real difference between Northern Alliance and Taliban," according to its lead reporter.[105] At least, in visual terms they will become easier to distinguish in future. Northern Alliance members have been fitted out with brand-new American combat uniforms. As the labels with the country of origin have been removed, according to the BBC, the uniforms are ideal for bartering with the Taliban, of course. So the "bad guys" will soon be appearing in the uniforms of the "good guys."

Where this kind of chaos reigns at the base among the Pashtuns in the field in Afghanistan, is it safe to ascribe clear structures and solid loyalties to the administrative and executive levels in Islamabad? It seems that the Pakistani ISI supported the Taliban and bin Laden while also stage-managing the murder of Northern Alliance leader Ahmed Shah Massoud.[106] That the CIA not only maintained contact with its former mercenary leader bin Laden but was even "pro-Taliban" until recently seems just as apparent. But what calculations could drive these services, or factions, to carry out the 9/11 attack?

Naturally, President Bush and the CIA benefited from the attack; naturally, Israel also has an interest in drawing the US into a war on Iraq and the Arab world; naturally, Unocal, Halliburton and "Wall Street" want to build a pipeline through Afghanistan; naturally, bin Laden hates the US-backed feudal regime in his home country – if it were not for

American support of the monarchy, the billionaire's son might have as good a chance to be president of Arabia as his adversary Bush had in the US. Yet, are we really supposed to imagine that one of these factions, each of which has a first-class motive for the attack, called on Mr. Atta in the spring, commissioning him for the 9/11 job?

Maybe I'm still too much of a nice person, but I find it difficult to believe that Mr. Bush or Mr. Bin Laden or any of the others named above are capable of such premeditated evil. It seems to me that from a psychological point of view the emotional escalation, the immeasurable anger, the disappointed child is missing here. There does seem to be some measure of disappointment on the part of General Gul, the former chief of ISI, secret superchief of all Mujahideen, bin Ladens and heroin factories and best friend of America, who was replaced during the Bush Sr. and Nawaz Sharif administrations."[107] And he is surely not the only former godfather who still has professional terror contacts.

So it's still possible to conceive of the 9/11 escalation as a pure act of revenge by disappointed ex-generals, operating outside of any official CIA-ISI-bin Laden axes of influence but with the latter's professional means. Cooked up by old foxes, humbled men of power, fundamentalist machos with no regard for the losses – and carried out by people belonging to that troop of "Jihad" robots that were once bred by the CIA and left to their own devices in the 1990's. In a way, the attack could then be described as fallout from the Cold War, that era when all means were justified in the holy war against "Communism," even terror and drug trafficking on a large scale, requiring the services of nifty sons of bitches like General Gul, who can't just be left out in the cold afterwards with their marauding terror fighters.

Indeed, even if such unofficial Dr. Strangeloves like a resentful secret service chief are the actual cause and the preparations went through his old channels, they still couldn't have remained concealed either from the Pakistani ISI nor from his mentor the CIA. The timeline of CIA foreknowledge that the researcher Mike Ruppert compiled on his website[108] leads to one inevitable question about the US secret services: if they weren't involved themselves, then what were they doing instead?

The question what the secret services with their $30 billion budget actually did to prevent this attack cannot be asked too loudly because it would "compromise the internal security of the United States." Equally, there is no need to fear that the Congressional inquiries will dredge up anything from the shady world of covert investigations, secret agents and *operations. The CIA budget was increased further after the attacks, but no official took personal responsibility, and everyone kept their jobs.*

The hunch about disgruntled generals outside the mainstream bears a resemblance to the rogue network behind Operation Northwoods (see page 204), which is the thesis of Tarpley's 9/11 Synthetic Terror.

11/20/01
Friends or Foes? The Bush-Bin Laden-Connection

The Saudi Bin Laden Group, or family holding company of Osama and the 40 thieves (or was that 24 brothers? Same thing...) sold its $2.5 million share in the Carlyle Group at the end of October.[109] Since the biggest US investor in the arms industry is coming on boom times now, it's unlikely that economic motives prompted this move by the alleged terrorist clan. Far more likely the Saudi billionaires were quietly asked to leave by a representative of the Carlyle Group: George Bush Sr. A lid has to be kept on the embarrassment over the close business relationship between the Bush and Bin Laden clans. This relationship is only the tip of an iceberg in which the longstanding connections between the two families and US secret services with Islamic terrorists are frozen.

We have already mentioned that Bush Jr. got the capital for his first company from James R. Bath, fund manager to the bin Ladens (see "9/14/01: Osama bin Laden"), and that his father had been acting for the arms investor Carlyle,[110] with which the Bin Laden clan was likewise involved until recently. It is also old news that Osama led the Saudi contingent into the Afghan Jihad against the Soviets.

Sure enough, the official version says the CIA and bin Laden parted ways over ten years ago, because of the latter's opposition to the presence of US troops on Saudi soil. The family, too, has allegedly spurned the black sheep, who after a sojourn in Sudan is pursuing his foul deeds as a terrorist monster in the caves of the Hindu Kush. It didn't take a report in *Le Figaro* about Osama's hospital stay in July and friendly visits from family members (blood relatives as well as the CIA) to raise doubts about such a version of events. New documents on BBC's *Newsnight*[111] indicate that the FBI was hampered in its investigations against the bin Laden family[112] long before 9/11 as well as afterwards.

Over 1,000 suspects continue to be held without *habeas corpus* in the USA and, if all goes according to Bush administration's plans, they will be prosecuted and even executed cloak-and-dagger-style by military courts. While the Talibanization of the USA's once-exemplary civil rights standards continued on its merciless march, eleven members of the bin Laden family left for Saudi Arabia undisturbed by the air travel embargo, just days after the attacks in New York. Among them was Abdullah bin Laden, a brother of Osama, who lived in a sleepy suburb of Washington where he headed among other activities the "World Assembly of Muslim Youth" (WAMY).[113] Although WAMY has long been held by the Indian and Filipino governments to be a financier and supporter of Islamic terrorism, as an ostensible youth club it is treated in the USA as a charitable body. Its bank accounts remain unfrozen to this day.

This is all the more astonishing since a secret FBI file which fell into the hands of security expert Joe Trento [114] shows that four of the alleged hijackers lived right in the street where WAMY had its offices, right near Abdullah's house where Omar, another brother of Osama's, was living. And it also emerges from the file that the federal police had this questionable club on the list of terror suspects since 1996, but was held back from in-depth investigations. Joe Trento on BBC *Newsnight*:

> The FBI wanted to investigate these guys. This is not something that they didn't want to do – they wanted to, but they weren't permitted to.

> They've had connections to Osama Bin Laden's people. They've had connections to Muslim cultural and financial aid groups that have terrorist connections. They fit the pattern of groups that the Saudi royal family and Saudi community of princes – the 20,000 princes – have funded who've engaged in terrorist activity.

> Now, do I know that WAMY has done anything that's illegal? No, I don't know that. Do I know that as far back as 1996 the FBI was very concerned about this organisation? I do. [115]

Well-founded words, as Michael Springmann confirmed in the same broadcast. Springmann was responsible for visas at the US embassy in Saudi Arabia in the 1980's under George Bush Sr.'s State Department and frequently received instructions to issue visas to unqualified individuals. His complaints on this matter were rebutted and ignored:

> What I was protesting was, in reality, an effort to bring recruits, rounded up by Osama Bin Laden, to the US for terrorist training by the CIA. They would then be returned to Afghanistan to fight against the Soviets.

> The attack on the World Trade Center in 1993 did not shake the State Department's faith in the Saudis, nor did the attack on the American barracks at Khobar Towers in Saudi Arabia three years later, in which 19 Americans died. FBI agents began to feel their investigation was being

obstructed. Would you be surprised to find out that FBI agents are a bit frustrated that they can't be looking into some Saudi connections?

http://news.bbc.co.uk/2/hi/events/newsnight/1645527.stm

It may well be that Osama's brothers and their association served purely charitable purposes for the advancement of Muslim youth, but then why were the police prevented by higher-ups from investigating? Attorney Michael Wildes, who represented one of the Khobar bombers in court, also spoke on the BBC program. A Saudi diplomat had given him access to 14,000 documents that provided a detailed exposure of the financing of terrorist activities by Saudi citizens and organizations. When Wildes tried to present the documents to the FBI, they told him that they were not permitted to read them: "Take it all away with you, we won't charge you for the copies, keep them or do something with them, catch a few bad guys."

It's likely that WAMY and Abdullah bin Laden featured in these documents, so it is no wonder that the brothers of the terrorist monster were allowed to go merrily on their way one week after the WTC attack, and the FBI was held back from doing anything about it. For what would the Osama brothers have done following their arrest? They would probably have unpacked such a mountain of dirty laundry that Bush Jr. would not have survived three more days in office, and together with his father would even have landed in court for "trading with the enemy," as Grandfather Prescott once did for his dealings with the Nazis.

In the wake of the Gulf War, Bush Sr. assigned the biggest military contract ever granted by the US army abroad – building and equipping US military bases in Saudi Arabia. Not less than $200 billion was spent, of which more than $65 billion on facilities and buildings.[116] The biggest construction company in the Arab world, the Bin Laden Group, came into play once again, carrying out a part of this huge contract. Now Osama was so offended by the presence of American troops in Saudi Arabia that it turned him into a terrorist, the official version goes – although his family's construction firm played a hefty role in keeping them there, cementing over the "holy earth" for infidel maneuvering grounds, bunkers, harbors and barracks. When the Khobar facility was bombed in 1996, Osama bin Laden was indeed named as the main suspect – and the contract for a new "super-safe" successor complex was awarded to none other than... the Bin Laden Group[117] (who else).

Foes one minute, friends the next? In 1996, Osama was sitting in the Sudan and could have been handed over to the USA, as the Sudanese defense minister General Erwa told the *Washington Post*. Washington turned down Sudan's extradition offer: the USA "feared uprisings" against the Saudi royal family if he were extradited, and recommended Sudan to request bin Laden to leave voluntarily. When Khartoum told the Americans that he planned to go to Afghanistan, US officials told General Erwa, "Let him go!" After he'd officially left, Clinton on a pseudo-hunt for Osama bombed Sudan's aspirin factory to bits...

The Bin-Laden Bush Business Connection

If the United States boosts defence spending in its quest to stop Saudi dissident Osama Bin Laden's alleged terrorist activities, his family may be the unexpected beneficiary, media reports said. "Among its far-flung business interests, the well-heeled Saudi Arabian clan, which says it is estranged from Laden, is an investor in a fund established by the Carlyle Group, a well-connected Washington merchant bank specialising in buyouts of defence and aerospace companies," *The Wall Street Journal* said in an investigative dispatch. It said "through this investment and its ties to Saudi royalty, the Bin Laden family has become acquainted with some of the biggest names in the Republican Party... In recent years, former president George H W Bush, ex-secretary of state James Baker and ex-secretary of defence Frank Carlucci have made the pilgrimage to the Bin Laden family's headquarters in Jeddah (Saudi Arabia). "Ex-president Bush makes speeches on behalf of the Carlyle Group and is senior advisor to its Asian Partners Fund, while Baker is its senior counsellor and Carlucci is the group's chairman," the journal said.

Hindustani Times, *9/28/01*

The *Washington Post*[118] commented on this behavior with the sinister lines: "And there were the beginnings of a debate, intensified lately, on whether the United States wanted to indict and try Bin Laden or to treat him as a combatant in an underground war." It's quite apparent that this "debate" back then led to the latter conclusion: "to treat him as a combatant in an underground war." And this is how he remains to this day: a combatant. His terror troops were deployed in Kosovo[119] and Macedonia[120] for American underground interests, they were active in Chechnya and other former Soviet republics, and now the Master himself is providing the A1 excuse for an illegal oil war against Afghanistan – even though he apparently got out of there a long time ago.

During the summer when preparations for the WTC and Pentagon attacks were coming to fruition and beginning to give off a rotten odor, did US officials react just like they did in 1996, when they told a too-cooperative Sudan to "Let him go!"? Were the FBI's investigations into

Osama's brothers and their dubious WAMY banned from then on, so
that the combatant in the underground war could go scot-free? What
happened to the warnings from foreign secret services that flight student
Atta and friends, who were also under FBI surveillance, were planning
the main attack on the WTC? Were they dismissed with an internal
memo: "Leave them to it!"?

The Al-Qaeda / Ladenistic conspiracy theory and the Afghanistan
connection were born ten minutes after the attack, to rise to the rank of
Fact not by proof but by shrill repetition, while ten miles away from the
Pentagon the Air Force squadron responsible for protecting the capital's
airspace stays on the ground and gives the hijacker one more easy chance
to get his approach angle just right[121] before he could hit his target spot-
on: it all looks more like dirty pool than a chain of tragic coincidences...

11/24/01
In Memoriam John O'Neill – the Cold-Blooded
Bin Laden Hunter, Killed in the WTC

In the last installment we reported that the FBI has been prevented from
making in-depth investigations against bin Laden's network at least since
1996 and that his US-resident and long-term terror suspect brothers were
assisted to leave unhindered after 9/11. In a book that appeared in France
at the beginning of the week by two intelligence experts and editors of
the internet magazine *Intelligence Online,* Jean-Charles Brisard and
Guillaume Dasquié,[122] the following forbidden truth was confirmed: John
O'Neill, the FBI department head in charge of investigations against bin
Laden since 1993, resigned a month before 9/11 in protest against these
hindrances. "The main obstacles to investigate Islamic terrorism,"
O'Neill told the authors, "were U.S. oil corporate interests and the role
played by Saudi Arabia in it."[123] It sounds like a Hollywood plot to say
O'Neill took a job as head of security of the WTC after his resignation –
and lost his life in the 9/11 attack, but it is tragic reality. The authors
dedicated their book to John O'Neill.

Julio Goday sums up some of Brisard and Dasquié's hypotheses in his
review:

> The authors say the U.S. government's main objective in Afghanistan was to
> consolidate the position of the Taliban regime and thereby obtain access to
> the oil and gas reserves in Central Asia. They say that until August, the U.S.
> government saw the Taliban regime "as a source of stability in Central Asia

that would enable the construction of an oil pipeline across Central Asia," from the rich oilfields in Turkmenistan, Uzbekistan, and Kazakhstan, through Afghanistan and Pakistan, to the Indian Ocean. Until now, says the book, "the oil and gas reserves of Central Asia have been controlled by Russia. The Bush government wanted to change all that." But confronted with the Taliban's refusal to accept U.S. conditions, "this rationale of energy security changed into a military one," the authors claim.

"At one moment during the negotiations, the U.S. representatives told the Taliban, either you accept our offer of a carpet of gold, or we bury you under a carpet of bombs."

http://globalresearch.ca/articles/GOD111A.html [124]

The bomb carpet has since been rolled out no problem, thanks to 9/11. It availed little that the Taliban got themselves a PR representative in Washington in the spring to polish their image: no bearded "assassin" with horn-rimmed spectacles and / or eye patch like the ambassador in Pakistan, but professionally smooth Laila Helms,[125] daughter of an Afghan former minister and – would you believe! niece of former CIA chief Richard Helms. Brisard and Dasquié depict her as a Mata Hari type who had been unofficially orchestrating dealings between Taliban and CIA since the beginning of the year. Helms brought Taliban leader Mullah Omar's closest advisor to Washington so that they could negotiate at the highest level.

The UN embargo had been putting ever stronger pressure on the Taliban from the start of the year, and right after Bush's slither into power, the US administration stepped up efforts in matters of Taliban and pipeline. Under the umbrella of the UN and moderated by Francesc Vendrell, Kofi Annan's personal representative, a number of discreet "6+2" talks took place at the beginning of the year, at which the six neighboring countries plus the USA and Russia discussed the Afghan situation. Representatives of the Taliban were also present at some of these meetings, including a meeting in July in Berlin at which, according to reports from former Pakistani foreign minister Niaz Naik, the focus was on the "formation of a government of national unity."

"If the Taliban had agreed to it, help would have flowed in straight away," and as Naik added in an interview on French TV, "the pipelines from Uzbekistan and Kazakhstan could have become reality." The US chief negotiator at these meetings, Tom Simons, allegedly threatened the Taliban and Pakistan quite openly: "either the Taliban behave as they ought to, or Pakistan convinces them to do so, or we will use another option."[126] "The words Simons used were 'a military operation.'" Such are the reports of Pakistani foreign minister Naik, as quoted by Brisard and Dasquié, on the negotiations that began to founder further and deeper in July, to be broken off on August 2nd after the final meeting between the Taliban and Assistant Secretary of State Christine Rocca. The Taliban might still have expressed their readiness to hand over bin Laden under certain conditions in February, but in July, according to Brisard and Dasquié, the USA – more interested in their pipeline than in Osama – began to consider military action.[127]

Was it the same game in February 2001 as in 1996, when Sudan offered to extradite bin Laden but the US government declined because, according to the *Washington Post,*[128] it wanted to make use of him as a useful combatant in their underground war? Did the same considerations lead to holding back the FBI's inquiry into the bomb attacks on the Khobar Towers in Saudi Arabia in 1996 and the USS Cole in Aden Harbor in October 2000, and likewise the investigations against members of the bin Laden clan living in the USA and their activities for "charitable" bodies? Was John O'Neill – the "best terrorist catcher in the USA" as the *New York Post* once called him – so painfully embarrassed by this institutionalized inactivity that he, a veteran with 30 years' service, threw in the towel?

At the beginning of the year the US embassy in Yemen had blocked O'Neill's return for further investigations – including at the birthplace of bin Laden's father, where one of the suicide attackers on the USS Cole came from – for "diplomatic reasons": his investigators would behave "like Rambos." "I wouldn't want to be the terrorist he was hunting. John O'Neill can move heaven and earth," the anti-terror head of Scotland Yard eulogized his internationally respected colleague.[129] A stubborn sniffer dog then, John O'Neill, just the man for hunting fanatical terrorists – so long as they are not under the wings of the CIA and oil diplomacy. His "pig-headedness" and "aggressiveness" often brought him into conflict with the secret services and the State Department, the *New York Times* reported.[130]

He resigned in August under the shadow of an internal investigation: while attending a meeting in Florida he had left a briefcase containing sensitive FBI documents behind at the hotel, which disappeared but turned up again unopened the next day. Even though he had reported his *faux pas* immediately, the investigations against him were proclaimed far and wide – a "smear campaign" according to many of his colleagues, since O'Neill had, without pushing for it, been put forward for a National

Security Advisor post. So he ended up after a glittering FBI career and in his prime at age 50 as mere head of security at the Twin Towers, where he started work on September 1. After the first plane hit he phoned his son to tell him that he was out in the open and in safety – then went right back into the building to help with rescue efforts, and lost his life. His remains have since been recovered.

Director Oliver Stone has put the Kennedy and Watergate conspiracies to film; if he were to portray the WTC conspiracy, he would have two eminently suitable protagonists in George W. Bush, who conducts oil wars on the back of the hunt for terrorists, and in John O'Neill, the real hunter of Osama bin Laden.

The New Yorker *painted an extensive posthumous portrait of John O'Neill.*[131] *There is even an internet site dedicated to his memory.*[132] *As a little boy John O'Neill already wanted to join the FBI, and he fulfilled his ambition so successfully that he would later enjoy saying with a grin: "I* **am** *the FBI." He left his dream job a frustrated, broken man. If he had been left to do it, terrorist havens Saudi Arabia and Yemen would not have been sacrosanct in the Bush government oil Monopoly game, and Bin Laden & Co. might have landed behind bars before 9/11. O'Neill noticed too late that they were under the protective guidance of the secret services and the State Department – otherwise he might not have made the mistake of letting himself get frustrated by it and resigning. Although his case is without doubt one of the most tragic of all those who died on 9/11, O'Neill's death barely got a mention in the US media. Best to let it lie – after all, public awareness, once stirred, can take an ugly turn.*

11/30/01
The Al-Qaeda-Ladenist World Conspiracy

What are the "sleepers" up to, then? Weren't we told in the days after the attack about the "Bin Laden" conspiracy theory and his "terror network" Al-Qaeda, whose members mingle among us unknown, ready to strike mercilessly at one code word from the caves of the Hindu Kush? Why do these heinous assassins continue to snore away while their leader is on the run and Afghanistan has been bombarded for weeks? Could it be the Al-Qaeda network of dormant terrorists doesn't exist at all?

Saad Al-Fagih for one, a medical doctor and Saudi dissident living in England, "really has to laugh" when he hears the tales about Al-Qaeda, terror network of bin Laden. His work as a doctor took him to Afghanistan and he knows the backdrop of *Jihad* every bit as well as he knows the situation in Saudi Arabia. Bin Laden had opened a recruitment office in Peshawar, Pakistan, in the 1980's for young Arabs who wanted to take part in the Afghan war. Initially these recruitments took place without any written records, but since more and more worried families were enquiring about the whereabouts of their sons, bin Laden had entry and exit lists started in Peshawar to record names and dates. Al-Fagih on the subject in an interview with TV magazine "Frontline":

Well, I [really] laugh when I hear the FBI talking about Al Qaeda as an organization of Bin Laden... [It's really a] very simple story. If Bin Laden is to receive Arabs from Saudi Arabia and from Kuwait – from other regions – he is [to] receive them in the guest house in Peshawar. They used to go to the battle field and come back, without documentation... no documentation of who has arrived. Who has left. How long he stayed. There's only [a nice general reception]. And you go there. And you join in the battle field... Very simple organization. Now, he was embarrassed by many families when they called him and ask what happened to our son. He don't know. 'Cause there's no record. There's no documentation. Now he asked some of his colleagues to start documenting the movement of every Arab coming under his umbrella... It is recorded that [they] arrived in this date and stayed in this house... And then there was a record of thousands and thousands of people. Many of them had come only for two weeks, three weeks and then disappeared. That record, that documentation was called the record of Al Qaeda. So that was Al Qaeda. There's nothing sinister about Al Qaeda. It's not like an organization – like any other terrorist organization or any other underground group. I don't think he used any name for his underground group. If you want to name it, you can name it "Bin Laden group." But if they are using the term Al Qaeda... Al Qaeda is just a record for the people who came to Peshawar and moved from there back and forth to the guest house. And moved back to their country. And if they want to follow the number, they must be talking about 20, 30 thousand people. Which is impossible to trace. And I think most of those records are in the hands of the Saudi government anyway, because people used the Saudi airlines, [at] a very much reduced fare. Twenty-five percent of the total fare of a trip to Islamabad...[133] *[Note. The primary meaning of "al Qaeda" is "record" or "register," but has been embellished to "The Base" by Western intelligence services; of course, it would be inconveniently incongruous to have to declare war on a guestbook. – Ed.]*

So much for the dramatic truth about the diabolical terror network, the latent storm troopers from the Empire of Evil that threaten our civilization: Al-Qaeda – a bunch of no-frills fliers with tickets subsidized by the CIA. Recruits for the trip to Peshawar were drummed up in over 30 US recruitment bureaus and at the previously-mentioned Jihad World Conference in New York alike. The prospect for young Muslims from around the world was an "all-inclusive" adventure camp under the esteemed leadership of charismatic Kalashnikov-clutching organizer Osama bin Laden. Old hat, yet since 9/11 it is being sold to us as the super-clandestine mega terror network of the 21st century – more threatening and more insidious than all known terror organizations and freedom fighters put together. A State terrorist like Sharon (see 3/3/02: "The Kosher Conspiracy") can currently have murderous mayhem carried out daily, with the cynical aim of forcing the Palestinians into submission, and be certain that this terror is being packaged and accepted in the West as "targeted killing." Thanks be to Al-Qaeda and bin Laden as the new spawn of latent Evil.

"If this were a dictatorship, it'd be a heck of a lot easier, just so long as I'm the dictator," said George W. Bush on December 18th, 2000[134] – a sentence worth taking note of, even if everybody laughed at the joke. Robert A. Wilson commented at the time: "With this sentence he convinced me, after 30 years of opposition to the National Rifle Association: I want a shooter!"[135] meanwhile Bush has all but trammeled the constitution, carried out hastily-staged military trials and begun a war which is extremely shady under international law – all thanks to the al-Qaeda-Ladenist world conspiracy. They're thinking about measuring noses and cheekbones in Germany again: for interior minister Schily at least, "biometry" is a suitable means of fighting terrorism:[136] the last time triage by German and non-German was the order of the day was during the struggle against the "Judeo-Bolshevik" world conspiracy.

Yet it is not Saddam, not bin Laden, or any other bearded terror monster – it is Bush Jr., after his insidious creep to power and the WTC Reichstag fire, who emerges as Hitler's true zombie. Over 1,100 foreign nationals in the USA continue to be held under martial law without charge since 9/11, with no access to lawyers, no visiting rights. Many have simply disappeared, their whereabouts a mystery. There's no mention of them in the mass media, whose patriotic confession is carefully scrutinized – or at best it's only because 52 Israelis are among them, which the *New York Times* [137] calls strategically stupid because it gives anti-Semitic propaganda to the enemy. The extremely wide-ranging and unconstitutional monitoring and control mechanisms of the new "Homeland Security" and counter-terrorism laws got through the

House of Representatives almost unanimously without even being read,
as CNN reported (and not with a critical, but a proud reporter's tone).
For Francis A. Boyle, professor of international law in Illinois, all this
amounts to an attack on the Constitution and a "coup d'état": "The
critical question is: When will the FBI, the CIA and the National
Security Agency start to turn these powers that they have under the
Ashcroft police state bill against American citizens?" [138]

The Patriot Act and Freedom Lost

**In forceful and unyielding testimony, Attorney General John Ashcroft
today defended the administration's array of antiterrorism proposals and
accused some of the program's critics of aiding terrorists by providing
"ammunition to America's enemies."**

**Emboldened by public opinion surveys showing that Americans over-
whelmingly support the administration's initiatives against terrorism,
Mr. Ashcroft told the Senate Judiciary Committee, "To those who scare
peace-loving people with phantoms of lost liberty, my message is this:
your tactics only aid terrorists."**

Neil A. Lewis, New York Times, *December 7, 2001*
http://www.nacdl.org/public.nsf/newsreleases/2001mn067?

The Disappeared, as they are known under Latin American military
dictatorships, are now on the agenda in the USA as well and, if John
Arshcroft goes through with his interrogation request for a further 5,000
foreign nationals, there could soon be internment camps too. Some are
even thinking aloud about allowing torture. All this under the banners
"War on Terror," "Infinite Justice" and "Enduring Freedom" – if this
were not the terrifying reality, you would almost believe that David
Zucker had made a new banana republic spoof: "Naked Dictator $2^{1/2}$."

Bush as Hitler's totalitarian zombie? Like his archetype he is
beginning his rise to great dictator with an ideological fiction – the Al-
Qaeda-Ladenist world conspiracy – and with the aid of an apparatus
organized largely as a secret association. Except for Ollie North, all of
the expelled and sometimes indicted "Iran-Contra" gangsters[139] among
his father's old terrorist-weapons-and-drugs cronies are back on board
and on duty. And the great thing is this: if you make the slightest hint
about the lack of taste of all this, right away you're anti-American. Like
the power to decide what the term "terrorism" means, where humble
guest lists from camps for part-time fighters are stylized as the script of a
tightly-organized world conspiracy, the Bush propagandists and their
vassals on the media front have taken over the term "Americanism" as

their own. "We decide what is German!" was once the motto in the Goebbels ministry. Being against Hitler then had no more to do with being anti-German than protesting against Bush's anti-constitutional decrees today has to do with being anti-American. Bushism no longer has anything to do with "America" or anything the name stands for.

Unfortunately, my November "Bushist" forecast turned out to be all too true – even understated.

12/07/01
Castle Gambit in Geopolitical Chess?

"Ever since the continents started interacting politically, some five hundred years ago, Eurasia has been the center of world power... The global hegemony of the US depends directly on for how long and how effectively we are able to maintain our superiority on the Eurasian continent and hinder the rise of any rival, opponent or potential enemy... Eurasia is the chessboard on which the struggle for global primacy continues to be played."[140]

Two towers were lost – but the center of the world chessboard changed hands. Not only the opening sentences of Zbigniew Brzezinski's 1997 work *The Grand Chessboard* read like the script of the war on Afghanistan, dubbed the "war on terrorism." It would be naïve to think that after his exit as Jimmy Carter's security advisor, Brzezinski was a foolish old professor (born 1928) being led by the nose. As an architect and co-founder of the Rockefeller think tank, the Council on Foreign Relations (CFR)[141] and of the Trilateral Commission,[142] he still has considerable influence. On Vice President Cheney, for example, who announced in 1998: "I cannot think of a time when we have had a region emerge as suddenly to become as strategically significant as the Caspian..."[143] At the time Cheney was still boss of Halliburton, the biggest equipper of the US oil industry, which had just planned the pipeline project through Afghanistan. For Brzezinski, vast reserves mean "the pipeline issue is of central importance for the future of the Caspian Basin and Central Asia." In his prophetic chapter entitled "The Eurasian Balkans" he continues:

If the main pipelines to the region continue to pass through Russian territory to the Russian outlet on the Black Sea at Novorossiysk, the political consequences of this condition will make themselves felt, even without any overt Russian power plays. The region will remain a political dependancy, with Moscow in a strong position to determine how the region's wealth is to be shared... It follows that America's primary interest is to help ensure that no single power comes to control this geopolitical space and that the **global community** has unhindered access to it. **Geopolitical pluralism** will become an enduring reality only when a network of pipelines and transportation routes links the region directly to the major centers of global economic activity via the Mediterranean and Arabian Seas, as well as overland. [144]

The emphasis on "global community" and "geopolitical pluralism" is mine and typical of a jargon which merges the interests of the USA, those of the global community, and Washington's dominance into one shorthand term called "pluralism" by Brzezinski and his colleague Samuel Huntington, whom he cites in this book: "The sustained international primacy of the United States is central to the welfare and security of Americans and to the future of freedom, democracy, open economies, and international order in the world." No empire, of course – just a sort of great co-prosperity sphere.

It's not a big leap from there to the battle cry, "either with us or with the terrorists." Andreas von Bülow hints that works commissioned by the CIA, geostrategic studies like Brzezinski's *Chessboard* or Huntington's *Clash of Civilizations,* usually have a public part which is left fairly general, and a secret appendix with concrete proposals and directives. 9/11/2001 gave a glimpse of the latter with a "probability bordering on certainty": "Covert operations by the secret services [are] the tools of choice for the realization of American major power and economic interests, while the deployment of military power remains rather unpopular."[145] A CFR spokeswoman confirms this in a current BBC broadcast: covert operations are regarded as being "less expensive" and often "more effective" than official military deployments.

What we are dealing with here is a hidden war, a shoot-out in the best cowboy tradition with "dead or alive" posters, calls for lynching justice, and the introduction of military courts. The Americans wanted to handle even a monster terror gang like the Nazis by constitutional means after the war. Why not with one arriviste Saudi billionaire turned Terror Prince bin Laden? Why was there never even mention of an attempt to bring him before the International Court in The Hague? Why was Interpol's first arrest warrant for bin Laden in 1998 not issued by Washington, London or Berlin, but by Tripoli, by none other than Muammar Gaddafi himself, who blamed Osama for supporting Islamist terror attacks in Libya, which also left two German secret service employees among the dead? Why are our new friends from the Northern Alliance, the brutal butchers who destroyed the country before the Taliban, now allowed to return as bloodthirsty avengers? Doesn't this mean, as Robert Fisk says in the *Independent*,[146] that we have finally switched over to the side of the war criminals? Why do statements by the Afghan women's organization RAWA pointing to this horrific absurdity not find their way into the media, let alone their representatives to the negotiating table in Petersberg [a Bonn suburb]? Why does oil giant Unocal, after years of intense pipeline negotiations with the Taliban, feel the need to issue a statement that it did not support and coddle students of Islam at any time?[147] Could it be that all this has to do with a form of politics that John Pilger,[148] chief correspondent at the British *Mirror*, labels the "geopolitical fascism" of the USA?

> Richard Falk, professor of international politics at Princeton, has explained this. Western foreign policy, he says, is propagated in the media "through a self-righteous, one-way moral/legal screen with positive images of western values and innocence portrayed as threatened, validating a campaign of unrestricted political violence."

> The ascendancy of Rumsfeld and his deputy, Paul Wolfowitz, and associates Richard Perle and Elliot Abrams means that much of the world is now threatened openly by a geopolitical fascism, which has been developing since 1945 and has accelerated since 11 September.

> The present Washington gang are authentic American fundamentalists. They are the heirs of John Foster Dulles and Allen Dulles, the Baptist fanatics who, in the 1950s, ran the State Department and the CIA respectively, smashing reforming governments in country after country – Iran, Iraq, Guatemala – tearing up international agreements, such as the 1954 Geneva accords on Indochina, whose sabotage by John Foster Dulles led directly to the Vietnam war and five million dead. Declassified files now tell us the United States twice came within an ace of using nuclear weapons.

> The parallels are there in Cheney's threat to "40 to 50" countries, and of war "that may not end in our lifetimes." The vocabulary of justification for this militarism has long been provided on both sides of the Atlantic by those factory "scholars" who have taken the humanity out of the study of nations and congealed it with a jargon that serves the dominant power. Poor countries are "failed states"; those that oppose America are "rogue states"; an attack by the west is a "humanitarian intervention." (One of the most enthusiastic bombers, Michael Ignatieff, is now "professor of human rights" at Harvard). And as in Dulles's time, the United Nations is reduced to a role of clearing up the rubble of bombing and providing colonial "protectorates."

> The twin towers attacks provided Bush's Washington with both a trigger and a remarkable coincidence. Pakistan's former foreign minister Niaz Naik has revealed that he was told by senior American officials in mid-July that

military action against Afghanistan would go ahead by the middle of October. The US secretary of state, Colin Powell, was then travelling in central Asia, already gathering support for an anti-Afghanistan war "coalition." [149]

In chess, when the loss of a piece brings a strategic advantage, it is called a sacrifice. Sacrifice strategies are difficult to recognize for the layman, especially when apparently indispensable figures are lost, like two castles. The grandmaster can easily imagine sacrificing two castles on the home front in order to gain a firm foothold in the opposing half of the board and an unbeatable strategic advantage or "world dominance" that more than compensates for the lost "hardware." There is plenty to indicate that the geopolitical chess champions in Washington foresaw the Taliban attacks on their two castles – or towers – and even sandbagged aggressive runners like bin Laden's FBI hunter John O'Neill in order not to disturb the opposition's preparations.

Intellectual forerunners like Brzezinski and Huntington – who made a name for himself as CIA advisor for the repression of uprisings following the fall of dictators – would simply not have been doing their jobs if they did not evaluate such sacrifice strategies in specific scenarios in the secret parts of their reports. And we would simply be blind if we did not see the "Great Game" programmed to victory and dominance at any price, behind the hypocritical jargon of "geopolitical pluralism," "human rights," "free world" and "humanitarian intervention."

The suspicion that Osama bin Laden may be an active "unofficial employee" of the British and American secret services becomes clear from the story of his arrest warrant. At the time of the first WTC attack in 1993, as well as the African embassy bombings and the attack on the USS "Cole" in Yemen, bin Laden was already counted among the main suspects – yet no international arrest warrant was put out for him. He had to be targeted instead by a "rogue" from the "Axis of Evil," namely Gaddafi, which makes sense. Since the Anglo-American Seven Sisters were driven out of the oil fields by the Libyan revolution, the British and Americans have been using Islamist forces like bin Laden's "Al-Qaeda" to destabilize the Gaddafi government. [150]

The conclusion is clear: al Qaeda is a subsidiary of Anglo-American intelligence...

In an appearance on the popular Al-Jazeera program "The Opposite Direction," Qaddafi condemned the 9/11 attacks, and referred to bin

Laden's Arab Afghans as "stray dogs" and terrorists. But then Qaddafi began to talk about the support network for al Qaeda:

I am actually puzzled. I mean, if America were serious about eliminating terrorism, the first capital it should rock with cruise missiles is London.

Interviewer: London!?

Qaddafi: London. It is the center of terrorism. It gives safehousing to the terrorists. I mean, as long as America does not bomb London, I think the US is not serious, and is using a double standard. I mean, on the contrary, London is far more dangerous than Kabul. How could it rock Kabul with missiles and leave London untouched? (Al-Jazeera, Qatar-Tripoli, October 25, 2001)

From 9/11 Synthetic Terror *by Webster Tarpley, Progressive Press, May 2005.*

A Reuters report on February 9th [151] that Pakistan's military leader Gen. Musharraf and Afghan president Karzai had agreed to resume the pipeline project sank significantly without a trace in the German press – just like the news that Karzai had been a consultant on the Unocal payroll before his Gucci-wearing career as interim and then loya-jirga-elected president. Karzai previously made himself useful in the struggle against the Soviet occupation of Afghanistan, as a middleman between CIA and Mujahideen in the distribution of arms, among other things.[152]

12/11/01
The Bush Putsch

Three months after the attacks on the WTC and the Pentagon, and still no proof of any connection with bin Laden or Afghanistan. By now not even the most trusting observers believe in the secret evidence that must be withheld from the public to protect sources. With the new secret military tribunals, evidence will be superfluous even if bin Laden is arrested. And thanks to his new laws on "national security," Bush Jr. has now classified all records from his father's term in office, too.

Like every suspected criminal, bin Laden and his people deserve a trial, or if we're at war, then the Geneva Conventions for prisoners of war apply. However, according to Attorney General Ashcroft in the *New York Times,*[153] it cannot be expected that any suspects caught in Afghanistan will enjoy the luxury of a trial in the USA. "Are we supposed to read them the Miranda rights, hire a flamboyant defense lawyer, bring them back to the United States to create a new cable network of Osama TV or what have you?"

Of course, a TV duel between Dubya and Osama – broadcast throughout the world by CNN and Al-Jazeera (courtesy of the Carlyle Group, the "family-run firm" of the Bush and Bin Laden clans)[154] – could probably finance the entire reconstruction of the WTC plus Afghanistan from ad revenues – and the propaganda effect would be so evenly matched, given equal time, that viewers would be able to decide for themselves. Then comes the sentencing of bin Laden if there is evidence against him, preferably before the new UN court of justice which the US is striving to sabotage, fearing to be hauled into court themselves for sponsoring terrorism. That would provide much better arguments for "Western values" – human rights, freedom and democracy – than underlining them with "smart bombs" in this crusade. That would dispel the magic of mega-terrorist bin Laden at a stroke.

Bush's policy of covert operations guarantees just the opposite: it transforms bin Laden into a hero and a martyr, and boosts Islamic terror worldwide as the new "Empire of Evil": exactly what the World's Only Superpower so urgently needs after the collapse of communism. Abroad, to justify its geopolitical chess moves as "humanitarian intervention" and "war against international terrorism"; at home, to paper over the recession and the threatening collapse of the global financial system, to draw the wagons in a patriotic circle in Al-Qaeda-induced panic and forge a lean, mean society by gutting constitutional freedoms.

Even former president Jimmy Carter speaks of a "putsch" on TV, and Scott Nelson, Richard Nixon's one-time lawyer, said at a recent Senate hearing that "Tricky Dicky" Nixon's notorious secretiveness was "child's play" compared with what is now going on in the White House.[155] Of course, the Attorney General will brook no criticism: "To those who scare peaceloving people with phantoms of lost liberty, my message is this: your tactics only aid terrorists, for they erode our unity and diminish our resolve."[156]

The call to blind obedience could hardly be expressed more directly, and demagogy reaches an extreme thought to be extinct in the West since the time of McCarthy in America and Hitler in Germany. There is no nationwide outcry as yet because the Gestapo-like wiretap and search laws apply "only" to the 20 million non-US citizens living in the USA, much as after the Reichstag fire, few "regular Germans" protested against Hitler's oppression of Jews, communists and foreigners.

"Lost liberty" is anything but a "phantom" for the over thousand "suspects" jailed without charges for months; or for the 68,000 documents from the Reagan era and Bush Sr.'s vice presidential term, which had been waiting expectantly for the light of day in January at the end of the customary twelve-year period, until Bush Jr. hastily changed the law on November 1 to keep them locked up. He also spirited his own records from his term as governor of Texas into secrecy in his father's "presidential library." Why? According to John Dean, former legal advisor to the White House:

> The Executive Order suggests that President Bush not only does not want Americans to know what he is doing, but he also does not want to worry that historians and others will someday find out...

> If President Bush continues with his Nixon-style secrecy, I suspect voters will give him a Nixon-style vote of no confidence come 2004. While secrecy is necessary to fight a war, it is not necessary to run the country. I can assure you from firsthand experience that a president acting secretly usually does not have the best interest of Americans in mind. It is his own personal interest that is on his mind instead.[157]

Dean, a stalwart Republican, speaks from experience. As Nixon's advisor he was involved in the Watergate cover-up and was even jailed for contempt of court for withholding evidence against his boss. Yet even loyal troopers like Dean count as supporters of terrorism according to Ashcroft's latest dictum – not to mention critical intellectuals like Noam Chomsky, whose collected interviews have just appeared as a book in the USA under the title *9-11*: "We should recognize that in much of the world the U.S. is regarded as a leading terrorist state, and with good reason."[158]

It is precisely for this reason that Bush Jr. has to hide the records of the Reagan presidency. Nearly all of the notorious culprits from the Iran-Contra affair[159] and the BCCI banking scandal[160] are back on board with Bush – and next to Bush Sr. in a central role in that $50 billion drugs, arms, money-laundering and terrorism operation of the mid-80's stands none other than Salem bin Laden, Osama's eldest brother. Through his US fund manager, Bush buddy James R. Bath, who invested in Bush Jr.'s first oil company "Arbusto,"[161] and banker Mahfouz, whose BCCI acted as a laundry for "Iran-Contra" drugs and arms dealings, Salem bin Laden had been connected with the business and politics of the Bush family since the 1970's. The "deep politics" of oil, drugs and terror, as Berkeley professor Peter Dale Scott[162] describes them, were already established then, and we are now experiencing their visible excrescence in the current "war on terrorism."

Drug Dealing for Strategy and Profit: a Global Opium War

Drugs, Oil and War explores the underlying factors behind the US strategy of indirect intervention in Third World countries through alliances with the biggest international drug traffickers. The strategy was ostensibly developed in the late 1940s to contain Communist China; since then, the US government has repeatedly used it to gain control over foreign petroleum resources. The result has been a staggering expansion of global drug traffic and the mafias associated with it, a problem that will worsen until there is a change in policy.

Peter Dale Scott, Drugs, Oil and War. The Deep Politics of US Interventions in Afghanistan, Colombia and Indochina (2003).

The consequences that even a veteran conspirator like John Dean foresees for Bush's covert politics – that the people will lose their trust in Bush by the next elections – inspire little hope for the world's future. Following his creep into power, so extremely successful until now, if his star threatens to fade, he can always take a flight forwards – into war.

Numerous institutions and archives have meanwhile submitted complaints against Bush's new policy of secrecy. Yet one good reason was not known then for his insolent sweeping of his governorship papers under the "presidential family carpet": the woes of his biggest election campaign contributor Enron, whose meteoric rise on the stock market began with the "deregulation" of energy laws by Bush Jr. in Texas. Business got so good that Enron alone anted up $4 million to install the "successful" Texas governor as president.

12/15/01
Facts, Fictions, Fakes...

A demonstration of how to create reality fiction by heaping up meaningless facts was given by the weekly newsmagazine *Der Spiegel* in its series "What Really Happened." The drama of the WTC collapse is recounted with punctilious pettifoggery as if a gushing description of symptoms alone could explain the cause of the "illness." Not one of the dozen open issues and contradictions about the execution and background of the attack is mentioned in the process.

The one-time German "flagship of investigative journalism" has joined the media phalanx of propaganda gum-chewers and armored fog-throwers – and if old Rudolf Augstein[163] had not had a few lucid moments now and then, one might have thought all the inmates at *Der*

Spiegel had lost their senses, fallen afoul of conspirators who had slipped Prozac into the editorial coffee machines, or some other "take-it-easy" psychopharmaceutical that nips every critical thought process in the cerebral bud and transforms it into a star-spangled pop-up ad. What a clueless vacuum spills over the pages – the whole disgurgitation has meanwhile appeared as a book[164] – already showed in the "original reporting" in the weeks following the attack. Hastily, and beyond the bounds of press codes and professional ethics, suspicions and assumptions were hoisted into the realm of facts and actual proofs. "What do facts matter, when there's hate": clearly not even editors themselves, as Uwe Galle so beautifully demonstrated in a documentary for the Swiss magazine *Zeitfragen,*[165] are immune to this motto, which *Der Spiegel* used as a headline for a profile of Mohammed Atta's father.

No wonder then about our footnote that *Spiegel Online*, translating a long essay by Indian author Arundhati Roy, dropped precisely those ten lines in which she mentions the arms concern Carlyle Group; until recently Bush Sr. was its representative and the Bin Laden family were investors. For where would an examination of these circumstances lead? Not to Afghanistan, but to Saudi Arabia; not to a global phantom organization like "Al-Qaeda," but to discreet networks of oil, military and intelligence activities; not to medieval "subhuman beings" set loose on a shooting spree, the Taliban, but to the fat-cat variety of this medievalism, the deeply undemocratic, misogynistic and corrupt feudal system of the elites; not to lowly, brain-washed flight students, but to their perfidious and thoroughly organized string-pullers; not to the catastrophe-crazed piecing together of the last minutes on board the hijacked aircraft or in the towers, but to the screaming question: why interceptors just a few miles away from the Pentagon never left the ground.

On October 17 I cited the report in the *Times of India* that named the reason for the surprising resignation of the head of the Pakistani secret service ISI, General Mahmud Ahmed: by telephone monitoring, the Indian secret service and the FBI had discovered that shortly before 9/11, one of Ahmed's closest colleagues had transferred $100,000 to Mohammed Atta. Compared with the wild assumptions and speculations concerning the string-pullers, which up to then had been trumpeted as possibilities, probabilities and truth, this seemed to be a real nugget of information, a hot lead; but apart from a few scant mentions, no investigative journalist in the Western media saw the need to pursue this scoop. It would have drawn attention away from Afghanistan to Pakistan, not to the young, remote-controlled village preacher and "Head of State" Mullah Omar, but to those who created and manipulated him; away from the poverty-stricken Afghan opium growers and straight to the heroin laboratories operating under the supervision of ISI and CIA; away from the bogeyman of fanatical Islamists and straight to their trainers, financiers, exploiters and masters.

In 1919, after spending decades in libraries searching for unusual phenomena and noting the available evidence and eyewitness accounts on index cards, author Charles Fort published his *Book of the Damned*, an encyclopedia of news items about inexplicable events that were doomed not to come to light – not because they hadn't taken place, but because their occurrence did not harmonize with prevailing ideas about the laws of nature or common sense. Radical rationalist Fort ("I think, therefore I had breakfast")[166] was a researcher of outcast facts that, in spite of being covered up, skipped over, ignored or explained away, have a peculiar ability to crop up again, like irritating weeds in a suburban lawn. For example, CIA researcher and onetime narcotics officer Mike Ruppert has a whole list on his website of condemned facts about the criminal machinations of the US secret services that simply will not be beaten down. He offers a $1,000 reward to anyone who can prove any error on his timetable of foreknowledge about the WTC attack[167] Anti-conspiracy conspirologists can thus earn an extra Christmas bonus – and *Der Spiegel* (along with Germany's main broadcasters and newspapers) can start an attempt at rehabilitation by finally looking the condemned facts in the eye.

The haste of the German media after 9/11 to fall lockstep into toeing the party line, far more than say in France or England, was worthy of a thorough investigation. In *The Mass Psychology of Fascism,*[168] the (also condemned) psychoanalyst Wilhelm Reich described fascist systems as neurotic combinations of a yearning for freedom with the fear of freedom, of freedom-loving phrases with authoritarian leadership principles. "What was new about fascism," he wrote, "is that the masses practically consented to their suppression and brought it about. The need for authority proved to be stronger than the will for independence." The very same thing seems to be happening to the consenting, self-subjugating Bushists and belligerents of our times – and for petty hacks, all will to think independently seems to have blown away in the wind. The froth of "freedom-loving" phrases doesn't stop, though...

After three months an amateur video was "found" by the CIA in which bin Laden (or somebody looking something like him) supposedly confesses to an unknown turban-wearer that he knew about the attack, and is congratulated for it – a scanty accidental find indeed after a quarter year of systematic investigation, even if the video, if it does turn out to be genuine, may stand as evidence of bin Laden's foreknowledge. Of course, it raises more questions than it answers: why did the super-terrorist, who hitherto took care to deliver his statements in military garb, denied his involvement and blamed the attack on a Jewish world conspiracy make his casual confession in this manner – instead of with his trademark Kalashnikov on TV station Al Jazeera?

Or did he not publish this tape at all, it just "accidentally got left in a house in Jalalabad," like Atta's bag with his last will at the airport, like the Koran and the Arabic flight manuals? But who is interested in videos in Arabic in Afghanistan, where nobody speaks Arabic? If it was for distribution throughout the Arab world, why then in this shabby quality? If it is a private video diary by bin Laden, not for publication, where are the other volumes? How many more were "found" by the CIA? Doesn't this example of bin Laden's diabolical cynicism on parade – the tantalizing explanation, that apart from the pilots none of the co-perpetrators knew of the suicide mission – contradict the version of the "finds" up to now, of the "last will" and the exact directions given to the group? The pitiful picture quality, shoddy sound and dubious origins of the new video evidence once again provide the media with everything they need to make realities out of possibilities and facts out of fictions. Yet the condemned, unwanted news items won't stop coming.

The video was torn apart after an unseemly short interval by the TV magazine "Monitor," and turned out to be obviously manipulated in picture and sound – quite different from the confessional video that emerged shortly after the attacks, in which bin Laden denied any involvement. The dubious "video evidence" that popped up in the following months proved nothing either.

12/29/01
Office Computers Survive WTC Crash, Black Boxes Don't!

Besides dealings in put options on airline shares (see "10/20/01: The Money Trail" and "10/26/01: The Money Laundromat") which still have yielded no conclusive trail back to the robber baron strongholds of the banking system, a new suspicion has now emerged that the WTC attack was anticipated, and that this foreknowledge was used for criminal financial speculations on an even greater scale.

Since last week the German firm Convar, a data recovery specialist,[169] has been working around the clock to confirm or dispel a suspicion that puts prior indications of 9/11 financial speculations in the shade. In the hours before and during the attacks an unusually high number of credit card transactions were funneled through companies based in the World Trade Center, far exceeding the normal Tuesday morning turnover. It is rumored that over $100 million in fraudulent billings were charged to computers in the WTC on September 9. Convar now has the task of recovering the data from hard disks found in the ruins to track down the culprits who apparently hoped all traces of their transactions would be erased by the destruction of the central computers.

"Of course it is also possible that there were perfectly legitimate reasons for the unusual rise in business volume," said Convar Director Peter Henschel. "It could turn out that Americans went on an absolute shopping binge on that Tuesday morning. But at this point there are many transactions that cannot be accounted for." The company told Reuters that it has received 32 computers, with up to 40 gigabytes of data stored on each one. To the total surprise of the disk doctors, "the hard drives were in good enough shape to retrieve the data."[170] Although the drives were heavily contaminated by dust which had infiltrated under high pressure, the data were 100% recoverable.

When the official line is that seven out of eight black boxes of the ill-fated aircraft were completely destroyed, this announcement from an internationally-known data recovery firm sounds pretty sensational. How can ordinary office computers survive the destruction of World Trade Center without a scratch to their delicate magnetic memories, while bomb and fire-proof "indestructible" black boxes do not?[171]

Against this background, the suspicion that the black box records were not really destroyed but concealed because their condemned data undermines the official legend can not be simply dismissed as malicious mistrust. Every surviving WTC disk drive recovered by Convar specialists in Germany with their laser technology is another indication of something hidden about the black boxes, and speculation about "controlled demolition"[172] gains ground.

Indeed, skepticism is in order about the possibility that data resurrected from the WTC computers might break open the case, even if the suspicions of $100 million in illegal transfers prove true, and if the transfers are traced to the string-pullers behind the scenes. There is as little likelihood that the police will be let loose upon them as there is of a thorough criminal investigation of the put-options. Either attempt would likely sink in the moat of the money banks' robber-baron fortresses offshore. The hounds are not baying at the trail uncovered by the *San Francisco Chronicle* on September 29, which found that some of the pre-9/11 option orders were handled by the Alex Brown Bank, closely connected to the secret services through its director "Buzzy" Krongard.

When it was taken over by Deutsche Bank, Krongard came over to the No. 3 spot at the CIA this March. It's not hard to guess at the qualifications that open the door to a banker for a top secret service post overseas. The gray zone of unofficial foreign policy – the terror, arms and drugs business – requires the handmaiden of discreet financial transactions, or to put it bluntly, a money laundry. Krongard is also known as an advisor on investments in software and hardware firms specializing in products for the secret services.

Journalist Tom Flocco tried to research the close connections between secret services, banks, the stock exchange regulatory commission and the dawdling or completely dropped investigations in this case. As could be expected, he could find no new hard evidence about the prescient speculators, but his report on the illegal activities of the Alex Brown Bank – and on the recent money-laundering conviction of former Wall Street head trader of Deutsche Bank Kevin Ingram – speaks volumes. Just like the almost unscathed hard drives from the WTC building…[173]

The never-published black box data, just like the radio communication with the hijacked aircraft that was only published in a few extracts, brings the suspicion of a cover-up a step closer.[174] There is no reason for these data to be withheld except that the already clearly obvious inconsistencies of the official version would come to light. How could office PC's remain intact while "indestructible" black boxes were totally vaporized – that this mystery went unmentioned in the media astonishes just as little as the absence of investigative reporting on the speculative transactions handled by Alex Brown and other banks.

1/04/02
Where was the Fire Department?

"We're pretty good if the threat's coming from outside. We're not so good if the threat's coming from inside," declared General Richard B. Myers before the Senate on 9/13/2001 at a hearing on his nomination as head of Joint Chiefs of Staff, America's highest military rank.[175] Journalist Jared Israel, who documents the mysteries of September 11 on his website,[176] compares this to a hypothetical fire chief near the Canadian border:

> Consider this, by way of comparison. Imagine that one night a Canadian arsonist slips into Buffalo, New York, and using a new incendiary device, starts fires in four elementary schools.
>
> People pull fire alarms near two of the schools. A neighbor calls the fire department when he sees smoke billowing out of the third school. and there is a fire station right across the street from the fourth school.
>
> Yet not one fire truck arrives until after the schools have burned to the ground.
>
> When asked why, the Buffalo Fire Chief explains, "We're good at dealing with Buffalo arsonists, but nobody expected some guy to sneak in from Canada!"
>
> The Chief would be laughed out of court. People would say, "When the alarms came in, how could anyone in the Fire Department have known that these fires were started by a Canadian arsonist? And even if they did know, why wouldn't they just follow their normal procedures – you know, slide down the pole, put on their coats, climb into the fire truck, turn on the siren. Why didn't they at least show up and try to put out these fires?"
>
> The same holds true for 9-11.[177]

The "fire trucks" to monitor the most sensitive piece of airspace in the United States, the no-fly zone above the Washington government district, are stationed only ten miles away from the Pentagon, virtually across the street, at the Andrews Air Force Base: military jets that can take off on command "in the highest state of readiness" to escort off-course aircraft, exercise pressure on erratic and uncooperative pilots and force them into landing if need be, and protect the presidential aircraft Air Force One, which also takes off from Andrews AFB. Air surveillance professionals have their routines and regulations for all these "firefighting-type" duties. Yet by the way things were looking on 9/11, even a pilot like Matthias Rust, who once landed on Red Square in a light aircraft, could have dumped a batch of bombs over the White

House in perfect serenity, or landed on a peace mission on the lawn out front without any kind of "fire department" even mobilizing. He would have just had to take off from any American airfield and would have been just as little hindered as American Airlines Flight 77, which was given all the time in the world to make just one more wide approaching loop to get its aim at the Pentagon just right.

What would happen if a passenger flight from a foreign airline came from Berlin, Moscow or Peking and veered off course toward the government buildings in Washington? Did the interceptors stay on the ground on 9/11 just because the threat came from domestic aircraft?

Brave Interceptors

On Sunday, September 16th, Vice-President Richard Cheney was interviewed on NBC TV's *Meet the Press*. During that interview he created the impression that the military would have needed presidential authorization to scramble fighter jets to intercept American Airlines Flight 77 before it hit the Pentagon.

Mr. Cheney did not present this lie in a straightforward manner.

Instead he did two things. First, he avoided discussing the failure to intercept Flight 77. Instead he talked only about the choices Mr. Bush supposedly made after the Pentagon was hit.

Second, he took it for granted that presidential approval was required to intercept a commercial jet, as if this were an accepted fact. Then based on this false foundation, he emitted a fog of emotional misinformation to confuse the millions of Americans who wanted to know: why didn't jet fighters scramble to intercept Flight 77 before it crashed into the Pentagon? Doesn't the U.S. have radar and an Air Force anymore?

It is common for officials attempting to cover-up a capital crime to put the blame on a subordinate. However Mr. Cheney used a different approach on *Meet the Press*. Relying on his skills in public deception, Cheney tried to create the impression that nothing improper had occurred, that faced with horrendous choices a brave President had done the right thing.

http://emperors-clothes.com/indict/indict-2.htm

Apart from the crucial question over the attack's real string-pullers, probably the biggest mystery in this case is the no-show by the "fire department," the question why Flight 77 was able to take a detour and steer toward the Pentagon unchallenged for over half an hour. The most credibility-stretching happenstance of all is that the black boxes were completely unreadable after this crash which, technically speaking, was totally typical of an accident where a plane hits a four-story office building. The apparent oddity that the passport of one of the alleged hijackers was discovered intact two blocks from the WTC appears completely self-evident by contrast: a passport can fly if it is rocketed into the air by an explosion, but an "indestructible" black box cannot burn under the utterly normal circumstances of the Pentagon crash. And just in case it should happen after all – since Murphy's Law applies to black boxes too – then just to be sure there are two of these appliances on board.

Yes, the cover story put forward by Vice President Dick Cheney – where he parried the failure to attempt an intercept with excuses about a shoot-down, which is quite a different thing – was readily swallowed by all, but the fire department analogy makes the scam clear. The question is not "why the fire wasn't put out," but why the fire department stayed away so long that eventually it was far too late.

Even the debate over the "Pentagon mystery" that emerged from February 2002 – the claim that the destruction at the Defense Department could not have been wrought about by a Boeing jetliner (see "The Mystery of the Pentagon," page 174) – remains irrelevant as long as the crucial question is not answered: how could a large aircraft maneuver completely unhindered for half an hour in the most sensitive "no-fly-zone" in the USA, especially after three other hijackings were already known?

1/10/02
The American Way of War

After the mass murder of some 3,000 people in the World Trade Center nothing is the same, so they say. One thing is sure to continue, though, even if the lockstep media do refuse to take notice: mass murder. A report by Marc Herold,[178] professor of economics at New Hampshire University, will probably have little chance of filtering into the public mind. According to his count, 3,767 civilians were already murdered by the American bombardment of Afghanistan between October 7 and December 10, 2001.

The famous biblical saying "an eye for an eye, a tooth for a tooth" is not, as is often misunderstood, a call to revenge, but on the contrary a reminder to be moderate in retaliation. If the West's crusade were really led by morals or Christian values, then a halt to the bombardments was due by early December. Yet in Bush's America only addled TV preachers mumble confusedly about charity and the Bible's commandments. The same applies to the fundamentalist ideologues in the Bible Belt as to the ultra-orthodox mullahs and rabbis in Palestine and the Arab World: rouse the rabble to murder and assure them divine support in the process.

Who is going to be so petty as to count bodies when it's a fight against the ultimate evil; who will be gnawed by moral scruples when it comes to halting the Antichrist on his final advance, or installing Allah's theocracy throughout the world? Marx's criticism of religion as the "opium of the masses" seems to be in need of an update, since at the beginning of the 3rd millennium, religiosity is evidently less effective as a dream-inducing tranquilizer than as ideological amphetamine: speed for war, for the inducement of activist tunnel vision.

Such doping of the mass subconscious may be the only way to explain the shoulder-shrugging indifference, the ice-cold ignorance, with which the murdered children, women and men in Afghanistan are being whited out of media coverage – in the very media which on 9/11 were so completely shocked by the merciless murder of "7,000 innocents." The fact that the number of WTC victims has meantime halved, while it is increasing on a daily basis in Afghanistan, is apparently not even worth a mention any more. Sure enough, the first US soldier to be killed under enemy fire made world headlines. One soldier sacrificed for 4,000 civilians murdered – a formidable statistic. The alleged 19 hijackers who set a new standard in murderous efficiency on 9/11 were robbed of their record just a few weeks later. And the new "American way of war"[179] will ensure that no one will be in a hurry to try and push the USA off this top spot.

What to make of a sheriff who on his search for a murderous gang lays waste to the whole town and, instead of tracing the culprits, has one innocent citizen after another killed? How is an allied village deputy who continues to deliver "unlimited solidarity" with such a sheriff to be judged? And how the newspaper and media cartel that hails this brutally berserk behavior as indispensable medicine and a civilizing measure, and doggedly indoctrinates the population about the despicable mob and the heroic sheriff, while the culpability of the former remains unproven and the "heroism" of the latter turns new victims into innocent corpses daily? What third-rate western are we in here, or to put it another way, what kind of mass-psychology operation, massively dumbed down to earn the title of the "biggest brainwash of all times?"[180]

A shocked public does not need this blanket brainwashing program forced onto it: all it asks for is simple and comprehensible explanations, and the more complex and disconcerting the reality is, the simpler the explanations are permitted to sound – and the more effective is the work of an ultra-simple conspiracy theory. A glaring example is the theory of an Al-Qaeda-Ladenist world conspiracy, backed to this day by no proof that would stand up in court, and which Bush Jr. has to thank for a popularity not achieved by any president since Roosevelt. And it enables the USA to take military control of the world's oil resources without a riposte.

Mighty military bastions on the Persian Gulf were created with the "liberation of Kuwait"; with the "liberation of Afghanistan" or the "destruction of Al-Qaeda," the same is now being done in Uzbekistan and Afghanistan. However, the scenario will not play without some heckling from the gallery, at least if a resolution[181] is passed by the US Senate with questions that are bound to become louder and louder as they go unanswered. Since they are a good summary of the remarkable circumstances discussed in this diary, herewith a list:

1. thousands of put options on United Airlines shares that were bought in the days before 9/11,

2. financial transactions of over $100 million that were processed via computers stationed in the WTC,

3. the black boxes of the four crashed planes,

4. the cell phone calls made by hijacked passengers that did not appear on their phone bills,

5. all conversations from air traffic control on 9/11,

6. the eyewitness accounts that Flight 93 (Pennsylvania) exploded before the crash, as well as the wreckage found seven whole miles away from the crash scene,

7. the role of Unocal in the construction of a pipeline through Afghanistan and the plans implemented for that purpose before 2001,

8. the role of the Carlyle Group in the coordination of Unocal goals and the plans implemented for that purpose before 2001,

9. the role of remote control in the 9/11 crashes,

10. George W. Bush's possible foreknowledge of the 9/11 attacks,

11. the role of the Northern Alliance in the flourishing production of opium following the US intervention.

As the 12th point I would add the question regarding the no-show of the "fire department" (see page 144) and promise to give up my job as a part-time conspiracy theorist straight away if these questions are answered for us with conclusive proof and the government's seal in a tidy PDF document in a few weeks' time. Only point 10 allows for a certain amount of circumspection, since the foreknowledge of the Dubya marionette is downright dubious. Just a year ago he still thought "The Taliban" were a rock group...

Reprise

When a journalist asked Governor Bush during the 2000 election campaign what he thought about the Taliban:

"He just shrugged his shoulders, bemused. It took a bit of prompting from the journalist ("discrimination against women in Afghanistan") for Bush to rouse himself: "Taliban in Afghanistan! Absolutely. Reprisals. I thought you were talking about some rock group."

Cited in War and Globalisation: the Truth behind September 11, *by Michel Chossudovsky, p. 5.(revised edition:* America's "War on Terrorism"*)*

Not one of the these questions, posed on January 10, is any closer to an answer today. The financial speculations remain just as unexplained as the black box data and radio communications. The mystery of the apparent cell phone conversations has become even more murkier, at least as far as Barbara Olson is concerned: she allegedly called from an on-board telephone, something which, however, as Joe Vialls demonstrates – see note to the 9/16 entry – is fairly improbable. As first-hand eyewitness accounts, telephone calls from the hijacked planes ought to be playing an important role: who telephoned whom when, and what exactly was reported? Together with tapes of the radio communication this would produce a pretty accurate definitive run-down of the hijackings. Instead the telephone conversations were only used to present the emotional drama of the hijackings and the heroic attempt to overwhelm the hijackers of the Pennsylvania plane. And above all the mystery of the alleged box-cutters still awaits elucidation.

Mid-January President Bush asked Congress not to instigate any in-depth investigations into the background of 9/11, as this would "jeopardize national security."

1/18/02
Enrongate

The tragic tale of John O'Neill, the USA's top terrorist hunter, who resigned his job out of frustration over the obstacles to his investigations of bin Laden only to lose his life in the World Trade Center, has meanwhile made waves in the US, too. Even CNN felt obliged to touch on his case, and the aforementioned book by Jean-Charles Brisard and Guillaume Dasquié that revealed it.

Richard Butler was the expert whom CNN consulted on the matter. He is a former UN weapons inspector and currently on the payroll of the Rockefeller Council on Foreign Relations. (Scott Ritter has since depicted him as a card-carrying creature of the war party who manipulated the inspections process into a pretext for the second war on Iraq.) He made no particular effort to dismiss or criticize the book's hypotheses – which is even more astonishing given that Brisard and Dasquié, among others, cite John O'Neill's view that bin Laden's capture was prevented so as not to jeopardize American oil interests: following the attacks on the US barracks in Khobar and on the battleship USS *Cole*, O'Neill and his FBI team were restrained from pursuing culprits in Saudi Arabia and Yemen. And during the pipeline negotiations, the reason US representatives rejected the Taliban offer to hand over bin Laden is that the Afghans were demanding a higher share of pipeline profits in return. Butler comments on this fairly laconically in the CNN interview:

> And you've got oil, and this is a fundamental thing. Let us not lose sight of this basic reality. The population of the United States of America represents 5 percent of the population of the world. Yet, we use 40 percent – 40 percent of the world's oil. So oil is a big issue, and as we were saying yesterday, there is very substantial oil in Central Asia. And to get that out to the sea, the best possible way to do it would be to build a pipeline across Afghanistan. So that's the web, Paula, and I don't think we're being told all of the facts. There are denials, claims that meetings didn't take place, when clearly they did. The most interesting thing those French authors told us today is that they had seen archives. We couldn't quite understand their accent, but I know what that means. That means records of diplomatic conversations that took place. [182]

Yet even without an insight into diplomatic dossiers, it is becoming clear that when all is said and done the agenda of the so-called "war on terrorism" boils down to a three-letter word: OIL! Hamid Karzai, who was appointed head of the Afghan interim government on Bonn's Petersberg mountain, played a role in the pipeline talks with the Taliban on behalf of the US oil company Unocal;[183] the new UN Special Commissioner in Afghanistan, Zalmay Khalilzad,[184] who arrived in Kabul in January, was for years also on the Houston payroll of the same multinational oil giant. Khalilzad, a naturalized US citizen born in Kabul, served under Bush Sr. as Assistant Deputy Under Secretary of Defense for Policy Planning, and as a Unocal man from the mid-90's onwards, he played a considerable part in the pipeline negotiations. As early as 1997, when the regime's human rights offenses were already apparent, he wrote in the *Washington Post* totally in the spirit of his employer: "The Taliban does not practice the anti-U.S. style of fund-amentalism practiced by Iran. We should be willing to offer recognition and humanitarian assistance and to promote international economic reconstruction... It is time for the United States to reengage."[185] Now, at his first press conference in Kabul, Khalilzad described the Taliban as sponsors of international terrorism and announced that the USA would step up its campaign until they and their allies were neutralized in bin Laden's Al Qaeda network. OK, that was then, this is now... Of course the last thing one needs on a billion-dollar construction project is a band of suicide bombers or potential saboteurs. But looking at the who's who of top government and US embassy positions, one would have to be blind not to notice that it's about the construction jobs and other contracts of the participating companies first and foremost – and not really about the world's liberation from terrorists at all.

The Bush Family Afghan

Working in turn for Unocal as a lobbyist, for the RAND Corporation as a consultant and for the State Department, Khalilzad was able to bend public policy and opinion to suit oil company objectives, while advancing his own career through Washington's revolving doors. His reward: "Zalmay Khalilzad was appointed to the National Security Council as a special assistant to the president and senior director for Gulf, Southwest Asia and Other Regional Issues. Bush's 'Afghan policy' would ultimately be his brain child."

"Zalmay Khalilzad – Bush's Theorist," in Enemies by Design: Inventing the War on Terrorism, *by Greg Felton, Progressive Press, 2005, pp. 212-218.*

And as if these indications were not yet enough to expose the oil-dripping agenda of the latest Afghan war, even on the domestic front the well-lubricated connections between Bushist politics and the oil business cannot remain undisclosed for much longer: "Enrongate," the scandal surrounding the biggest bankruptcy in American history,[186] leads straight into the conspiratorial swamp of nepotism, corruption and betrayal, that Bush Jr. appears to have shaken off after his dubious election victory thanks to the "war on terrorism," and all the way back to his own insider dealings as managing director of oil drilling firm Harken Energy at the beginning of the 1990's. As with Enron, where the directors lost no time in cashing in before the bankruptcy, George W. Bush also sold his shares for just under $1 million just a few weeks before Harken "unexpectedly" went bust at the start of the Gulf War.[187]

Just as Enron constituted a major source of Bush Jr.'s campaign funding, Harken's investors counted among the most important bankrollers of Bush Sr. And just as documents concerning the fraudulent transactions disappeared at Enron, investigations into the Harken insider deal were shut down by his father. Bush Jr. has now liquidated the "Freedom of Information Act"[188] at a stroke, preventing the future release of documents from Bush Sr.'s term. The teams from the audit and trustee firms now investigating the Enron fraud[189] have been packed with Bush-men more intent on obfuscation than illumination.

Tom Flocco and Michael Ruppert researched more parallels in the third part of their series "Profits of Death."[190] For them the Harken case is "the mother of all Enrons." Two banks that were once involved in those dealings, the Faysal Islamic Bank of Bahrain and the Kuwait Finance House, now feature on the list of institutions suspected of financing terror – but only on the lists of European investigators. So far they remain unscathed by George W. Bush's asset freezes. Both these suspect banks have their correspondent accounts with precisely the same major bank whose US affiliate Alex Brown struck an unpleasant chord with speculation on 9/11: Deutsche Bank.

If even CNN is now reporting on the background to the resignation of top bin Laden investigator John O'Neill, is it not time for German TV news to start investigating Deutsche Bank?

If one compares the gigantic investigative effort in the Whitewater scandal and Bill Clinton's affair with an intern, which clocked up $70 million in costs, to the kid-glove handling of the far more significant scandal surrounding Enron, the biggest contributor to the Bush campaign, a striking "double standard" in media attentiveness becomes apparent. The present president can evidently count on impunity thanks to the "war on terrorism."

The "Freedom of Information Act" was not "liquidated at a stroke" as directly as noted above, but the Justice Department is instructing all authorities that from now on they are authorized to withhold documents at their discretion under reference to national security.[191]

TV station CNN is taking similar liberties. The quote from Richard Butler recorded above disappeared swiftly from the specified CNN transcript. However this text was provided in that form on 10/1/2001, around 9 a.m. Eastern time. Unluckily, I quoted from the online document and only printed out a copy two hours later. The document must have been "updated" by CNN in the meantime, because my printout already contains the now-published version. Since the quote is not one that decides the outcome, and Google produced no results on the search for the original, I did no further research on it. It does show how carelessly candid statements by insiders are tidied up afterwards – and how fleeting the freedom of the press can be.

2/02/02
From Al Capone's Turf to Pipelineistan

Inter arma silent leges – In wartime, the laws fall silent. Cicero's famous epigram from the heyday of the Roman Empire holds true for the American Empire today. When we see pictures on TV of prisoners of war at Guantánamo Bay (under the nose of Fidel Castro of all people, himself a long-standing entry on the CIA's assassination list), stuck in cages that even chickens don't suffer in politically correct zones these days, we may well doubt whether civilization really has developed at all in the last 2,000 years.

True, unlike in ancient Rome and Greece, slavery has since been banned by law. In reality, however, the "civilized" West shipped off its rights-deprived human beasts of burden surreptitiously into the sweatshops of the Third World. It may be that according to all the world's democratic constitutions the people are sovereign and corruption is illegal. In reality Enron demonstrates that in the final analysis, whoever has political influence can write the laws, e.g. on energy, and buy the most politicians. It is true that in the name of humanity and human rights war and violence are supposed to be the last resort; in reality, they are the usual continuation of these corrupt dealings by forceful means. There's no business like war business.[192]

Inter arma silent media: in time of war the media are silent. The media did not yet have a major role in the age of the Roman Emperors; if they had, Cicero would have noted their silence too. This unwritten law would hold completely true under Caesar George W. Bush were it not for the little virtual village that, like the Gauls of Asterix' stronghold, fiercely resists the Romans and the noisy silence of the media – and shares suppressed news on its internet marketplace round the clock.

Take Sherman Skolnick[193] for example, investigator in a wheelchair like "Ironsides" of TV fame. He has been on the trail of corrupt judges and politicians for years, and in the fourth part of his "Enron-Black Magic" series[194] he takes us into one of the powerhouses of the American empire, where the validity of Cicero's dictum is known very well: to Cicero, Chicago. This is the part of town once notorious as Al Capone's patch, where the American secret service contrived the 1944 invasion of Italy with the Mafia elite and laid the foundation for the CIA-Mafia-Vatican "rat-lines."[195] Also resident as Archbishop in the 1970's was Paul "Gorilla" Marcinkus, who as subsequent head of the Vatican Bank is one of the most colorful criminals that ever infested the Holy See. Skolnick was already on the trail of the secret service and Mafia coalition in Marcinkus' time, when millions disappeared from the accounts at the First National Bank in Cicero (for purposes including the financing of terror) – and the judges refused to examine the case for "national security"[196] reasons. They were equally inert in 1992 when Cardinal Marcinkus fled a European arrest warrant to his old homeland where he could enjoy a contemplative dotage.

A senior member of the bankruptcy supervisory board who was to testify in court as a witness about the frauds and cooked books at the First National Bank was found shot dead one day before Christmas 1991. Audits at the Rockefeller-affiliated bank, which frequently changed its name and whose alter ago was the money laundry BCCI, were carried out by Chicago-based Arthur Andersen[197] – the same auditors who covered up losses and shredded files in the current Enron case. Of course, it could be purely accidental that the latest man who knew too much and met a curious death[198] was former vice chairman of Enron Clifford Baxter;[199] yet day by day it is becoming more obvious that in the end Enron means the same thing for US mobsters as Gazprom did for the Russian mafia.[200] For the Americans, of course, the slush funds tap not only national, but world oil reserves: at the end of the 1970's Enron bought itself a governor to "deregulate" the Texas energy supply, and at the end of the 1990's a president to carry out similar deregulation, by sharper means henceforth if necessary, in Pipelineistan too.[201] Since the media can't completely hush up the collapse of the Enron giant, some sort of light ought to fall on the background to 9/11 – and onto the economic depression about to hit the freshly-installed president, which thanks to war can be skated over for the time being.

Meanwhile news is cropping up again on the vast plains of the Internet about Delmart E. Vreeland, this little agent of the Navy secret service whom we already profiled (see "11/04/01: Osama meets CIA") as someone who possibly knew about the WTC attacks in advance, and/or as a wannabe James Bond. One of the cryptic notes that he handed to prison officers at the beginning of August has just been published[202] as part of the trial against Vreeland – and namely the one that begins with the list: "Sears Towers, Chicago? World Trade Center? White House? Pentagon?"[203]

Confirmation worthy of a detective novel emerged during the trial that Vreeland clearly remained a secret service employee and was not, as the US Navy claims, dismissed in 1986. To verify the identity of his client, the lawyer made a live phone call in the midst of the courtroom: he dialed the number of the Pentagon, got connected with the "Department of Defense," and asked for the office of Lt. Delmart Vreeland. One moment later the operator confirmed Vreeland's name, his room number and the direct extension. The prosecutor objected to this startling proof: the accused (imprisoned for months) had obviously found the means to hack the Pentagon's telephone directory by remote computer...

So Vreeland will continue to be a potential candidate for the inevitable leak in every conspiracy. His lawyers are convinced that they can stall, if not completely defeat, the US extradition request (rather untypical for a case of alleged credit card fraud) for years to come. If Vreeland stays in jail his whole life – one never can tell – and further details of his foreknowledge are published, then that could become even more valuable to the quest for truth in the WTC incident. Since Canada is not at war, the laws and the media there are not quite so silent...

2/11/02
The Forbidden Truth

The book we cited in connection with the tragic death of bin Laden hunter John O'Neill, *The Forbidden Truth* by French authors Jean-

Charles Brisard and Guillaume Dasquié, has now also been published in German.[204] In Switzerland one of Osama's brothers, Yeslam bin Laden, who lives there and has become a citizen, is trying to block further distribution of the book with a court injunction.

"All the answers, all the keys to dismantling Osama bin Laden's organization can be found in Saudi Arabia,"[205] said FBI anti-terror chief O'Neill in an interview with the authors in July 2001. He also named the reason why he then resigned his job as a top terrorist hunter: "The main obstacles to investigating Islamic terrorism were U.S. oil company interests and the role played by Saudi Arabia." In the first part of the book, the two intelligence and finance experts draw on secret service documents, eyewitness accounts and diplomatic sources to describe how these interests led to the installation of a pipeline-friendly regime in Afghanistan and secret negotiations with the Taliban on the pipeline up until August 2001. Especially clear is how the UN-led multilateral talks with the Afghan government were making good progress up to the end of 2000, then went into reverse when Bush Jr. moved into the White House.

At the end of September 2000 the Taliban's deputy foreign minister gave a speech in Washington promising concessions on human rights and the bin Laden problem – which was generally interpreted as a clear warming in relations. The desired stabilization of the country appeared to be at hand. Yet the tone and ground rules changed when Bush came into office. Alongside the "6+2" group talks (Afghanistan's neighboring countries plus the USA and Russia) Washington resumed direct bilateral discussions with the Taliban. "Presumably so as not to get out of practice," comment Brisard/Dasquié wryly. Then a few months later, at a final meeting in Berlin in July 2001, the US representative openly threatened the Taliban with military action.

In the second part of the book the authors develop a background scenario of central importance not only in explaining what happened on 9/11, but also for the containment of terrorism in the future: the Saudi-Arabian networks of Islamic fundamentalism. Besides the multi-billionaire empire of the royal family and its 4,000 princes, the financial sources of this "kingdom of dangers" are fed also by the financial and investment network of two families, the bin Ladens and the bin Mahfouz, each worth billions. Clan chief Khalid bin Mahfouz (born 1949) is connected with Osama bin Laden via several businesses. The luxurious second home of Khalid bin Mahfouz since 1981 has been suitably located in Houston, Texas – and long before he had dealings with Osama, it was not only the Bush family who counted among his early banking clients. He also managed the private accounts of General Noriega, Bush Sr.'s nifty S.O.B.

The Saudi Bin Laden Group, the family holding company from which Osama is officially cut off, is linked with the Mahfouz empire via a great number of businesses and interests, including the Geneva-based Saudi Investment Company (SICO) headed by Osama's brother Yeslam – the same Yeslam bin Laden who has filed to stop the further distribution of *The Forbidden Truth*. It continues to be available in Germany and, says the publisher, additional supplies should be on their way to Switzerland soon. As the authors strictly document all their sources in this book and refrain from speculative claims, the book appears legally watertight – to such an extent that the precise lists of names, addresses, interests, and cross-holdings can confuse the reader. However, these connections could be of great interest for criminologists and investigators should they ever get a chance to do what was denied to John O'Neill: to rap the knuckles of the Gulf oil monarchy and its fundamentalist sheikhs.

Conventional terror groups like Germany's Red Army Fraction in the 1970's, which had to raise funds by robbing banks, look almost like Robin Hood compared to this gigantic, oil-fed financial network. Clans like the bin Mahfouz or the bin Ladens are among the richest families in the world – and in another chapter Brisard/Dasquié make short work of the fairytale of Osama as an estranged rebel, the black sheep and lost son of two dynasties. How little the "renegade" myth fits Osama bin Laden is laid bare by the fact that the first international arrest warrant against the terrorist supposedly active since the early 1990's was not issued until 1998 – and not by Washington, London or Berlin, but by Tripoli. Gaddafi's officials accused bin Laden and collaborators in Al Muqatila, a radical Sunni group, among others, of the 1994 murder of two employees of the *Bundesamt für Verfassungschutz*, the German Federal Office for the Protection of the Constitution, Silvan Becker and his wife. The office is responsible for monitoring extremists and foreign spies.

The background to this story reveals how the West is entangled with its alleged enemy: not only was British Petroleum (BP) driven off the oil fields by the Libyan revolution, but Colonel Gaddafi also stood for a liberal, enlightened form of Islam; this led in turn to a coalition of interests between Islamic fundamentalists and British intelligence who planned Gaddafi's murder in 1996 using Al Muqatila fighters, Brisard and Dasquié report. Ever since the 1980's, when bin Laden led the Saudi contingent of holy warriors against the Soviets in Afghanistan, the West has worked closely with Osama and used him, if not as a direct agent, then as a tool for the violent implementation of its foreign policy goals.

Brisard believes it is wrong to describe bin Laden as a "creature of the CIA:"

> America's support for bin Laden was in large part the involuntary consequence of its own ambitions in the region. Saudi Arabia's support, on the other hand, was a calculated policy, clear and unambiguous, concerning its brand of Islam in the world. In light of these revelations, Osama bin Laden appears, above all, to be a product of Wahhabism and an instrument of the Saudi kingdom."[206]

So long as this kingdom's backing of terrorism supposedly can't be touched without disturbing America's oil supply, and the decades-old business connections between the oil-drenched Bush administration and the Saudi dictatorship remain a taboo subject, there is little prospect of real success in the war on Islamic terror. The taboo has now at least been broken with the publication by Brisard and Dasquié, already the Number 1 bestseller in France. According to the publisher more than 20,000 copies of the German edition were delivered in the first two weeks. No publisher has yet been found – unsurprisingly – in the USA, but judging by the attention it has been getting in Europe this will not be long in coming.

It remains to be seen whether its indications strike home with readers and also with the international community's decision makers. A demand on the USA is long overdue to dredge not just the safe harbors of terrorism that happen to be in convenient place on the geopolitical chessboard, but above all those that supply the material and ideological backing for the most dangerous arm of terrorism.

The well-documented report by the two French authors makes it quite plain that the wellspring of Al Qaeda terror can only be drained in Saudi Arabia – just as the late lead investigator O'Neill tried to do, but was prevented. Progress in this direction up to now has been zero. After the removal of the Taliban, the most backward Islamic regime in the world is the Saudi monarchy – even fundamentalist Iran is a bit more democratic – yet it continues to enjoy outstanding support thanks to US protection. The profound and long-standing business connections of the Bush family and US oil industry with the region guarantee permanent membership in the "Axis of Good" for undemocratic rogue state Saudi Arabia and the other feudalistic oil dynasties in the neighborhood.

However, that the USA mostly accidentally built up Saudi dissident Osama bin Laden into what he became – as Brisard and Dasquié claim – and that he is a tool of Saudi Arabia, seems rather doubtful to me.

Yeslam bin Laden is not loosening his grip in Switzerland. He has temporarily renewed the distribution ban on The Forbidden Truth *through a court of appeals, and the Pendo publishing house is taking the case to the supreme court. It has since been published in the United States, but like Thierry Meyssan's two books, it was never a front-runner on the US market against the indigenous 9/11 exposés.*

2/18/02
Propaganda Myths From the Führer's Bunker

25 years ago Bob Woodward became a hero of investigative journalism when he scooped the Watergate scandal in the *Washington Post*, but his insider log on 9/11 now shows the hero of yesterday churning out sycophantic society pages today.

My distrust of the official explanations of 9/11 was less an attack of intellectual clear-sightedness than a subjective feeling of unease from the start. Something just did not seem right to me, though I did not know what. The conspiracy-theory slant on events was born more of this need than of the intention to prove any kind of conspiracy, it was more of a groping attempt to find my way in the fog than a targeted, planned attempt to shed light. So it was neither desired nor planned that this commentary should extend to a practically never-ending story, but there is one simple reason why it did: the inconsistencies of the official version became bigger by the day – and the apparently "crazy" conspiracy-theory perspective turned out to be far more realistic and closer to the "truth" than the "sober," allegedly objective perspective of the mainstream media.

Meanwhile I am convinced that the real 9/11 conspiracy theorists did not spring up on *telepolis* and on other pages on the Internet but went public via CNN, Time magazine, the network and newsprint news, and all the other public channels: to this day the explanation they present us about the attacks on the WTC and the Pentagon has consisted of nothing but an Al Qaeda-Ladenist world conspiracy, for which five months after the event there is still not one piece of evidence that would stand up in court. In the midst of all this the world's "public enemy number one" personified has disappeared from the news without a murmur, and whether he's "dead or alive" no longer matters now. The scapegoat condemned in absentia has done his duty as bogeyman of Evil. Al Qaeda, the "worldwide network" of dangerous kamikazes and "sleepers" – what are they really up to, who are they waiting for, why won't they wake up, have they no alarm clock? The 30,000-names-long guest list from bin Laden's guesthouse in Peshawar is becoming ever more insignificant as a scenario, and has given way to a completely abstract "terror" threat and most recently an "Axis of Evil."

The day after, on 9/12, when I tried to imagine the "unimaginable" as a "choreographed catastrophe," I must have belonged to a radical minority. Meantime it is all looking rather different, and the actions of the United States are making it clear: it is not a matter of solving the case and catching the culprits, but a sequence of military moves on the geo-political chessboard. Key questions about 9/11 slip into a tomb of silence, drowned by the drumming of war, weapons, stars and stripes.

The president's remarkable impassiveness as his assistant whispered the news to him at the school has meanwhile found an explanation: Bush was already informed of events in New York before his school visit. But evidently there was no hurry. There was equally little hurry for the country's highest military figure, General Richard Myers, who was having breakfast with a senator in Washington. The pair just carried on chatting while the two WTC towers were hit and a hijacked plane crashed into the Pentagon. The reason why the Chairman of the Joint Chiefs of Staff, the US army's highest commander, was not informed in such an event can only be that no urgent need for action was seen.[207] The only person who seemed to be in a hurry that morning, when he learned of the attacks by telephone, was Secretary of State Colin Powell. He cancelled breakfast with Alejandro Toledo, the new Peruvian president, and flew straight home. And Vice President Dick Cheney was meanwhile rushed to the White House bunker by secret service agents.

In his "insider log," Bob Woodward, Watergate luminary of the *Washington Post*, summarizes the activities of top government members from September 11 to September 20, on the basis of direct interviews and notes by the participants. A phone call came in for Cheney in the bunker from President Bush on Air Force One: "We're going to find out who did this and kick their ass."[208] Apart from sound-bite gems like this, Woodward's extensive report contributes little to solving the case. One almost gets the impression that just as information fell conveniently into his hands when he was a young reporter, which led to the revelation of

Nixon's "plumber's unit," as a star journalist nowadays he gets the dope from intelligence circles, mostly doing service to obfuscation and legend-creation around Bush's war cabinet.

One of the most blatantly obvious questions from the 9/11 drama – why air defenses let the Pentagon aircraft steer unchallenged towards its target for almost an hour, even after two hijacked jets had already flown into the WTC towers – is smoothed over by Woodward's meticulous log in the following manner:

> In the White House bunker, a military aide approached the vice president.
>
> "There is a plane 80 miles out," he said. "There is a fighter in the area. Should we engage?"
>
> "Yes," Cheney replied without hesitation.
>
> Around the vice president, Rice, deputy White House chief of staff Joshua Bolten and I. Lewis "Scooter" Libby, Cheney's chief of staff, tensed as the military aide repeated the question, this time with even more urgency. The plane was now 60 miles out. "Should we engage?" Cheney was asked.
>
> "Yes," he replied again.
>
> As the plane came closer, the aide repeated the question. Does the order still stand?
>
> "Of course it does," Cheney snapped.
>
> The vice president said later that it had seemed "painful, but nonetheless clear-cut. And I didn't agonize over it."
>
> It was, "obviously, a very significant action," Cheney said in an interview. "You're asking American pilots to fire on a commercial airliner full of civilians. On the other hand, you had directly in front of me what had happened to the World Trade Center, and a clear understanding that once the plane was hijacked, it was a weapon." [209]

That's it. Astonishingly there's no hurry in the bunker either. The hijacked aircraft approaches Washington, the aide asks once, twice, three times, receives clear answers each time, but nothing happens. Instead of resolving this Kafkaesque situation and broaching the fire department's no-show (see "1/4/02: Where was the Fire Department?" on page 144), Woodward leaves Cheney to rehash his inner turmoil again, like in a bad Hollywood film. And cut. From here the article then pans to the crash of the Pennsylvania plane.

The meeting in the bunker on the evening of 9/11, which brought together Bush, Cheney, Powell, Rumsfeld, Rice and CIA director Tenet at 9:30 p.m., provides Woodward's starting point for his minutes of "America's chaotic road to war." "Intelligence was by now almost conclusive that Osama bin Laden and his Al-Qaeda network, based in Afghanistan, had carried out the attacks." There is no mention where this conclusion came from – not even in the third part of the series about the next day, on which "for (CIA director) Tenet, the evidence on bin Laden was conclusive – game, set, match."[210] The only "reason" given is that links to Afghanistan were allegedly discovered in the case of three of the hijackers. That's it. Otherwise the issue of evidence implicating the alleged culprits, on which after all the case for war hangs, is of little importance nowadays for erstwhile hero of investigative journalism Bob Woodward. A quarter of a century after Watergate he appears to have defected to the "plumbers'" side himself – and, fed with exclusive interviews from top officials, is cobbling together propaganda myths from the Führer's bunker:

> The war cabinet had questions, no one more than Rumsfeld.
>
> Who are the targets? How much evidence do we need before going after al Qaeda? How soon do we act? While acting quickly was essential, Rumsfeld said, it might take up to 60 days to prepare for major military strikes. And, he asked, are there targets that are off-limits? Do we include American allies in military strikes?
>
> Rumsfeld warned that an effective response would require a wider war, one that went far beyond the use of military force. The United States, he said, must employ every tool available – military, legal, financial, diplomatic, intelligence.
>
> The president was enthusiastic. But Tenet offered a sobering thought. Although al Qaeda's home base was Afghanistan, the terrorist organization operated nearly worldwide, he said. The CIA had been working the bin Laden problem for years. We have a 60-country problem, he told the group.
>
> "Let's pick them off one at a time," Bush replied.
>
> The president and his advisors started America on the road to war that night without a map.

Main point war, main point a big war, main point an "enthusiastic" president who wants to "pick them all off." Were it not terrifying reality you could believe you'd erred into a re-make of Chaplin's classic *The Great Dictator*. In this respect you could even thank Bob Woodward, now mutated into an uncritical court reporter, for his relentless portrayal. It matches the background that it's concealing perfectly.

Die Welt *reproduced Woodward's propaganda fake in three installments starting Dec. 2 with the following introduction: "The series makes it clear how surprised the US were by the Al Qaeda attacks. It also makes it emphatically clear that whoever believes that the Afghanistan*

maneuver is going to remain the only riposte to 9/11 is mistaken."
Of course the paper doesn't ask how it comes to be that somebody who is
so totally surprised suddenly has a bunch of answers ready. Shortly after
the attacks the Springer newspaper chain inserted a preamble into all its
journalist contracts directing that NATO and US policies be supported in
every article. The last person who managed to rally such anticipatory
obedience from the German media was a certain Herr Goebbels.

2/24/02
The Biggest Heroin Fiefdom of all Time

The rise of Britain's East India Company into the Empire's globe-
spanning financial concern in the 18th and 19th centuries was due
primarily to the illegal opium trade into China (see 10/10/01: Uncle
Sam's Junk). Continuation of the trade was secured by military force in
two Opium Wars. The honourable society of merchants in London
always waxed especially indignant over the degrading opium trade each
time they set about to trigger a new war against China, in order to secure
and expand their opium monopoly there. George W. Bush continues this
time-honored tradition with his latest announcement of a new offensive
in the "war on drugs."

   One of the main reasons why the events of September 11 are so
resistant to inquiry is that their background leads into a taboo zone which
vested interests do not care to divulge. One of these taboos is the direct
and indirect financing of US foreign policy via the illegal drug trade.
Thus the "heroinization" of Pakistan after 1979 was seen not only as
inevitable collateral damage in the struggle against Communism, but was
still useful after the end of the Cold War so that Pakistan could pay for
weapons purchases and debt servicing to the IMF. By the end of the
1990's, the revenue of the shadow economy heroin business in Pakistan
was 30% greater than the government budget.[211]

   In October we foretold that a US invasion would not halt the
flourishing heroin business in Afghanistan, which is controlled by the
ISI, Pakistan's secret service and the CIA's most important partner in the
region. According to Adam Porter on the Guerilla News Network
(GNN), the appointment of General and druglord Rashid Dostum to the
new Afghan cabinet cemented the biggest heroin regime of all time.[212]
Outside of government, too, the warlords and drug dealers are back in
business.[213] The Northern Alliance, which unlike the Taliban never took

steps to curtail the cultivation of opium, now controls wide sectors of the country. Pakistan has released one of the big smuggling kings of the Khyber from jail, and in Kabul, the drug control office which the Taliban set up has been evicted by the new government, their telephones and cars confiscated: "They didn't even leave us with a bicycle," complains the director of the agency, who now has only a room in the foreign ministry to crawl into.[214] Meanwhile the press agencies report that US Special Forces regularly visit the shops and bazaars on Opium Street in Kandahar[215] and leave behind demands to "change your business." Pro forma and for the illustrated newsweeklies, then, something is being done about the opium trade. In reality of course the economies of Afghanistan and Pakistan would collapse if the opium and heroin trade were really stopped.

George W. Bush is pushing on the home front to help ensure this never happens. His announcement of an escalation in the "war on drugs"[216] and a juicy increase in the particular war budget is balm for the price of opium and heroin, which fell into the cellar after the beginning of the war: "We'll be rich," crowed a young dealer[217] to the *New York Times*. A kilo of opium worth $300 in August was now asking only $150.

"When we fight drugs, we fight the war on terror" announced alcohol and cocaine abuser Bush in his "National Drugs Control Strategy." He brought this soggy message home in the most expensive TV ad slots the US government has ever paid for.[218] During the Superbowl football finals, two such 30-second spots consumed $3.2 million of taxpayers' money – and established virtually a direct connection between drug use and Osama bin Laden.

Whoever would rather not believe that the CIA and other US intelligence agencies are involved in the drug trade only needs to read their own report on the subject,[219] which gives at least a hint of the tip of the iceberg. Noam Chomsky also spoke on this in a recent interview.[220] Dan Russell explains in *Drug War: Covert Money, Power & Policy* (1999):[221]

> The centers of power responsible for dealing the drugs are the same centers of power disseminating the artificial hysteria necessary for their continued criminalization. That keeps the retail a hundred times higher than the natural value and the trade exclusively in the hands of the muscle. Another name for the muscle is military intelligence.
>
> Clandestine rule by the military-industrial complex means corrupt wars of conquest and the rule by drug dealers. As the world's traditional intoxicating plant substances were banned, they became as valuable as precious metals –

ones which could be planted and harvested. *Illegal drugs, solely because of the artificial value given them by prohibition, have become the basis of military power anywhere they can be grown and delivered in quantity.* To this day, American arms producers are effectively the biggest drug money launderers in the world."[222]

Small wonder then that the USA stubbornly resists the establishment of an International Criminal Court, and blocks every initiative for reform of drug policy, upholding the dogma of prohibition and repression. How else to keep this secretive business safe and lucrative in the hands of the "muscle."

A study by the UN drug control program UNDCP investigated the level of the traffic in different countries with different drugs, and the influence of prohibition. The result? Hard repression favors the sale of hard drugs:

> Thus, in the United States, 78 per cent of all drug consumers take cannabis, yet the market for it represents only 12 per cent of the total market for illicit drugs. In the United Kingdom, 89 per cent of drug consumers take cannabis, but the cannabis market represents only 29 per cent of the total illicit drug market. The Netherlands is an exception to this pattern: cannabis represents about 60 per cent of the total illicit drug market, clearly a result of the de facto decriminalization of cannabis.[223]

According to the UNDCP, the ratio of hard to soft drug sales is about 7:1 in the USA, but in the Netherlands, only 2:3. These UN figures show that the pragmatic, damage-reducing policies of the Dutch are much better suited than the repressive policies of the Americans to drying up terrorist funding sources. Since drug money is the most important source of financing for international terrorism, a truce in the "war on drugs" and a new pragmatism in narcotics policies would be the most important step in the struggle against terrorism. We are talking about $500 billion or more spent annually on products of the poppy, coca and hemp plants – the hugest black market of them all. If the aim really were to rein in this market, it could easily be done by legal production and regulated dispensing of these substances.

But then who will finance unofficial US foreign policies? The "Contras" in Nicaragua, the "Jihad" camps in Afghanistan, the death squads in San Salvador and Colombia, the KLA in Kosovo? Who will prop up indispensable allies like the heroin regimes of Kabul and Islamabad? How to finance the Islamist destabilization of Central Asia and Russia? The Mafia, military dictators and terrorists are addicted to drug money, but US geopolitics are dependent on these slush funds too.

Thanks to Bush's offensive in the "War on Drugs," the money will be flowing merrily again...

One of the greatest taboos in international politics is that drug dealing is one of the financial pillars of unofficial US foreign policy. To rock the boat on this issue would only distress the public. The President calls for a "war on drugs" on the homefront at the same time he installs a puppet government of drug dealers in Afghanistan, and counts the world's greatest heroin producer Pakistan as his most important ally – this must be counted as a fact. Yet whoever wants to publicize it, will be immediately written off as "anti-American" – and will have no chance of publication in our whoring media. If the truth would out that the "war on drugs" is a propaganda trick that finally causes far more suffering from drugs than it prevents, the question might not be long in coming: isn't the "war on terrorism" a similar chimera?

3/03/02
The Kosher Conspiracy

After the left-liberal political magazine *The New Statesman*[224] ran a lead story entitled "The Kosher Conspiracy" about the British government's slavish support for A. Sharon's policies, a storm of reproaches of anti-Semitism broke over the journal. Although one of the authors, the renowned Australian journalist John Pilger, has repeatedly distinguished himself for his investigative reporting on human rights violations like the genocide in East Timor, that did not save him from the blows of the Holocaust Club, which currently strike everyone who publicly criticizes Israel and its supporters. But a detail like 20,000 Jewish demonstrators who marched in New York last week against Sharon's terror policies, they scarcely appear in the mainstream news media...

"Cui bono?" Who benefits? A half year after the attacks, when one asks which countries and governments benefited, the list is short: only the USA and George W. Bush, with Israel and Ariel Sharon. Surely it would be jumping to conclusions to accuse these two as accomplices merely because they are the prime beneficiaries, but as the criterion of motive is central to every criminologist's preparation of the profile of a culprit, Bush and Sharon really ought to be pretty near the top of the list of suspects.

When someone is murdered in a detective story and the innocent gardener is suspected because the victim's will names him as the main heir, he will have an acute interest in a timely and complete investigation to discover the real miscreant. What would the reader think of a gardener who tells the police to drop their inquiries and to concentrate instead on preventing further murders? Yet this is just what President Bush and his VP Cheney did in late January: they called on the Democratic leader Tom Daschle not to start any more investigations of the events of 9/11, because according to Cheney, that would take resources and personnel away from the "war on terrorism." So now it's official: the US Government is covering up the background on 9/11.

To perfect the smokescreen, they have now established the Information Awareness Office: a disinformation and propaganda agency, whose grandest intelligence task is to tap all e-mails and phone calls in the USA for terrorist communiqués.[225] "The Information Awareness Office. You want to know what that is? Think, Big Brother is Watching You," says a columnist of the British *Guardian*, and adds: "You want to test it out? Text-message any American friend, "Bmb OK. Allah gr8.""[226] It gets better: as director of the nosy new agency Bush has named the old wheelhorse Admiral John M. Poindexter, who was Reagan's security advisor and then went to jail for cooking up the Iran-Contra scheme.

No investigation on that, please

Both President Bush and Vice President Dick Cheney urged Senate Majority Leader Tom Daschle four months ago not to push for an investigation into the events of Sept. 11, Daschle said on Sunday.

Appearing on the NBC program "Meet the Press," Daschle flatly contradicted Cheney, who last week denied he had warned Daschle off an investigation.

Daschle and other Democrats favor a special commission into the official handling of pre-Sept. 11 terror warnings. Both Cheney and Bush have in recent days argued publicly against the idea, opting instead for an ongoing inquiry by the intelligence committees of Congress.

Daschle, a South Dakota Democrat, said Cheney telephoned him on Jan. 24 to urge that no Sept. 11 inquiry be made, and that Bush had followed up on January 28 with a similar request during a breakfast meeting at the White House.

"I can tell you on January 24th, first, and on January 28th second, and on other dates following, that request was made," Daschle said.

"I don't recall the exact words. The motivation was that they didn't want to take people off the effort to try to win the war on terror. They were concerned about the diversion of resources, the diversion of manpower in

particular, and that was the reason given me by both the president and the vice president," Daschle said.

Last week on the same program, Cheney denied calling Daschle to argue against a Sept. 11 probe, saying, "Tom's wrong. He has, in this case, let's say a misinterpretation. What I did do was... say, we prefer to work with the intelligence committees."

Asked on Sunday about the apparent contradiction with Cheney, Daschle said: "It's an honest disagreement. I'm willing to accept the fact that they don't agree that was the right interpretation." But he refused to back away from his account.

Daschle last Tuesday said he would push for an independent commission after disclosures suggesting authorities missed a series of hints last year that critics believe might have helped prevent the attack.

House and Senate Intelligence Committees are investigating jointly the failure to uncover the plot to hijack four airliners and crash them into targets in Washington and New York on Sept. 11, killing more than 3,000 people.

But congressional Democrats have called for a special commission to probe, among other things, why the FBI failed to act on an agent's memo last summer recommending his superiors look for al Qaeda members training at U.S. flight schools.

"We are not making any accusations against the president, but we know that we have to do a better job," Daschle said.

Daschle said he thought they would be able to get the necessary votes in the Senate to back a special commission, adding the vote would take place some time in June.

He said the commission's inquiry could be broadened to look at other events, including the August 1998 bombings of U.S. embassies in Kenya and Tanzania that have, like the events of Sept 11, been blamed on Osama Bin Laden's al Qaeda network.

U.S. national security advisor Condoleezza Rice, appearing on "Fox News Sunday," said the administration opposed any probe outside the congressional intelligence committees because a war against terrorism was still underway.

"We worry about anything that would take place outside of the intelligence committees, and indeed, we think the intelligence committees are the proper venue for this kind of review."

Susan Cornwell, Reuters, 27.5.2002[227]

With such offensive team spirit in the surveillance and propaganda sectors, the explosive spy case which has been the hot potato of the US media for months may also be pushed under the rug, although it is probably the greatest wiretapping scandal in US history. After 9/11, about one hundred people were arrested in the USA on suspicion of espionage. Disguised as "art students," they had gained entry to various agencies and in some cases had connections to the US branch of an Israeli telephone company, which supplies America's police and intelligence services with wiretapping equipment. This bombshell is ignored for two reasons: for one, the jailed suspects have been linked to the events of 9/11, and moreover, they are Israelis.[228]

Murdoch's pro-Bush channel Fox News ("We report – you decide") broke the story in late December, but soon banished the text of the four-part series[229] from its website:[230]

> It turns out that Israel has had a potential wiretap on every phone in America for years, along with the ability to monitor and record who any person is calling, anywhere in America; information of great value even if one does not listen to the calls themselves. Amdocs, Inc., the company which subcontracts billing and directory services for phone companies around the world, including 90 percent of American phone companies, is owned by Israeli interests. Yet another Israeli company, Comverse Infosys, is suspected of having built a "back door" into the equipment permanently installed into the phone system that allows it instant eavesdropping on any phone in America.[231]

Press Conference with Mr. Ari Fleischer, White House spokesman, 2/25/02

Q: Ari, why would this administration choose a man for counterterrorism who is so associated with the dark side of the Iran Contra scandal, Admiral Poindexter?

MR. FLEISCHER: When you say, choose him for counterterrorism, can you be more specific?

Q: He's in the Pentagon, he's been appointed head of DARPA, which is a counterterrorist office, developing plans, demonstrations with information.

MR. FLEISCHER: I'm not aware of any appointment.

Q: Yet.

MR. FLEISCHER: Let me just say about Admiral Poindexter, Admiral Poindexter is somebody who this administration thinks is an outstanding American and an outstanding citizen who has done a very good job in what he has done for our country, serving in the military.

Q: How can you say that, when he told Colonel North to lie?

MR. FLEISCHER: Helen, I think your views on Iran Contra are well-known, but the President does believe that Admiral Poindexter served –

Q: It isn't my view, this is the prosecutor for the United States.

MR. FLEISCHER: I understand. The President thinks that Admiral Poindexter has served our nation very well.

Q: Really?

MR. FLEISCHER: That's the President's thoughts.

Q: Do you know his record?

MR. FLEISCHER: I'm sure you will inform me.

Q: I don't have to, all you have to do is look it up.

http://www.whitehouse.gov/news/releases/2002/02/20020225-16.html

Fox reporter Carl Cameron learned from FBI sources that some of the arrested suspects were employees of this telephone company; of course they admit to no wrongdoing.[232] Cameron's report continues:

> Investigators suspect that the Israelis may have gathered intelligence about the attacks in advance, and not shared it. A highly placed investigator said there are – quote – "tie-ins." But when asked for details, he flatly refused to describe them, saying, quote:
>
> "Evidence linking these Israelis to 9-11 is classified. I cannot tell you about evidence that has been gathered. It's classified information."

It's no secret that there are intimate connections between the wire-tapping specialists from Comverse Infosys and the Israeli government and its Mossad intelligence agency which may thus have had access for years to every telephone in the US – even the one in the Oval Office of the White House.[233] During Clinton's "Monicagate" hearings Ms. Lewinsky mentioned a remark by the President that their conversations might be overheard by a "foreign service." Oddly enough, after his affair with the White House intern hit the fan, Clinton put a stop to the high-pressure search for a bug in the White House. The little warning shot was evidently sufficient; one can easily imagine what further embarrassments a "foreign service" might be able to serve up after years of wall-to-wall eavesdropping. With such an arsenal of blackmail, it must be child's play to keep unflattering stories out of the papers, even a spy scandal of Enronesque dimensions.

This background makes sense of the famous retort of Ariel Sharon when foreign minister Peres criticized his aggressive policies in early October: "Every time we do something, you tell me Americans will do this and will do that. I want to tell you something very clear: don't worry about American pressure on Israel. We, the Jewish people, control America. And the Americans know it."

Sharon's remark came in a debate on October 3 on the radio station Kol Yisrael,[234] so even though the words were not subsequently confirmed by his spokesman, it was grist to the mill of the "Jewish World Conspiracy" and the *Protocols of the Elders of Zion*, a propaganda piece of unbroken popularity among Muslims and the radical right in the West. Hannah Arendt noted that Hitler imitated in practice the very conspiracy theory that he had set in motion as a propaganda instrument (see the chapter on "The Elders of Zion"); we can observe that Sharon more or less unconsciously carries out his policies on Hitlerian models.[235] When President Bush admonished Sharon in late September to halt the offensive against the Palestinians, Sharon compared him to Neville Chamberlain,[236] who had watched Hitler's annexation of Czechoslovakia without batting an eye – as if Israel, bristling with high-tech weaponry, were about to be overrun by Palestinian demonstrators with stones and Molotov cocktails. In fact Sharon has the same view on the Oslo Accords as Hitler did on the Treaty of Versailles: a document of dishonor that can only be cleansed from the world by war.

That such a politician should already be arraigned before a war crimes tribunal[237] – for the massacres of Sabra and Chatila 19 years ago[238] – is quite an understandable demand, and relatively easy to carry out, if he came from Afghanistan, Yugoslavia, Iraq or some such place. But he is from Israel, and only needs to pull the "wild card" of anti-Semitism to be left in peace. In the section on the brown-shirted past of the presidential dynasty (see "9/26/01: Skulls, Bones & Bush") I attributed it to the anti-Jewish traditions of the Bush clan that Sharon gave not a whit for the strenuous peace-making admonitions coming out of Washington. Yet the simmering wiretap scandal may explain not only foreknowledge of the attacks – with a possible connection to the speculative activity around 9/11, which was swept under the rug without an investigation – but also Sharon's aggressive chutzpah. Evidently he really does have suitable thumbscrews to bring Big Brother into line at any time.

Shouldn't one rather keep thoughts like this to oneself, since they aid the enemy – neofascists and fundamentalist Islam, who use the theory of the Jewish World Conspiracy as an important propaganda tool? In my opinion, the opposite is true. When conspiracies like the wiretapping scandal are papered over up and hushed up, this feeds suspicion of a "Kosher Conspiracy" rather than eliminating it, since keeping mum does not stifle the rumors. Of course, a debate on this issue is too much to expect. Anyone who points to today's fascist tendency in the USA is written off as "anti-American," and whoever criticizes Israel's violations of international human rights is immediately hit with the red card "anti-Semite" and is out of the game. As long as these Nazi rules of play – "What is un-German is, *we* decide" principles like "freedom of opinion," "democratic media" or "political consensus" decay into miserable rhetoric. The freshly established US agencies for propaganda and "Information Awareness" will only aggravate rather than end this.

The cover-up of the Israeli spy ring affair [239] *in the USA continues. In April, George W. Bush called Sharon a "Man of Peace"; in June, he called a nothing speech by Sharon historic, and stood by him in everything, when he was not busy absenting himself entirely from the scene of the crime. Iraq's refusal to re-admit UN weapons inspectors is blown up into a worldwide scandal, while Israel can refuse to let the International Red Cross into freshly occupied territories without fear of the slightest sanction.*

My comparison of Sharon's policies to Nazism brought me a number of protesting letters, which I then referred to an interview that the author Amos Oz published on Dec. 17, 1982, in the Israeli daily Davar. *That was after the massacre in Sabra and Chatila, for which Sharon must answer before a war crimes trial, when he loses his immunity as head of state. This interview circulated on the Internet as a conversation with Sharon, although Amos Oz had actually carried out these discussions with leading military officials of the Lebanon invasion on condition of anonymity, and published them without the names of the individuals. The passage cited below was attributed to "C," who is described only as a soldier with "a certain past." Notwithstanding, many commentators have linked these statements to Sharon – including Holger Jensen,*[240] *previously a reporter for* Newsweek, *who quoted from the "Sharon" interview in April for an article in the* Rocky Mountain News. *Following protests from Jewish circles, Jensen asked Amos Oz personally, who did not reveal the identity of "C," except to say that it was not Ariel Sharon. Jensen then apologized in a* mea culpa[241] *– and resigned from his position as editor "by mutual agreement."*

Even when the following viewpoint cannot be ascribed personally to Sharon, to me it seems that the remarks of his comrade-in-arms adequately portray the spirit, ideological context and philosophy of the sitting Israeli president:

You can call me anything you like. Call me a monster or a murderer. Just note that I don't hate Arabs. On the contrary. Personally, I am much more at ease with them, and especially with the Bedouin, than with Jews. Those Arabs we haven't yet spoilt are proud people, they are irrational, cruel and generous. It's the Yids that are all twisted. In order to straighten them out you have to first bend them sharply the other way. That, in brief, is my whole ideology.

Call Israel by any name you like, call it a Judeo-Nazi state as does Leibowitz. Why not? Better a live Judeo-Nazi than a dead saint. I don't care whether I am like Gaddafi. I am not after the admiration of the gentiles. I don't need their love. I don't need to be loved by Jews like you either.[242]

Here the mechanism known to psychology as "identification with the aggressor" seems to me very clear: people who suffer violence in their childhood become violent themselves; peoples and nations evidently likewise. By this analogy, the state of Israel, born under the duress of Hitler, archfather of violence, has now grown, psychohistorically speaking, into something like a violent hooligan who simply knows no other way to behave. How to convince Sharon and his fellow killers that there are other ways to survive than those they inherited from their brutal "Father?" With suicide bombers certainly not – these only provoke them into being "even better Nazis."

As regards anti-Semitism, Sharon's fellow combatant from the Lebanon campaign leaves no doubt in this interview that it is a strategic aim to incite world-wide hatred of Jews through violent land-grabbing and massacres:

Let me tell you what is the most important thing, the sweetest fruit of the war in Lebanon: It is that now they don't just hate Israel. Thanks to us, they now also hate all those gourmet Jews in Paris, London, New York, Frankfurt and Montreal, in all their holes. At last they hate all these nice Yids, who say they are different from us, that they are not Israeli thugs, that they are different Jews, clean and decent...

Soon their palaces will be smeared with the slogan: Yids, go to Palestine! And you know what? They will go to Palestine because they will have no other choice! All this is a bonus we received from the Lebanese war. Tell me, wasn't it worth it?

Soon we will hit on good times. The Jews will start arriving, the Israelis will stop emigrating and those who already emigrated will return.

But the better times never arrived, which must be why General Sharon and Co. have to stir up new wars and massacres. According to this conspirative logic, Neonazis and other racists who deface synagogues and brandish anti-Semitic slogans are the best helpers in settling Sharon's "land without people."

3/12/02
The Mystery of the Pentagon

Bit by bit, the mainstream media can no longer completely black out all the suppressed facts and unprecedented news. Last week in their cover story on Saudi Arabia, *Der Spiegel* mentioned in passing the arms conglomerate Carlyle Group and its representative, George Bush Sr. In October, *Spiegel Online* had censored an article by the Indian author Arundhati Roy (see "11/2/01: A long-planned War"), removing the mention of the Bush and Bin Laden families' investment in Carlyle.

So maybe the questions arising from the "Petition to the US Senate to Investigate Oddities of 9/11" (see "1/10/02: The American Way of War" on page 146) will also get a public airing – as well as the interview with Osama bin Laden in the Pakistani newspaper *Ummat* on September 28th,[243] in which he denies having anything to do with 9/11. As a piece of evidence, this interview seems to be at least as authentic as the retouched-looking home videos with his alleged confession.

Six months after the attack, and still no "sleeper" cells have awakened, still no suicide bomber from the Al Qaeda Network has befallen the western world. This could be counted as a success in the "war on terrorism" – or else as a simple sign that the "sleepers" were fiction, invented to spread mass hysteria. Without the suggestion of a continuing threat, the police manhunt for the culprits could not be immediately replaced by military action and within days by war; without inflating the effigy of a dangerous network of cunning and psychotic assassins menacing western civilization and the hearth of every home, the people could not have been driven into such a warlike frenzy.

To understand the agenda behind this propaganda – which it should be clear, after half a year, is definitely not to explain the circumstances of the attacks nor to capture the culprits and their backers – I recommended the books by Brzezinski (*The Great Chessboard*) and Huntington (*Clash of Civilizations*), which clearly define the geostrategic goals of the USA as well as the perceived enemies needed to attain them. These somber political considerations were anticipated by Carl Schmitt, theoretical and juridical architect of the Third Reich (and admired teacher of Leo Strauss, the philosophical godfather of the Neocons). Schmitt's *Concept of the Political,* published in 1932, has many passages that sound like they could have been written after 9/11/2001:

> An imperialism based on economic power will naturally attempt to introduce a worldwide condition in which it can succeed by using the unhindered use of its economic arsenal, including cutting off credit, raw materials embargoes, debasement of foreign currencies, and so on. It considers any attempt by a people to escape the reach of such "peaceful" methods as "anti-economic violence." It will also employ sharper measures, although still "economic" and therefore "unpolitical," essentially "peaceful" means of coercion like... the interdiction of food supplies to the civilian population, hunger blockades. Finally it also possesses technology for violent physical killing, technically perfect modern weapons, which its wealth of capital and know-how makes unprecedentedly effective, should they actually need to be used. For the implementation of this arsenal, a new and essentially pacifist vocabulary has been developed, which knows no war, only sanctions, punitive expeditions, international police and peace-securing missions. The adversary is no longer called an enemy but a violator and disturber of the peace, and is banished beyond the pale of humanity. A war waged to protect or expand the economic power position must, with an array of propaganda, become a "crusade" and a "war to end all wars," or "the last war of humanity."[244]

The "either with us or with the terrorists" of George W. Bush's headily received declaration of war echoes Schmitt's "concept of the political" as the distinction between friend and foe, just as the anti-terror tactics carried out with "unprecedentedly effective weapons" were also defined as a "Crusade" and a "Clash of Civilizations." The psychological shock of the unprecedented events plus the immediate launch of the Godzilla-billboard-sized Menace to Mankind Bin Laden made virtually instantaneous mobilization possible. Anyone who thought to ask first and shoot later, or who asked for proof of guilt, became themselves guilty of "cowardly thinking" and "unpatriotic behavior"; whoever aired doubts about the official version of events could be simply brushed off with the label of "Conspiracy Theorist."

Daniel Pearl, who dared to dig into some background details on location, such as the links between opium farming, the Pakistani intelligence agency ISI and its partner the CIA, was kidnapped and murdered. Coincidentally by none other than Umar Sheikh,[245] British subject, ex-student of the renowned "London School of Economics" and top agent of the ISI director Mahmud Ahmed, who was fingered by the Indian and US services as "terror pilot" Mohammed Atta's backer, to whom he is said to have transferred the sum of $100,000 last summer.

Did the media cartel of silence, evidently produced under pressure, sweep more than dozens of greater and lesser discrepancies under the carpet: perhaps a whole Boeing 757, which smashed into the Pentagon building?Already while watching the news on 9/11 I noticed that there were no pictures of the airplane that hit the US defense ministry. In the following days, a search for "Pentagon Crash Pictures" brought images of the burning building, but no airplane. In late February I stumbled on the French website "Hunt the Boeing,"[246] which unleashed days of debate on the Internet. The thesis was that a 100-ton Boeing would have left behind more damage and more debris than can be seen on official photos of the crash scene.

Critics of the supposed "French joke"[247] were quickly refuted,[248] and the debate that then flared up apparently led to the official release on March 8th of a series of alleged new pictures of the crash in many newspapers and on the Net. Yet remarkably enough, even on the retroactively produced photo evidence[249] there is no airplane, but only an explosion to be seen – and the date stamp on the photos is September 12, 5:37 p.m.! Is it possible that the security clocks and cameras in the Pentagon – after all not an insignificant building – run on lunar time? Or perhaps the entire Pentagon debate, as some bloggers think,[250] is another red herring – a false trail that distracts from the Israeli spy ring and its connection to 9/11?

Knowing the way around

The Pentagon is not very high, a pilot could come straight to the Pentagon like this to hit, he should have flown a lot in this area to know the obstacles which could meet him when he is flying very low with a big commercial plane to hit the Pentagon in a special place. Somebody has studied this very well, someone has flown in this area very much.

Hosni Mubarak, http://www.presidency.gov.eg/html/14-Sept2001_press_2.html

Be that as it may – compared to the photos of the WTC crashes, which were repeated hundreds of times, photo evidence of the Pentagon crash was rare on 9/11 and remained extremely sketchy afterwards. If the riveting attack in New York had not taken place first, the oddities of the later crash would have stuck out immediately. Neither the black box nor the radio traffic from this flight have been made public – although the responsible fire chief at the site was certain, in a press conference on Sept. 12th, that the black box of AA 77 would soon be found. This very secretiveness inspires suspicion and prepares the ground for every kind of disinformation, which is then susceptible to distract attention from the actual causes. The real Pentagon mystery is not the search for a giant Boeing and preoccupation with dubious photo evidence, but remains the question, how could an airplane intrude with impunity into the most sensitive "no-fly-zone" in the USA?

The oddities of the Pentagon crash then led to a wide-ranging discussion, which accelerated with the publication in April 2002 of the book by the French author Thierry Meyssan (L'Effroyable Imposture – The Big Lie). *According to its strident thesis, the Pentagon was not struck by a Boeing, but by a missile. Where the big passenger jet ended up, Meyssan naturally can't explain.*

My hunch proved correct that this would divert attention to a side show. Numerous articles use Meyssan's thesis as a convenient excuse to ridicule all critical inquiry into 9/11 as conspiracy theories.

3/22/02
WTC, the World Trade Conspiracy

Do you know what the World Bank does?[251] Or the IMF, the International Monetary Fund?[252] Both institutions claim they fight poverty and support the economies and currencies of developing countries with long-term financing. They do nothing of the kind. They use financing to get these countries under their control – and they support any government that will deliver, however corrupt, dictatorial or incompetent it may be.

So far is the criticism of these "august" institutions well-known and in such general terms also relatively fruitless. Yet Greg Palast,[253] one of the few leading investigative journalists who have not bent to the service of the propaganda machine after 9/11, is able not only to documentarily prove such general accusations, but to prove what criminal methods the IMF and World Bank are using in the example of the current Argentina disaster. Employment opportunities for independent journalists in the USA being rather modest, Palast works currently mainly for the BBC and British newspapers; yet when it comes to explosive documents from the US, he seems to have as good contacts as ever.

For example, he got a copy of Executive Order W199I, by which the Bush administration cut short the FBI investigation of Al Qaeda last summer, whereupon terrorist-hunter John O'Neill threw in the towel and resigned (see "11/24/01: In Memoriam John O'Neill...") The document will also play a role in the lawsuit filed by a still anonymous FBI agent against the US government with the support of the anti-corruption organization "Judicial Watch,"[254] for hindering the investigation of bin Laden.[255] On reading the interview with Palast about his researches and documents on the IMF and World Bank,[256] it appears Executive Order W199I may make still more waves. World Bank director Wolfensohn refused an invitation from CNN to debate with Palast on the air, after which the initially disputed authenticity of the internal "eyes only" document could no longer be questioned.

Palast says the documents are copies of secret agreements which countries like Argentina must sign before they get credits from the IMF or World Bank. One of the conditions is the "privatization" of public utilities – water and electricity, transport, telecoms networks, oil pipelines – to international corporations, and the "processing" of the responsible politicians, which Palast describes with an example of an Argentine Senator:

> I actually spoke to a Senator from Argentina two weeks ago. I got him on camera. He said that after he got a call from George W. Bush in 1988 saying give the gas pipeline in Argentina to Enron – that's our current president – he said that what he found was really creepy was that Enron was going to pay one-fifth of the world's price for their gas and he said how can you make such an offer? And he was told, not by George W. but by a partner in the deal, well if we only pay one-fifth that leaves quite a little bit for you to go in your Swiss bank account. And that's how it's done.[257]

Joe Stiglitz, head economist of the World Bank and a Nobel Prize medalist in economics, was fired after he learned details of these practices during his travels for the bank, and began to ask critical questions. Palast spoke with him at length and described the methods used to steal state enterprises from their people and bring them under the control of the IMF and World Banks:

> He told me, he went into countries where they were talking about privatizing and selling off these assets. And basically, they knew, they literally knew and turned the other way when it was understood that leaders of these countries and the chief ministers would salt away hundreds of millions of dollars...

> They hand it over, generally to the cronies, like Citibank was very big and grabbed half the Argentine banks. You've got British Petroleum grabbing pipelines in Ecuador. I mentioned Enron grabbing water systems all over the place. And the problem is that they are destroying these systems as well. You can't even get drinking water in Buenos Aires. I mean it is not just a

question of the theft. You can't turn on the tap. It is more than someone getting rich at the public expense...

The IMF and the World Bank [are] 51% owned by the United States Treasury. So the question becomes, what are we getting for the money that we put into there? And it looks like we are getting mayhem in several nations. Indonesia is in flames. He was telling me, the Chief Economist, Stiglitz, was telling me that he started questioning what was happening. You know, everywhere we go, every country we end up meddling in, we destroy their economy and they end up in flames. And he was saying that he questioned this and he got fired for it. But he was saying that they even kind of plan in the riots. They know that when they squeeze a country and destroy its economy, you are going to get riots in the streets. And they say, well that's the IMF riot. In other words, because you have a riot, you lose. All the capital flees from your country and that gives the opportunity for the IMF to then add more conditions...

After we were attacked on September 11, Bush ran out and said we got to spend $50 to $100 billion to save our economy. We don't start cutting the budget, you start trying to save this economy. But they tell these countries you've got to cut, and cut, and cut. And why, according to the inside documents, it's so you can make payments to foreign banks – the foreign banks are collecting 21% to 70% interest. This is loan-sharking. If fact, it was so bad that they required Argentina to get rid of the laws against loan-sharking, because any bank would be a loan-shark under Argentine law.[258]

Here in a nutshell are the main moves in this huge game:

Step 1: Tie the granting of credits by the IMF and World Bank to maximum "privatization" of public property, bribe the responsible officials and bring the key industries under control.

Step 2: Order budget cuts, austerity measures, dismantling of the social system as "consolidation measures" in order to keep up debt payments. A drastic drop in GNP, popular uprisings and capital flight are all part of it.

Step 3: When the economy is extensively destroyed and the country is no longer able to supply its own needs, take down all tariff barriers to foreign products and demand horrific prices and interest rates for all necessities of life, such as medicine.

Step 4: Install a militarized corporate government, which will run the business of the "colony" forthwith for profit and nip any eventual slave rebellions in the bud.

The name "Conspiracy" for this domineering form of world trade is fully deserved. This globalization regime goes on largely in the open and in plain view, aside from a few fragments of conspirative "agreements of understanding" such as Greg Palast was able to get his hands on. Pipeline negotiations were held with Mullah Omar and his Taliban government up until August 2001. Their assent to the American conditions would have brought them "carpets of gold" (in other words, new IMF/World Bank credits) – their refusal, and their evident disinterest in a fat bribe on a discreet bank account – earned them a "carpet of bombs," just as the US negotiator had threatened. And since then, with a onetime Unocal consultant as President, a "corporate government" too, or as the title of Palast's newest book puts it: *The Best Democracy Money Can Buy.*[259]

Whoever can't be bought for this sort of "democracy" must be convinced by insistent bombardment. Thanks to 9/11 and the new "war on terrorism," gunboat diplomacy no longer even needs to apologize. The Osama fraud that made this war possible is perhaps the latest and greatest conspiratorial action of the Bushist empire, which allows it to unsheathe its talons to their full extent, unhindered and at will. Whoever got letters from the late "land of the free" could clearly recognize the new imperial demand and the old tradition it rests on, from Caesar to Hitler to Bush – right on the postage stamp.

PART 3.
Ask Who It Was,
But For Heaven's Sake Don't Ask Why

At the present rate, within the next few years the Illuminati will have the American people under tighter surveillance than Hitler had the Germans. And the beauty of it is, the majority of Americans will have been so frightened by Illuminati-backed terrorist incidents that they will beg to be controlled, as a masochist begs for the whip.

Robert A. Wilson, The Eye in the Pyramid, *p. 198.*

(You've got real *problems when reality is indistinguishable from a 30-year old book apparently written after gargling with LSD.)*

The Never-Ending Story

The tragedy of Sept. 11, 2001, is a never-ending story that only future generations will be able to tell in its entirety. The real facts behind the 9/11 terror attacks will only be unearthed by future historians, just as it took over half a century before declassified government files made it possible to establish beyond doubt the foreknowledge of the "surprise attack" on Pearl Harbor. It has taken decades after John F. Kennedy's assassination for more precise outlines of this attempted coup to become discernible.[1] Not only has Bush Jr. withheld presidential files of his father's administration from the National Archives, but he has also sealed the files of successive presidents and those of his own administration, which means they won't be released for research after the usual twenty years under the "Freedom of Information Act." So it will be a long time indeed before the whole "truth," or what can be reconstructed of it, comes to light.

It seemed all the more important to me as a media witness and contemporary of this historical event to record in this conspirological diary the things that struck me as inconsistent and strange in the official portrayal of events. My aim was not to father yet another conspiracy theory, but to reveal the "bin Laden/al-Qaeda" theory that is blaring on all media channels for what it is – a conspiracy theory. Even eight months after the atrocity, no evidence that would hold up in a court of law has emerged to corroborate bin Laden's guilt. In half a year, the biggest police operation of all times has found no accomplice, no mastermind and not a single real suspect. From a criminalistic perspective, 9/11 is a case for the Guinness *Book of World Records* – the biggest unsolved murder case in history.

Robert A. Wilson has pointed out that conspiracy theories have an inherent self-defense mechanism which immunizes them by branding critics as members of the conspiracy.[2] Every argument against the conspiracy theory thus becomes an argument in its favor, and increases the scope and the threat of the alleged conspiracy. Critics of the official version of the attacks against New York and Washington experienced something similar. Anyone daring so much as to ask questions was labeled a "conspiracy theorist," "anti-American" and a supporter of terror. Here is the strong correlation between conspiracy theory and its theological counterpart, demonology – whoever denies the devil's existence must be possessed by him. And it also becomes clear how little, in times of crisis and emergency, our "enlightened" media age differs from the irrational, superstitious Middle Ages. Virtually overnight, "Osama" was installed as Satan incarnate, the new antichrist whose ubiquitous, world-spanning demons ("sleepers") threaten the entire world, and who can only be defeated in a global "crusade." The massive conjuring ritual on all major media channels in the days after the "attacks" made it nearly impossible to escape this brainwashing. Those who wanted to know instead of believe, those who wanted to understand instead of repeating blindly, those who demanded proof instead of conjurations, were flooded out by the mainstream of the media, which blanketed the entire world with the "bin Laden" theory.

The entire world? Not quite. A virtual yet global village – the Internet – put up resistance against media mimicry. And those privileged to access this Petibonum (the village of Asterix and Obelix that resists the Roman legions) could get the electronic druids at www.google.com to brew them a magical info-potion – alternative information that immunizes against the empire's simplifying and mind-dulling propaganda.

On an earlier occasion I described the Internet as an ideal environment and biotope for conspiracy theories. Never before have the conditions been more suitable for the dissemination of conjecture and rumor than on the World Wide Web. While most newspapers, television and radio stations are obliged not least by press law to document their news and claims and to be able to prove them if doubts arise, this kind of discipline is not enforceable on the Internet. After 9/11, of course, when practically all the media blithely discarded their code of independent, non-partisan and objective reporting, voluntarily offered their services for propaganda purposes and sold the "bin Laden" conspiracy theory as factual reality, the Internet, that "conspiracy biotope," turned out to be the last oasis for seeking the truth.

The questions mainstream journalists no longer asked about the course of events, about the failure of air defenses, etc. were raised here: the story of Osama bin Laden as double agent and instrument of US intelligence; the business ties between the bin Laden and Bush families; the pipeline plans and geostrategies of the Anglo-American oil companies; the secret negotiations with the Taliban up until August 2001; the meeting at the American Hospital in Dubai, where the local CIA representative visited the patient Osama bin Laden in July 2001; the drug trade as financial pillar of unofficial U.S foreign policy. All this taboo information which is barely or not at all compatible with the official conspiracy theory could be researched on the Internet – with the help of the search engine Google. By entering two or three names or terms, anyone no longer trusting TV and newspaper reports was able to compile their own news bulletin and tune out of the announcements emanating from the "Ministry of Truth." In future, scientists and beha-vioral researchers will find it worthwhile to study the interaction of media, manipulation and mass psychology in this example of what is probably the biggest brainwashing operation in history – and to draw attention to the paradox that although such pervasive propaganda can only achieve its direct "live" effect in a networked media society, it is the culmination of networked media technology, the Internet, that ultimately provided the only means of escape from the machinery of manipulation.

As a journalist, I have learned over the past two decades to appreciate the technology of networked computers. In 1981, I joined the editorial staff of *taz*, which was founded in response to media mimicry on Germany's hunt for RAF terrorists during the "German Autumn" of 1977, and was also the first newspaper to be produced digitally. Although *taz* editors didn't make a lot of money, there were two invaluable advantages – working for an absolutely independent newspaper, and the latest computer technology. Long before the Internet became a reality, we *taz* reporters used to make a stir at press conferences with our Olivetti M10's, the legendary precursor of today's notebooks, which transmitted data to our editorial office via an acoustic coupler fitted onto a telephone receiver. Ever since I installed the first modem at home in the mid-1980's – and "pope of the hackers" Wau Holland held the founding meeting of the "Chaos Computer Club" in the *taz* offices – it was clear to me that the computer revolution was not the personal computer, but the inter-personal computer, the networking of computers and data banks. Even if the rate of transmission of 1.2 kilo-bytes back then more closely resembled the speed of a jungle drum than today's DSL, I have used this technology to retrieve information ever since, and increasingly so; but never have I found it to be so necessary for survival, so absolutely essential for my sanity and independence as after Sept. 11, 2001.

Without the Internet my brain inevitably would have suffered the same soft-soaking as hundreds of millions of TV-only consumers. The Web provided things like GNN – the Guerilla News Network – as well as CNN. The online morning paper could be from India, Pakistan or the Arab world, "fresh from the printers." Beyond the narrow spectrum of the views of the US military and the CIA, one could also hear critics and skeptics of the official version. In short, thanks to the Internet there was an escape route from the reality tunnel cemented by propaganda and the clamor of war.

In the 48 hours after the attacks, the incomprehensible and highly complex 9/11 event was simplified by the corporate media into three basic premises:

- Osama bin Laden and his "al-Qaeda" network carried out the attacks.
- Their base is in Afghanistan and must be eliminated by war.
- The war must be extended to other countries that "harbor terrorists."

These three tenets have dictated US policy ever since Sept. 12, and in his first speech to Congress after the attacks, President Bush elevated them to unquestionable absolutes – "Either you are with us or you are with the terrorists." At the time, such menacing words were hardly necessary to extract support – a wave of sympathy, compassion and solidarity with the residents of New York and the American people swept the globe. But Bush's advisors who fed him the phrase seemed to anticipate on what thin ice their al-Qaeda-bin-Ladenesque global conspiracy theory rested. With one forceful sound bite, doubts were pre-empted before they could arise.

We know from the behavior of primates and other mammals living in herds or packs that when threatened by danger, they follow whichever alpha male is the first to offer a way out, a solution. The solution the US president offered to the millions of domesticated primates, shocked and disoriented by the unprecedented events, couldn't have been any simpler. "It was Osama!" and he lives in the Tora Bora cave complex, and that's why we will destroy it, and if he's not there then we will hunt him down wherever he is. Nothing could undermine the success of the "It was Osama" theory – not the lack of evidence to substantiate bin Laden's guilt, nor the fact that he himself denied any participation in the attacks – in a video generally accepted as genuine, and in a Sept. 28 interview with Pakistani newspaper *Ummat*[3] – nor the fact that the sort of "evidence" presented in the days and weeks following the attacks to corroborate bin Laden's guilt and his connection to the alleged hijackers would never hold up in court.

Constant repetition on all channels hammered the message home and systematically blacked out any questions and doubts. To voice skepticism meant excommunication, and the anathema was "conspiracy theory." President Bush pronounced it before the U.N General Assembly on Nov. 10, 2001: "We must speak the truth about terror. Let us never tolerate outrageous conspiracy theories concerning the attacks of September 11th – malicious lies that attempt to shift blame from the terrorists themselves, away from the guilty."[4]

In this way any alternative point of view of the events was eliminated *ex cathedra* as "outrageous" – sacrilegious, abominable, criminal. With this master stroke the al-Qaeda-bin-Ladenesque conspiracy theory has been victorious. Not because those questioning, doubtful and skeptical views lacked sufficient grounds for suspicion – compared with the baby-soft evidence for the official version, the evidence for some of the inconsistencies appears downright bone-hard – but because they were shut out from the start as intolerable "conspiracy theories" of the Axis of Evil. And because the mainstream media blithely followed this dictate.

The Myth of Free Media

The myth that in democratic states the "free press" functions as a fourth power, a balance wheel in political crises, has never been so mercilessly shattered as by the news reporting after 9/11. The lofty insignia of "independence," "non-partisanship," "fairness," and "objectivity" with which the media pathetically flatter themselves lay utterly in tatters, at the very latest by the time the World Trade Center lay in ruins. Of course it would have been naïve to expect anything else. Media science has long recognized that press principles are thrown overboard even during far less significant scandals. The media are inclined to exaggerate and dramatize events when facts are unclear, as Communications Professor Mathias Kepplinger illustrated based on a number of recent scandals, such as mad cow disease, neo-Nazi attacks and the German CDU party funding scandal. Kepplinger traces this to the "way we communicate in situations of great uncertainty." The process of establishing a consensus at such times is based less on rationality than on group dynamics. "If several people in a group describe their observations one after another, their judgements quickly come to resemble one another because a group norm, a viewpoint generally accepted within the group, is established."[5]

Necklace patriotism

US news anchor Dan Rather is considered a paragon of journalistic integrity. For 20 years the now 70-year-old has presented the most important news program on CBS... Since the terror attacks on Sept. 11,

"patriotism running amok" is threatening US journalism and is preventing representatives of the media from asking the government critical questions, Rather warned in the BBC television program *Newsnight.* **He too has refrained from asking the government tougher questions out of fear of appearing unpatriotic.**

The situation in the US after the attacks on Manhattan and Washington is similar to the situation in 1980's South Africa, said the New York journalist… "There was a time in South Africa that people would put flaming tires around people's necks if they dissented." The fear of such "necklacing," of having a flaming tire of lack of patriotism put around your neck, is what keeps him and his media colleagues to this day from asking tougher questions about the "war on terror."

The biggest problem is journalists' self-censorship, said Rather. "It starts with a feeling of patriotism within oneself." At some point, you find yourself saying: "I know the right question, but maybe it's not exactly the right time to ask it."

Frankfurter Rundschau *02/18/2002,*
www.blackcommentator.com/106/106_rather.html

The striking media conformity after the attacks can be attributed to this herd instinct, which demands a clear-cut friend/foe dichotomy in an emergency (true to the spirit of Carl Schmitt) and not a rational, critically objective assessment of the facts. The notorious keyword "conformity" shouldn't immediately bring to mind an Orwellian or Goebbelsian "truth" and propaganda apparatus. Although this classic type of censorship undoubtedly exists since 9/11, it doesn't explain the media's adherence to the official version of events that prevails for over half a year now. The entrancing repetition of the "bin Laden" conspiracy theory, without a single differentiating idea to disrupt it, cannot be blamed on legions of censoring bureaucrats who filter the news behind every desk. Instead, blame it on the fact that even though we live in a highly technological and networked society, we haven't shed the rudimentary responses of primates. This is true for the psychology of small groups – like reporters, editors and commentators – and even more so for mass psychology.

The media's ability to sell as fact for so long a conspiracy theory unsupported by any sound evidence cannot be explained solely on the basis of its huge dissemination and penetrative force, but above all by the positive feedback the media's message has encountered. When even reporters and journalists – a group that is the best informed and most familiar with different viewpoints – were thrown into utter uncertainty by the incomprehensible event and carried away by the slogan "It was Osama," it is hardly surprising that the mass of media consumers gratefully absorbed the message.

The reaction of two elderly ladies, my mother and an aunt, with whom I watched a program about the "war against international terrorism" around Christmas provided a real eye-opener in this respect. When Osama bin Laden was shown, I mentioned that according to French reports he last met with a CIA agent in July 2001; when the Pakistani secret service ISI was described as the "CIA's partner" in the region I added that the alleged terror pilot Atta was financed via the ISI ... and here and there I added a few more comments. "So tell me, is it really true what you're telling me?" my mother asked me skeptically, and I answered: "I think it's at least as true as what we get to see on the news." Her reaction: "Well then, you better stop going on about this. It's getting too complicated for me. I'd rather stick to what they're saying on TV... and the young Mr. Bush doesn't cut such a bad figure." This response seems typical to me not only for old ladies but for the overwhelming majority of the population.

The psychological shock; the number of casualties, initially estimated to be around 50,000; the incomprehensible, Babylonic-apocalyptic event constantly repeated in slow motion; the unhinged world of "nothing is as it was"; the deep and widespread confusion triggered by this chaos; all this cried out for an explanation, for a quick appraisal of the situation, for a plan. And this is what George W. Bush delivered in a way that was perfect because it was simple. He presented a culprit and declared war on him and on his supporters. It was no coincidence that the president's congressional speech was met with rapturous cheers reminiscent of Nazi party conferences. Indeed, the moment endowed him with the halo of a leader and savior as he lifted the spirits of the fear-paralyzed masses. The cathartic effect was in no way weakened by the fact that he was selling a simplistic conspiracy theory as the basis for a declaration of war – as you know, Hitler never had anything else to offer either.

Maybe as domesticated primates we have something of a scapegoat reflex genetically implanted into us, which in times of catastrophe and chaos provides us with an emotional outlet for fear, while guaranteeing the cohesion of the pack by focusing on a common "enemy." It seems to me the success of Bush's war policy can only be explained on the basis of such an instinctive reflex, of a reaction that is based more on an archaic herd instinct than on individual reason. The more dramatic the event and the more confusing the situation, the greater the pressure to resolve the situation. Had Osama and his 40 robbers not existed, another enemy like him would have had to be invented then and there for reasons of group dynamics alone.

What would a more intelligent, less primate-like response have looked like? The decisive factor driving the whole event is horror and the fear it triggers. Whoever masterminded the attacks, their calculations were based entirely on the fear and horror they unleashed. Yet the very thought that the perpetrators are counting on a panic reaction is a sign of more sophisticated reasoning, of a wider realization. Not only the horror is perceived as real, but those causing it and their intentions are also taken into account. This awareness, the conspiratorial, skeptical, paranoid perception, opens up the possibility of a whole range of responses to the horror, above and beyond panic. Herd panic reacts to disaster with cries for action for action's sake, be it even blind action – so George W. Bush was generally described as "prudent" in the days following the attack, merely because he didn't drop a few nuclear bombs here and there.

The New Inquisition, which has a monopoly on the "truth about terror" and calls for a fight against "outrageous conspiracy theories," was proclaimed, for very good reasons, in mid-November. In the preceding days, French media reported that the last meeting between bin Laden and the CIA took place as recently as July 2001 in the American Hospital in Dubai (see "11/04/01: Osama meets the CIA"). This threatened to debunk the myth that cooperation with Islamic terrorists had ended a long time ago. According to a report by CBS correspondent Barry Petersen,[6] US intelligence probably knew bin Laden's whereabouts around 9/11; the evening before, he was taken to a military hospital in Rawalpindi for dialysis treatment. So the mastermind of the most audacious terror attack in history is hanging on a Pakistani military drip and is saved from kidney failure during the final countdown. Hopefully, this should make for a very nice scene when the terror spoof "The Naked Cannon 23.5" is filmed in the near future.

"Well, but what do you really believe now?" Those who asked this question in the seminars of "Cybernethics" professor Heinz von Foerster had to pay a dollar into the seminar kitty; for the word "truth," the fine was doubled to two dollars. "The term truth means war," says von Foerster. "It creates the lie, it divides people into those who are right and those who are wrong. I once said truth is the invention of a liar."[7]

In regard to 9/11, I advocate that all observations should be inextricably linked to the observer. As I deal with these matters, I sometimes find myself in the same situation as the quantum physicist who is plagued by the particle/wave paradox. The more thoroughly you focus on one aspect of the system, the more you lose sight of another. But aren't Schrödinger's cat and Einstein's mouse irrelevant in a state of emergency? Wasn't it a matter of having to open the box and establish certainty in order to take action? If that is so, if the frightened herd cries out for action, the primate mob clamors for revenge and a clear-cut friend-foe image must be created, and the time has come for those gruesome "truths" that mean war: then there is only one counter-strategy. The "outrageous conspiracy theories," the "malicious lies" and the diversion from the "real culprits" must be further exposed and publicized.

Cui bono?

If truth means war, what have the "bin Laden conspiracy" stylized as "truth" and the declaration of war based upon it done for us to date (July 2002)? Has the "war against international terrorism" that has been waged for half a year made the world any safer? Were dangerous terrorists locked up to protect the public? Did sacrificing thousands of civilian lives, accepted for Afghanistan as "collateral damage" and as a blood toll for the 9/11 attack, make any "sense"?

No doubt, it is a sign of progress that people in Kabul can listen to music again, that girls are allowed to go to school and that men are shaving. Whether this justifies months of bombardment is debatable, however, especially since the Taliban regime introduced its backward fundamentalism with the blessing and the support of the very people who now eliminated it militarily. As recently as July 2001, during the last secret pipeline negotiations with the US in Berlin, Mullah Omar was allowed to keep his medieval theocracy provided the Taliban agreed to the project (and to their assigned share in the profits). Let's recall the alternatives offered by the United States, a "carpet of gold" or a "carpet of bombs." In October, Afghanistan was buried beneath the latter.

When we put two and two together – US geostrategic interests in the region and the pipeline plans launched in the early 1990's by Unocal and other oil companies – and second, 9/11 and the subsequent war against Afghanistan – are we jumping to conclusions by assuming a direct cause and effect for which there is no hard evidence? This could be so – and the example shows why the question "who benefits?" is a favorite with conspiracy theorists. It represents one of the classic traps of conspiratorial thought, because by emphasizing the motive for the act it hopes to gloss over the lack of tangible evidence. Whoever benefited most must have done it.

The US intelligence services and the military-industrial complex were able to book enormous budget increases and profits in the wake of the attacks – so they must have something to do with it!

Under the shelter of the "war on terrorism," Israel was able to launch a new campaign of conquest with impunity – so the spooks from Mossad must have been pulling the strings!

George W. Bush was in danger of going down as an electoral thief, and the impending bankruptcy of his biggest bankroller Enron threatened to trigger a stock market crash. This called for a war to cover up the domestic and economic crisis!

Geopolitically, it is vital for the US to gain control of Central Asian oil reserves if it wants to secure its global hegemony in the 21st Century. The government staged 9/11 as a "surprise attack" to drive a reluctant nation into a war that could turn out to be the "mission of a generation" (to use Defense Secretary Rumsfeld's words).

Osama bin Laden hates the United States because of its military presence in Saudi Arabia. He carried out the attack to rally the world's Muslims to fight the infidels!

Five motives, all of which bear a certain logic. Of course, many more could be cited, but no tangible evidence leading to the mastermind exists for any of them, even if the media continue to pretend as if bin Laden had been convicted. The question of motive helps investigating criminologists to focus their field of investigation. Crimes without motive are rare, so the victim's circumstances are examined for any motivating interests. But motives alone, as we know from any whodunit, do not constitute hard evidence. They are not enough to convict the culprit.

Spy vs. Spy

"Spy vs. Spy" was the name of a famous *Mad Magazine* series, and if one heeds historian R. J. Blackburn (see "Appearances are Deceiving," page 29) then this mad game is played at the center of all powers and states, which constantly feel threatened by potential enemies from inside and out. Secret services, conspiracies and plots are their true life blood.

"Anybody in Washington who isn't paranoid must be crazy." This pearl of wisdom is attributed to Henry Kissinger, whose corollary activities as Secretary of State and national security advisor have led to consequences for him personally. He is now hardly able to leave the country without an arrest warrant for war crimes being shoved under his nose, accusing him of responsibility for those terror attacks on Sept. 11, 1973 that bombed Chilean President Allende out of government. A strange case of date magic $(9+11+1+9+7+3 = 1\ 1\ 1\ 1)$, which exemplifies, however, how the fundamentally paranoid and secretive politics of states in turn give rise to a secret, unofficial foreign policy with terrorist tendencies.

> We removed the government of Guatemala, when its leftist orientation displeased us; we tried to instigate a civil war against Sukarno in Indonesia; we intervened to put the Shah back on the throne in Iran, after (the elected prime minister) Mossadegh had broken the monopoly of British Petroleum over Iran's oil; we tried to start a counterrevolution in the Bay of Pigs in Cuba; we even waged a secret war in Laos and paid members of the Meo tribe and Thai mercenaries who fought for us there. All these operations were begun without the knowledge and consent of Congress. No land was too small, no leader too insignificant, to escape our attention. We sent poison to the Congo in a plan to infect Lumumba with a deadly disease; we armed dissidents in the Dominican Republic, although we knew of their plans to kill (the head of state) Trujillo; we took part in a military coup in South Vietnam, which toppled the very government that we had promised to defend... for years we tried to murder Fidel Castro and other Cuban leaders. The various attacks were spread over three US administrations, and included a broad cooperation between the CIA and the Mafia.[8]

This catalogue of sins is not the work of a raging anti-American conspiracy theorist. It was compiled by the chairman of the Senate Select Committee on "Alleged Assassination Plots Involving Foreign Leaders," Senator Frank Church, introducing the 350-page investigative report with a few words on the "morass of American foreign policy."

That was in 1976 – and in view of the appalling facts outlined in the Senate report, President Ford immediately issued an official ban on such assassinations. This does not mean, however, that since then all has been above board – in Nicaragua, Grenada, El Salvador, Panama, Iraq and Afghanistan. The list may show, however, that a state whose basic stance is one of chronic paranoia is led to feel threatened even by banana republics and is "compelled" to eliminate that "threat" by force and terror if necessary. Those who scent secret conspiracies by "enemies" everywhere – "left-wingers," "liberals," "Communists," "terrorists" – cannot envisage any other course of action than to hit back with equally secretive and conspiratorial methods. This tendency to combat real or imaginary conspiracies does not, however, lead to the containment of conspiratorial behavior, but actually generates and promotes it.

"God is not Neutral"

So, with regard to 9/11, we have a range of motives as well as a number of suitable suspects. It's the same story as in any decent whodunit, and not everyone with a dubious past automatically qualifies as the culprit. It's a foregone conclusion that bin Laden and his organization fit the suspect profile because of their terrorist past, but secret services like the CIA and Mossad fit just as well, especially with regard to staged "surprise attacks." Just look at the 1954 Lavon Affair, in which Israeli agents carried out attacks against British and American installations in Egypt and successfully blamed it on Islamic fundamentalists.

This had the desired result: British and French troops (together with Israeli ones) attacked Egypt in the Suez Crisis of 1956. This kind of fake terror is all too common. Due to their tradition, as well as their basic attitude marked by paranoia and a penchant for violence, secret services differ very little from terror organizations, even if they are officially classed under the "axis of good" and are even meant to abide by the law and the constitution.

But the paranoid and conspiratorial orientation almost automatically generates a mechanism that heedlessly overrides ethics and morality. This short-circuiting mechanism works as follows: my enemy's enemy is my friend. In the battle against an imaginary (or real) archenemy it becomes irrelevant whether this "friend" is also an outright criminal, a "son of a bitch" or a "rogue state." This explains how the US backed the build up of Koranic schools and terror camps in Pakistan and Afghanistan. The "holy warriors" churned out in fast-track, intensive training courses were meant to lure the Soviet archenemy into a pre-emptive invasion of its "own Vietnam" (in the words of then security advisor Brzezinski). And from the mid-1980's onward, Israel helped the radical Islamist movement Hamas gain a foothold in Palestine in a bid to undermine the diplomatically successful archenemy Arafat and his PLO.

In this "spy hunts spy" game, the worst of rogues are welcome as tools and coalition partners. All means are acceptable for the sake of a sacred cause, or against the threat posed by a supposed great conspiracy.

Israel and Hamas

It's an open secret well known to all those familiar with Middle East politics that Israel supported the establishment of Islamist Hamas since the late 1970's. The Israeli government granted Hamas hundreds of permits to build and run "religious" institutions, schools, health services, etc., knowing full well that this Islamic brotherhood had a fundamentalist, terrorist background. Reports on this subject are usually only found in independent media like the alternative *New York Press* or with independent reporters like Robert Fisk, the senior correspondent of Britain's *Independent:*

"Remember that when Arafat was still regarded as a superterrorist, before he became a superstatesman – of course he's reverting back now to superterrorist – remember that the Israelis encouraged the Hamas to build mosques and social institutions in Gaza.

"Hamas and the Israelis had very close relations when the PLO was still in exile in Tunisia. I can remember being in southern Lebanon in 1993 reporting on the Hamas, and one of their militants offered me Shimon Peres' home phone number. That's how close the relations were! So let's remember that the Israelis do have direct contact with those they label even more terrorist than Arafat.

"In the cowboy version of events, they both hate each other. In the real world, they maintain contact when they want to."

In an interview with Italy's *L'Espresso* on 12/19/01, Yasser Arafat said:

"Hamas was constituted with the support of Israel. The aim was to create an organization antagonistic to the PLO (Palestine Liberation Organization). They (Hamas) received financing and training from Israel. They have continued to benefit from permits and authorizations, while we have been limited, even (for permits) to build a tomato factory. Rabin himself defined it as a fatal error."

http://www.nypress.com/15/17/taki/2.cfm, http://www.thirdworldtraveler.com/ Fisk_Robert/MiddleEast_AccordingFisk.html

It would be worthwhile thoroughly investigating why these "sacred" causes are apparently so essential to form a society and practically indispensable for its mobilization, and why they are usually pure conspiracy theories – starting with the assumption that there is an invisible, almighty creator of all things who pulls all the strings, normally abbreviated by the code name "God."

This is where we need to apply critical conspirology like a skeptical science of perception to make clear that it's sheer madness to jump at each other's throats over an unproven (and unprovable) conspiracy theory. And yet it seems humans have done nothing else for millennia than to beat the living daylights out of one another over the "truth" of this conspiracy theory. Were it not for "conspiracy theory," that great simplification, which allows *Homo sapiens* to hallucinate a "truth," a "sacred" cause, driving him to mass murder wouldn't be so easy. But once he has swallowed the pill of simplification, he is capable of anything.

Must GOD, as the *sole*, central conspirator has been known ever since monotheistic conspiracy theorists reformed the jumble of gods, perhaps be portrayed as an unquestionable truth, because this is a conspiracy theory for which there is definitely no commonly accessible evidence?

If you're wondering what all this has to do with the mysteries of 9/11, please recall not only George W. Bush's remark that "God is not neutral," but also his above-mentioned anathema against "outrageous conspiracy theories," as well as the definition of the "war on terrorism" as a "crusade" in the context of Operation "Infinite Justice." How archaic is that? Invoking an unquestionable, sacred and godly "truth," Bush II marched into war to ward off the terrorist horror, and within a matter of days he rose from presidential oaf to prudent and wise leader of the Western world.

A Return to "Clean" Journalism via a "Dirty" Theory of Knowledge

As I write this, the "outrageous conspiracy theories" have found their way into Congress, despite their denunciation as anathema by Bush. At the beginning of April, Congresswoman Cynthia McKinney demanded an investigation into possible foreknowledge by the Bush Administration and its links to defense companies, like the Carlyle Group. Not only is Mrs. McKinney a woman, she is also black and a Democrat, pretty much the polar opposite of the governing Bush and his oil men, who practically all belong to the WASP elite. And given that her own party beat her up about her statement, the chances of her demands being met are less than promising. Yet it should be recorded for the sake of the history books that distrust of the official version of 9/11 spread not only on the right and left fringes of the social spectrum, but was now also putting out shoots amongst the middle classes, and that not even stigmatization and demonization as a "conspiracy theory" could stop the voicing of suspicions and demands for an official inquiry.

Congresswoman Cynthia McKinney's statement

The need for an investigation of the events surrounding September 11 is as obvious as is the need for an investigation of the Enron debacle. Certainly, if the American people deserve answers about what went wrong with Enron and why (and we do), then we deserve to know what went wrong on September 11 and why.

This is not a time for closed-door meetings and this is not a time for secrecy. America's credibility, both with the world and with her own people, rests upon securing credible answers to these questions. The world is teetering on the brink of conflicts while the Administration's policies are vague, wavering and unclear. Major financial conflicts of interest involving the President, the Attorney General, the Vice President and others in the Administration have been and continue to be exposed.

This is a time for leadership and judgment that is not compromised in any fashion. This is a time for transparency and a thorough investigation.

http://globalresearch.ca/articles/MCK204B.html

In the short history of reactions to 9/11, the conspiracy theoretical approach has become presentable against all odds. The scorn heaped upon the "nutballs," "crackpots" and "conspiracy wackos" seems to be the last line of polemical defense. Years ago, it may have been enough to muzzle the odd "wacko" in order to push through an official version of controversial events with propaganda, but in the age of the Internet – when millions of "wackos" can publish undesirable news – this is virtually impossible.

Of course, the Internet churns out untold quantities of misinformation, too, which has given the largely uncontrollable WWW a bad name as an unreliable rumor shop. But 9/11 has come to the rescue by showing all those observers who have managed to preserve their sound judgement that in times of crisis the "respectable" media are also nothing but a dubious rumor shop that cooks up conspiracy theories and spreads propaganda fairy tales with abandon and no critical detachment. That is why it's no longer possible to gain an accurate picture of reality through the media without one's own conspiratorial perspective. Conspiracy-theoretical thought has shifted from its marginal position as the dirty black sheep of epistemology, the theory of knowledge, into the center of sober political analysis.

Had the media endeavored to fulfill their constituted role by equipping themselves with the tools of a critical conspirology, of skeptical, even of paranoid perception, then the near total lack of any investigative or probing journalism striving for objectivity would have been avoided. It is only because conspiracy-theoretical thinking is taboo that the identical, unquestioned propaganda is blaring on all channels. But I dare to venture that after the experience with the reception of 9/11 this might change, and the "dirty" epistemology of conspiracy thinking will become increasingly indispensable as a tool of "clean" journalism.

On the heels of Cynthia McKinney's initiative, the journal of record in her state, the *Atlanta Journal-Constitution,* carried out a poll in mid-April in its online edition, asking readers whether they thought the Bush Administration had foreknowledge of the attacks or not, and whether this question should be pursued further. Only 2% out of more than 23,000 respondents advocated breaking off all investigations, 46% were convinced that the government knew of the attacks beforehand, and 52% believed the government had no idea. The newspaper pulled the poll after only half a day, before the percentage of the trusting could sink below the 50% mark. Apparently, so much critical headwind simply hadn't been expected.[9]

Robert Fisk, the Middle East correspondent of Britain's *Independent* – with Ahmed Rashid one of the last journalistic authorities in the Middle East who hasn't surrendered his common sense to the consensus machinery – had a similar experience on a lecture tour through the USA.

> And for the first time in more than a decade of lecturing in the United States, I was shocked. Not by the passivity of Americans – the all-accepting, patriotic notion that the President knows best – nor by the dangerous self-absorption of the United States since 11 September and the constant, all-consuming fear of criticizing Israel.
>
> What shocked me was the extraordinary new American refusal to go along with the official line, the growing, angry awareness among Americans that they were being lied to and deceived. At some of my talks, 60 per cent of the audiences were over 40. In some cases, perhaps 80 per cent were Americans with no ethnic or religious roots in the Middle East – "American Americans," as I cruelly referred to them on one occasion, "white Americans," as a Palestinian student called them more truculently.
>
> For the first time, it wasn't my lectures they objected to, but the lectures they received from their President, and the lectures they read in their press about Israel's "war on terror" and the need always, uncritically, to support everything that America's little Middle Eastern ally says and does.[10]

For me, the reactions that Fisk describes confirm the thesis that the conspiratorial subconscious is growing and that the masses won't let themselves be fooled by cheap conspiracy theories in the long run – at least not as easily as before the Internet revolution. Millions of private detectives, researchers, investigators, private eyes and snoops all around the world are investigating the inconsistencies of 9/11 on their own out of mistrust of the official proclamations of truth. Perhaps it's naïvely optimistic, but I do harbor hopes that this decentralized "Internet Intelligence" will ultimately trounce the "Central Intelligence Agency."

Of course, the official secret services are tilling the same battlefield, creating confusion with their disinformation. Of course, they produce cover-up stories, alternatives to deflect those who don't believe the official version from the real conspiracy. Of course, the spooks at CIA headquarters in Langley use their $30 billion budget not only to oust obnoxious presidents, bribe putschist generals and profit from weapons and drug trafficking; they also hire journalists, authors and media people to deny the fact. But the number of critical observers and the mass of skeptics also ensure a new quality that makes it more difficult for the neo-Orwellian Ministries of Truth to impose their propaganda messages.

During the Third Reich, radio became such a successful medium for the establishment of a dictatorship because it carried just one message, that of the Führer. Nowadays the Internet enables us to receive "enemy broadcasts" from all around the world and incorporate their data into our perception of reality. So it might not take half a century to uncover the plot of 9/11 after all... The criminal investigation of the case, which was stopped by the Bush Administration at the end of January, will continue on the Internet, and the blatant evidence of official lies and cover-up attempts that is already emerging will continue to grow and increase the pressure. Sooner or later, the public pressure arising from the Internet will force the mainstream media to emerge from their trance.

"The only logic," the great physicist James C. Maxwell once said, "is probability." So instead of simulating "truth" in the face of unresolved facts, it's a matter of working with the blurred vision of probabilities. As conspiracy theories do just that, they automatically develop immunity against debunkers and denouncers. "Is Bush behind it all or the aliens?" said one of those typical headlines in that phase.[11] The people's skepticism of the prevailing dogma, too great to be ignored any longer, is dealt with in the "funny pages" of newspapers and magazines as a kind of conspiracy entertainment. To see these "facts" thrown into the same pot as E. T. fairytales may sound like an affront to someone who thinks it's "absolutely clear" that Bush is behind it all, but it can't harm a transparent conspiracy theory that works with probabilities. On the conspiracy probability scale from 0 to 23, the likelihood that "aliens" are behind it all could perhaps be ranked at 0.05, while the Bush clan should come in at least at 15 based on the latest information. A new find like the Reuters report[12] dated Feb. 9 (typically, it was drowned out in the German press) that Pakistan's military ruler Musharraf and Afghanistan's president Karzai have agreed to resume planning for the interrupted pipeline would mean another half percentage point for Bush, because this moves the oil interests motive into the foreground.

"Let One Happen, Stop the Rest"

We must return once more to the strange case of the shady undercover agent Delmart "Mike" Vreeland, arrested in Canada in December 2000, who passed a message on to his prison guards in August 2001 warning of a big attack on exposed targets in the USA (see "11/04/01: Osama meets CIA" and "2/02/02: From Al Capone's Turf to Pipelineistan"). A Toronto court has released the 35-year-old Vreeland on bail, and he is fighting a legal battle to avoid extradition to the US, which he fears he wouldn't survive for more than a few hours. He has written an open letter[13] to David Corn of *The Nation*, who described him as a "conspiracy nut," and he has also answered 35 questions in an extensive interview with Mike Ruppert.[14] According to this, Vreeland was arrested in Toronto after arriving from Moscow and first learned of the planned attacks in early December 2000 from documents held by a US agent, who had been passed a warning that Russian President Putin supposedly got from Saddam Hussein's son in Iraq.

After the Canadian authorities denied Vreeland's request to speak to military intelligence, he wrote his ominous and hasty message in August. The sealed envelope was then handed to his guards to be kept with his belongings, and not until Sept. 14 was it opened again. Apart from a list of buildings – WTC, Sears Tower, White House, Pentagon – the note also contains the strange sentence "let one happen, stop the rest." This remark reads like an instruction to a group of undercover agents after they have relayed their plans back to headquarters. In response to Mike Ruppert's question whether this statement implied that the CIA or some other intelligence agency had achieved complete penetration of the terrorist cells, Vreeland answered:

"That goes without question. Sometimes certain governments design, create networks like Al Qaeda, which was really the government in Afghanistan. Those entities create specific problems at the creating government's direction."
"Do you know who had achieved this penetration?"
"I cannot comment on that."
"Is it possible that the terrorist cells were being 'run' without knowing by whom?"
"Absolutely."

For me the story of this low-ranking agent seemed plausible from the start: a wannabe James Bond who used his Navy-backed credit card to order champagne by the crate and pretend to be a yacht buyer. It's also believable that on his spying trips to Moscow he heard a forewarning of the attacks from colleagues. It also makes sense that he would use this knowledge to save his skin now that his employer is pulling the plug on him and his credit card excesses. Secret services use trumped-up accusations and other tricks when needed to put "hot potatoes" among their undercover agents out of circulation – and to deny ever having had anything to do with them.

Let's assume for a moment that Vreeland is really nothing but a common criminal and credit card fraudster. In that case, what good would it do him to come out with a hare-brained secret-service story like the one he told the Canadian authorities? If he is really clinging to an invented identity as an agent, shouldn't he expect to be locked up in the closed section of some nuthouse rather than to be set free? No, this low-ranking, semi-criminal, undercover snoop, a regular "freelance" for Navy intelligence since his official dismissal from the Navy, who was being paid $4,260 a month for his shady undertakings, this Lieutenant Delmart "Mike" Vreeland is for real. But what compels him to warn his prison guards in August 2001 of a terror attack, and to scribble the names of the designated buildings on a piece of paper? It's understandable that he doesn't answer the crucial questions in his interview – as a "whistleblower" he must already fear for his life as it is. But thanks to his case we can add another variation to the foreknowledge scenarios.[15]

A terror group, let's call it al-Qaeda to keep it conventional, plans a series of attacks with passenger aircraft on exposed buildings in the US. The planning and preparation does not remain undetected. In June 2000, according to Vreeland, the Iraqi secret service finds out about it, and in November it passes on the information to friendly Russia. At this point at the latest, the American secret services also find out about it, but don't seem to take any action. Instead, they pronounce the slogan "let one happen, stop the rest." That is what US agent Vreeland, arrested in December 2000, writes in August 2001 in a warning note that lies dormant among his belongings until Sept. 14. And anyone who wants to can safely interpret this comment as a stage direction.

The question is, through which channels was it possible to infiltrate these unofficial collaborators into al-Qaeda. Here the Pakistani secret service ISI fits into the picture as the closest CIA partner in the region which supplied Mohamed Atta with $100,000 in July, among other things, according to the *Times of India*,[16] citing Indian sources and the FBI. Is al-Qaeda infiltrated by unofficial collaborators in the same way as the board of Germany's extreme right NPD party is infiltrated by intelligence agents? Was Osama, the double agent par excellence, promised a peaceful retirement after playing the part of whipping boy – be it in some Saudi oasis, be it shaven with a new passport in Florida?

Seriously now, it wouldn't be the first time that a terror group is penetrated by government intelligence and manned with informers or an agent provocateur. Whether Red Brigades or RAF, Jihad or Hamas, wherever terror is part of the game, the state intelligence services sooner or later get involved directly or indirectly. In the case of bin Laden, whose Mujahideen were recruited for battle against the Soviets with the help of the CIA, it can hardly have been any different. And when I read and thought about Vreeland's scribbled note "let one happen, stop the rest" it "clicked": this case is probably no different. It also seems the only plausible explanation for the otherwise incomprehensible secrecy of the Bush Administration, for the failure to respond to the multitude of forewarnings, for the failure to investigate the unanswered questions regarding the course of events, for the failure to pursue hard leads, for the restraint shown by the investigators toward Saudi Arabia and the bin Laden family, for the lack of any tangible evidence on the ringleaders of the attackers, or a link to al-Qaeda. We are working with probabilities, and what is more than likely is this: al-Qaeda was and is infiltrated by double agents, al-Qaeda was and is the instrument of unofficial US foreign policy, and al-Qaeda was and is funded by Saudi sources.

At this point, it is hardly possible to trace complex events like the 9/11 attack and its consequences back to *one* cause or *the* mastermind – unless it's simply for the sake of countering the official conspiracy theory "bin Laden" with an unofficial one called "Bush." The hypothesis that these two apparently mutually exclusive theories secretly belong together seems quite plausible. The US secret services (or certain parts of them) knew of al-Qaeda's plans, their preparation and execution; they didn't react to the forceful warnings by President Putin and by other countries, because they had more accurate and direct information about the plans of attack; that's why on 9/11 a "window" was kept open in America's most sensitive "no-fly" zone, and that's why only one day after the alleged surprise attack, it was possible to deliver the list of 19 culprits.

The Axis of Suspects

Almost all observers and experts agree that such a complex undertaking as the attacks of 9/11 couldn't have been carried out without secret service and military support. The tall tale that the attack was planned and carried out from an Afghan cave by an autonomous gang is no longer taken seriously, not even by the most gullible, given the zero results of the manhunt so far. So, if the terrorists were supported at least indirectly by state entities, then what states come into question? Do they belong to those which Bush Jr. defined as the "axis of evil," particularly Afghanistan, which has been "liberated" in the meantime? Hardly – they would have shot themselves in the foot by backing the attacks. Their governments ran the risk of removal by military force, like the Taliban – particularly Saddam Hussein in Iraq. In the search for governments that gained from 9/11, only Bush in the United States and Sharon in Israel actually fit the bill, and to a certain extent Pakistan's military dictator Musharraf, whose hold on office has been firmer since the start of the war. Although Saudi Arabia is not a direct beneficiary, it is remarkable how it managed to stay out of the line of fire fairly well, considering that the majority of the alleged attackers as well as Osama are Saudis.

A war only the US government wants

During the 17 months of the Bush administration just about everything has gone wrong for the US government in preparing the public for military strikes against Iraq. Convincing friendly governments and allies has not gone much better. Acts of terrorism against US facilities overseas and the anthrax menace at home could not be linked to Iraq. Evidence of al-Qaeda-Iraq collaboration does not exist...

Concurrently, a systematic disinformation and misinformation campaign, one of the biggest ever undertaken by the US authorities, is intensifying. The US and international public are being sedated daily with increasing doses of propaganda about the threat Iraq poses to the world in 2002. In the forefront advocating war against Iraq has been the US deputy secretary of defense, Paul Wolfowitz, who sees a military solution as the

only option. On July 14 he stated in Istanbul: "President Bush has made it clear how dangerous the current Iraqi regime is to the United States, and that it represents a danger we cannot live with indefinitely."

To make such statements without offering supporting evidence is irresponsible. It promotes government-induced mass hysteria in the US, and is meant to garner bipartisan support for military action...

The US Department of Defense and the CIA know perfectly well that today's Iraq poses no threat to anyone in the region, let alone in the United States. To argue otherwise is dishonest. They know, for example, that al-Dora, formerly a production center for vaccine against foot and mouth disease on the outskirts of Baghdad, and al-Fallujah, a pesticide and herbicide manufacturing unit in the western desert, are today defunct and beyond repair...

One does not need to be a specialist in weapons of mass destruction to conclude that these sites were rendered harmless and have remained in this condition. The truly worrying fact is that the US Department of Defense has all of this information. Why then, one must ask, does the Bush Administration want to include Iraq in its fight against terrorism?...

What was it that Paul Wolfowitz said at the west wing of the US Capitol on April 15? "May God bless all the peacemakers in the world." He still has a chance to be among them.

Hans von Sponeck, former U.N. humanitarian aid coordinator for Iraq, Frankfurter Rundschau *07/30/2002. http://www.fr-aktuell.de/*

So we could then juxtapose the "axis of evil" which quite clearly was not involved in the attacks, with an "axis of suspects," nations which facilitated this act of terror, didn't prevent it, or benefited from it.

The movie *Wag the Dog,* in which a US president stages a fake war against "the Albanians" to deflect attention from domestic scandals, was withdrawn from German TV in the middle of September out of diplomatic delicacy, and broadcast only three months later. Intelligence service expert and author James Bamford[17] (*The Puzzle Palace: Inside the NSA*) did not respect such tactful timing, and shocked the US public in early 2002 with details of "Operation Northwoods."[18] This was a scheme drawn up by the US military in the early 1960's to invent a war pretext by faking a series of terror attacks and blaming them on Cuba. The scenario involved attacks on US cities and the sinking of a passenger ship, until the operations in preparation were stopped by the newly-elected President Kennedy and his Defense Secretary McNamara – very much to the chagrin of some hawks and Commie-killers. Declassified documents show the operation consciously assumed civilian casualties, and was no game-theory exercize around the green table of a think tank, but a tangible undertaking by operational planning staff.

The timing of Bamford's revelations threw off many dewy-eyed contemporaries who could not believe that a freedom-loving, democratic country like the USA could plan such criminal operations. But where power, geopolitical influence and the imperial structure of a world power are at stake, some innocent victims are taken for granted. And when we look at the long list of official and unofficial wars the US waged in the second half of the 20th Century we can agree with Noam Chomsky when he describes the United States as the "leading terrorist state." We must also acknowledge, however, that it's precisely this strategy which allowed the USA to rise from global political insignificance a century ago to sole world superpower. The CIA was set up in 1945 according to the *Realpolitik* precepts of a hired top gun from Germany, Hitler's intelligence czar Gehlen. Its 50-year complicity with dictators, drug traffickers, arms pushers and other nifty sons of bitches has been a huge success, so the CIA and the various military intelligence services see absolutely no reason at all to abandon their proven methods. Who would build an empire must think in terms of imperial structures and must subordinate short-term moral scruples to the long-term goal.

Are President Roosevelt, his Secretary of War Stimson and their handful of faithful spooks who provoked and allowed the attack on Pearl Harbor guilty of a war crime and abetting murder for their sacrifice of 2,000 fellow Americans – or did they honor their official duty to do the best for their country by using this trick to lead their country into the extremely successful world war? From the point of view of conventional morality or democratic ideals, no end could possibly sanctify such murderous means. But in the realm of *Realpolitik* such means are used, and that's why the USA is at the top of the list of my personal "axis of suspects" – followed by the Saudi and Pakistani governments, its most important vassals in the plot. Billions of dollars from the Saudi oil feudals lit the fires of "Holy War" in the 1980's and built up mercenary leader Osama bin Laden. Pakistan delivered the ideological and combat armament for the Mujahideen in hundreds of Koranic schools and training camps, financed by the flourishing heroin trade. Everywhere in the Islamic world young Muslims were recruited for this brainwashing and holy-warrior program, all under the supervision of the USA, which also recruited holy warriors in dozens of American recruiting offices and even trained some of them in US army camps.[19]

With the US as supervisor, Saudi Arabia as financier and supporter and Pakistan's secret service ISI as local organizer, we have assembled the most important "havens of terror" that gave birth to the 9/11 catastrophe. The Israeli intelligence service Mossad must have got wind of the preparations for the attacks (and of the US services' foreknowledge) – as the hushed-up wiretapping and spy scandal involving a large Israeli spy ring in the US seems to suggest. But Mossad kept this information to itself, except for an official general warning to the US. After 9/11, however, it seems that Mossad secretly informed its CIA colleagues in Virginia and the White House about its explosive background knowledge, thereby gaining enormous leverage to extract US solidarity for Israel's renewed campaign of occupation. For me this kind of secret leverage is the only explanation for the United States' unlimited support for Sharon's state terror, which has even gone as far as denying access to the Red Cross and UN humanitarian missions to prevent the uncovering of possible massacres in Jenin and elsewhere.

In Saddam Hussein's case, denying access to UN weapons inspectors is grounds for war, while even if Ariel Sharon gives the finger to the Red Cross, George W. Bush calls him a "man of peace" – whether voluntarily or not, this should be investigated by an independent tribunal on 9/11 and its consequences. Besides the main protagonists, USA, Saudi Arabia and Pakistan, the "axis of suspects" should in any case also include Israel – at least as beneficiary and freeloader.

Welcome to Brainwashington D.C.

It's possible that I'm barking up the wrong tree with all this speculation, but speculation is all there is even for the vendors of the official version given the dearth of facts. On May 1, 2002, the BBC reported:

> US intelligence officials have admitted they failed to unearth any sort of paper trail leading to the 11 September attacks.
>
> In the most detailed account so far of the investigation, the head of the Federal Bureau of Investigation (FBI) said that after seven months of relentless work America had found no hard evidence mentioning any aspect to the attacks on New York and Washington.[20]

The short report did not create a sensation, let alone make it onto the front pages of the world press. "Biggest police operation in history unsuccessful," "Seven months of large-scale investigations – no leads," "Secret services, police and 9/11: deep sleep meets incompetence" – something along those lines should be the headlines. Because guess what

FBI director Robert S. Mueller gives as a reason for the spectacular flop of an investigation: "The hijackers had…no laptops, no storage media of any kind. They dressed and acted like Americans."[21]

Wow! What ingenious terrorists! They didn't run around with turbans and beards casting sinister fundamentalist glances, but instead were clean shaven and smiley, and to top it all they were so shrewd as not to save any of their plans on a computer hard drive or leave written notes lying around. Of course nobody was prepared for this kind of perfidious insidiousness, and that's probably why at press conferences nobody inquires whether it had ever crossed the minds of the FBI, CIA or NSA chiefs to resign in view of their abject failure in preventing or solving this case.

Nor does anybody ask how the authorities arrived at the conclusion that a Mr. Mohamed Atta and 18 other perpetrators carried out the attacks. As we know, they don't appear on any of the passenger lists released by the airlines. But if you're not on the passenger list[22] and you don't present some form of identification at check-in, then you can't even make it onto the aircraft.

And certainly no one asks about the real identity of the 19 alleged attackers, at least seven of whom used identification papers of people who were not involved. Who are they really, and what about the others, were their papers real? Besides, not a soul seems to be interested any longer in what the actual connection was between these 19 phantom attackers and Osama bin Laden and his al-Qaeda terror troops.

"The plans," according to the FBI director, "were hatched and financed overseas, beginning as long as five years ago." Again nobody asks how Robert S. Mueller can know about this long-term planning when after seven months of investigation no "hard evidence" has been found.

> The investigation was enormously helpful in figuring out who and what to look for as we worked to prevent attacks. It allowed us to see where we as a nation needed to close gaps in our security. And it gave us clear and definitive proof that al-Qaeda was behind the strikes.

The cynicism must be savored as it melts on the tongue. The biggest murder case in history remains wholly unsolved after more than half a year of investigations. Not a single mastermind was identified, let alone arrested, none of the hard leads from the stock market speculation were pursued, none of the accessories and profiteers were named, not to speak of the total lack of any "clear and definitive proof." And the police chief stands up and wants to make us believe that this debacle was "enormously helpful" for the prevention of further attacks. But nobody yells out, throws stink bombs at him in the name of the victims or just politely asks questions. Anyhow, it would be pointless, as the *Los Angeles Times* suggested in April.[23] "But the global search has produced virtually nothing in the way of hard evidence about the terrorists' planning, and authorities said Monday that they now face the growing realization that they may never know many key details."

Welcome to Brainwashington D.C.! Welcome to the biggest propaganda show of all times! Welcome to the consensus machine! Please leave your brain at the cloakroom, get in, enjoy yourself and have fun. Please beware of unattended questions, packages full of inconsistencies and other dubious items of luggage and immediately report any of these to the consensus authority. And don't forget to fasten your seat belt – World War III is hardly like a Sunday outing. For journalists and members of the media joining us on this trip, the press office has prepared a special leaflet drawn up by the doyen of the American press and former managing editor of the *New York Times*, John Swinton.

> There is no such thing, at this date of the world's history, in America, as an independent press. You know it and I know it. There is not one of you who dares to write your honest opinions, and if you did, you know beforehand that it would never appear in print. I am paid weekly for keeping my honest opinion out of the paper I am connected with. Others of you are paid similar salaries for similar things, and any of you who would be so foolish as to write honest opinions would be out on the streets looking for another job. If I allowed my honest opinions to appear in one issue of my paper, before twenty-four hours my occupation would be gone. The business of the journalist is to destroy the truth, to lie outright, to pervert, to vilify, to fawn at the feet of mammon, and to sell his country and his race for his daily bread. You know it and I know it, and what folly is this toasting an independent press? We are the tools and vassals of rich men behind the scenes. We are the jumping jacks, they pull the strings and we dance. Our talents, our possibilities and our lives are all the property of other men. We are intellectual prostitutes.[24]

Swinton's statement before the exclusive New York Press Club was not delivered after 9/11/2001, it hails from the year 1880 – yet it has probably never been as topical as now.

Nevertheless, I am not a pessimist. Even if we are on the way to World War III; even if the United States is storming towards a Fourth Reich with patriotic strides and destroying constitutional civil liberties for "security reasons;" even if the dollarization of the world economy and the raids by the IMF and World Bank constitute imperialism by another name; even if the biggest brainwashing operation of all times is underway since 9/11 and the masses are fed a simulated reality of al-Qaeda-bin-Ladenesque conspiracy theory; even if the matrix constructed by Washington, Wall Street and the ministries of truth of global media appears to be inescapable and the domesticated primates' stupidity corresponds to what mathematicians describe as "infinite;" even if all this and the media trance is leading up to what Austrian satirist Karl Kraus once described as the "end of the world through black magic" – no, I am not a pessimist. For, all the media's magic and all the power of printer's ink, four-color images and surround-sounds amount to nothing, if the gates of individual perception are not opened to them.

And never before in my life have I met more people who mistrusted the news and the headlines than in the weeks after 9/11, people of all ages and all political persuasions. Never before in my 20 years as a journalist and author of more than 500 newspaper and radio pieces have I had a greater response than to the articles of the WTC series – although they were only published on the Internet. Although? I reckon it's rather *because* they were only to be found in the Internet magazine *telepolis,* and soon after on thousands of websites and forums everywhere on the Internet, that they achieved this level of response and credibility. The response came from all those who turned away with incredulity and skepticism from the cock-and-bull story and the war noise of the media matrix, and who searched on the Internet for additional information and background knowledge, who wanted to know what was behind the glaring contradictions and inconsistencies, who didn't want to be duped and incited by a clumsy conspiracy theory and a propagandistic black-and-white portrayal of events.

Of course, these people, who trust their own judgement even in confusing and shocking situations rather than listen to simplifying slogans and insinuations, even if this initially increases the confusion even more, they are a minority, compared with the herd of TV slaves that willingly submits to the delicate wash cycle of propaganda. But in the case of this skeptical minority that thinks for itself the term minority needs to be "qualified." Despite its numerical inferiority, its power to subvert is great if it succeeds in drawing attention to its new quality, and this is precisely what the Internet has facilitated in a fantastic way. It provides every Google user who thinks for himself with the research facilities available to intelligence staffers, and also the means to disseminate information further. The pressure exerted by these decentralized, self-organized secret services won't subside, even, and especially, when civil liberties are curtailed in the name of reinforcing security, and any form of criticism, protest and demonstration against it is branded as "supporting terrorism." In the Internet age, unbelief can no longer be eliminated via an Inquisition, book burning and printing bans cannot suppress information in the network age, censorship and bans on assemblies cannot prevent free communication.

The New World Order

On Oct. 1, 2002, the world is divided up – divided up between the high commands of the United States military. For the first time in history, there is not a spot of land that doesn't fall under the responsibility of one of the US regional commands – not even in Antarctica. This alone reflects Washington's changed self-perception as the sole remaining superpower after the Cold War. But it also reflects a changed threat and risk perception. Dangers can be lurking anywhere for the superpower… Washington is planning an integrated command center for strategic – and also preemptive – attacks, strategic retaliation and strategic defense. This high command is supposed to plan and execute conventional and nuclear strategic operations, thereby symbolizing a new, second, very different age and understanding of deterrence…

Militarily the new, elemental experience of 9/11 couldn't be expressed any more clearly. An old American dream, the one of America's invulnerability, is over. Precautions against industrial society's vulnerability to asymmetric risks and threats are to be taken at all levels. The military initiative is complemented in the civilian sphere by the establishment of an "Office of Homeland Security" and a "Homeland Security Council" in the White House, as well as the planned – pending Congressional approval – establishment of a Department of Homeland Security on Jan. 1, 2003…

ACLANT, NATO's Atlantic command, is no longer necessary from the Pentagon's point of view. But ACLANT is not just any command. Ranking alongside NATO Allied Command Europe, it is one of the highest command authorities of the alliance. ACLANT is NATO's most important military bridgehead on the American continent. It has important responsibilities… Therefore, it would have serious consequences for NATO if its Allied Command Atlantic were disbanded or its importance significantly downgraded…

Put simply, Washington wants to be able to strike before it has been attacked. George W. Bush's administration most recently coined the phrase "defensive intervention" for this type of attack. This signals that the

US will in future interpret more loosely what constitutes the right to self defense under international law and will largely transfer the decision as to what constitutes a just war from the U.N. in New York to Washington. In early fall, these deliberations are expected to result in a public government paper, in a new "National Security Strategy."

What has been particularly alarming is the fact that preemptive nuclear attacks were explicitly not ruled out. The argument is that many potential targets – bunkers located extremely deep below the ground or in mountains, for example – cannot be safely destroyed with conventional weapons. Nuclear weapons, probably also new, specially developed, nuclear weapons, are the only appropriate means. Nuclear attacks against such targets – terrorists do not have a state territory – could also be launched against non-nuclear states. Yet again, international law would suffer a blow...

Political Washington is increasingly convinced that Europe is not interested in being a serious political or military partner in shaping world order; that Europe wants to shirk taking on global responsibility. The passivity of European states must be all the more astonishing since the Bush Administration's policy runs counter to the principle of European integration – the increasing legalization of international relations – and negates ever more clearly the basic interests of European foreign and security policy, multi-lateralism and multi-polarity.

Otfried Nassauer, director of the Berlin Institute for Transatlantic Security, "A new military division of the world," Frankfurter Rundschau, *07/15/2002. http://www.fr-aktuell.de/*

More and more people won't let themselves be duped by conspiracy theories and scapegoat propaganda and will demand that the biggest murder in history be cleared up – in the name of the victims and in the name of world peace, which is threatened far more by the "war against international terrorism" than by terror itself, certainly in terms of lost human lives. In the first six weeks of the war in Afghanistan alone, more innocent people died than in the terror attacks in the United States, but neither were the alleged mastermind bin Laden, and his gang tracked down, nor did the war make the world safer in any way. Instead of religious fanatics and fundamentalists, now corrupt warlords and drug dealers rule in Kabul, and the opium and heroin business flourishes more than ever.

This war has only brought more security for oil giant Unocal, oil services company Halliburton (fief of Vice-President Cheney) and a few other companies. They can finally build their pipeline through Afghanistan. The gun smoke had barely cleared and the start-up of the

$2 billion project was announced. You're a fool if you're thinking of conspiracy...

The rooster crows, the night is over and this book is also coming to an end. It left many questions unanswered, but it might contribute to the right questions being asked more clearly in future with regard to the secrets of 9/11, as well as with regard to conspiracies and conspiracy theories in general. We must accept conspiracies as the dark side of globalization – and develop the appropriate theories and methods to recognize, evaluate and direct them – if we want to defend freedom, justice and democracy and to ensure the planet remains inhabitable for what will soon be 7 billion people.

Never before in the history of mankind has more power been concentrated in the hands of so few people as in our times of global corporate rule. Never before have the possibilities been greater for the oligarchs to wield their power and influence, and thereby the danger that the democratic forum and the will of the people become a sham and the real decisions fall prey to conspiratorial power politics, shrouded in secrecy. Yet, never before have the opportunities also been better to see this, to communicate this knowledge and to exert pressure in public.

And what have we here, as if the author had ordered a final elegant touch to his work, the following report came over the news ticker one day before closing off this text: "The FBI warned of al-Qaeda attacks with airplanes – Was Bush informed beforehand?" In July 2001, when John O'Neill, the FBI's counter-terrorism director, resigned unnerved because he had been constantly hampered by the Bush Administration in his investigations against bin Laden, the FBI office in Phoenix, Arizona presented a dossier that warned of dubious flight students from Arab countries, and voiced the suspicion that attacks with commercial aircraft on buildings like the WTC were being planned.

Were these alerts ignored back at CIA and Pentagon headquarters, just like the warnings and intercepts of Japanese communications about the attack on Pearl Harbor? Of course, the president was "not informed in detail in advance," and of course, "he couldn't have prevented the attacks," because it was only a suspicion which the FBI voiced... and so forth, those are the wobbly statements tendered by his spokespeople. The predetermined break points – sloppiness, inaccuracy, lack of coordination – are outlined. Yet, even in the rear-view mirror, the obvious has been positively staring us in the face, the fuse of investigation is lit...

Afterword: In Praise of Anti-Bushism: a Defense of American Values

If asked the question: "What do you make of America?" at the moment I would have to declare myself an anti-Bushist. Since "anti-Bushism" is not yet a commonly-used term and "Bushism" has not yet been universally accepted as a danger, perhaps the anti-Bush stance needs explaining. To cut it short, you could say that the anti-Bushist is to the anti-American what the anti-Zionist is to the anti-Semite: the "anti" is not aimed at the people, its culture, values and religion, but at a certain form of politics and the means by which it is implemented.

Since in times of war distinctions like these only cause confusion, Bush II immediately made it clear after 9/11 that from now on people could be either Bushists or terrorists but nothing in between. Thus anti-Bushism was simultaneously declared a non-entity before its very birth. However, since the victims of the attacks on the WTC and the Pentagon became far more numerous on Afghan soil than on America's – and the sheriff never ceases to smash innocents to smithereens in his search for the ultimate bad guy – since then, if it wasn't already before, staunch anti-Bushism has become the number one duty of the citizens of the global village.

Just recently I sat at a podium with an executive editor of *Die Welt*, who pronounced as "self-evident" the new preamble in employment contracts at Springer Verlag in which journalists have to sign a declaration of loyalty to the USA and NATO. My objection, that not only was Bush currently behaving like Hitler after the Reichstag fire but also that newspaper heads stood to attention now as they did then, was rejected furiously. Perhaps he confused my anti-Bush attitude with the usual anti-Americanism. I had drawn my wisdom on this from a media analysis by Columbia University, which observed a decisive change in US war reporting: whereas military spokesmen in earlier wars apparently tended to express themselves jubilantly and positively, but the media in a more understated and critical way, nowadays the military seem to have become the prophets of doom and the media are the "cheerleaders."

Those who hop about and wave their flags, grinning away, naturally sign declarations of loyalty to the "team" blindly. It is true to say that the anti-Bushist, who once associated America with free speech, free press and the fundamental belief in the media as the State's independent fourth estate, turns away in horror.

Either-Or else

Americans should not expect one battle, but a lengthy campaign, unlike any other we have ever seen. It may include dramatic strikes, visible on TV, and covert operations, secret even in success. We will starve terrorists of funding, turn them one against another, drive them from place to place, until there is no refuge or no rest. And we will pursue nations that provide aid or safe haven to terrorism. Every nation, in every region, now has a decision to make. Either you are with us, or you are with the terrorists. (Applause.) From this day forward, any nation that continues to harbor or support terrorism will be regarded by the United States as a hostile regime...

This is not, however, just America's fight. And what is at stake is not just America's freedom. This is the world's fight. This is civilization's fight...

Some speak of an age of terror. I know there are struggles ahead, and dangers to face. But this country will define our times, not be defined by them. As long as the United States of America is determined and strong, this will not be an age of terror; this will be an age of liberty, here and across the world. (Applause.)

The course of this conflict is not known, yet its outcome is certain. Freedom and fear, justice and cruelty, have always been at war, and we know that God is not neutral between them. (Applause.)

http://www.whitehouse.gov/news/releases/2001/09/20010920-8.html

American armies of past centuries stood as a paradigm of modern media democracy due to their openness during frontline reporting, but since Vietnam ever stricter censorship has been applied, and by the time of Poppy's Gulf War, quite a lot was already happening behind the public's back. Today just one representative of the media is protesting against this: porn czar Larry Flynt of Hustler magazine. The wheelchair-bound publisher, who campaigned in the courts to establish the freedom of American citizens to gaze at a pubic hair in a newspaper, now files a complaint against defense secretary Rumsfeld for obstructing frontline reports.

Just as the world's best hockey players long since stopped coming from the sport's British motherland, but now come from Pakistan, India or Australia, American virtues and values seem to be more strongly rooted in the colonies these days than in America itself, where free speech, a free press and independent reporting survive only by going extraterrestrial on the Internet. The whole of the rest of the media, truth be told, is actively complicit in the biggest brainwashing operation in history. This is how CNN boss Walter Isaacson called on his employees in a memo to play down the suffering in Afghanistan: it was supposedly "sick to place too much emphasis on the incidents and suffering in Afghanistan"; if suffering civilians really had to be shown at all, then only "in the context of the terror attacks that caused great suffering in the USA." CBS news anchor Dan Rather unblushingly went one better: "George Bush is the President. He makes the decisions – and as befits an American, wherever he wants me, I'll stand in line, just tell me where."[25]

NOT IN OUR NAME

Let it not be said that people in the United States did nothing when their government declared a war without limit and instituted stark new measures of repression.

The signers of this statement call on the people of the US to resist the policies and overall political direction that have emerged since September 11, 2001, and which pose grave dangers to the people of the world.

We believe that peoples and nations have the right to determine their own destiny, free from military coercion by great powers. We believe that all persons detained or prosecuted by the United States government should have the same rights of due process. We believe that questioning, criticism, and dissent must be valued and protected. We understand that such rights and values are always contested and must be fought for.

We believe that people of conscience must take responsibility for what their own governments do — we must first of all oppose the injustice that is done in our own name. Thus we call on all Americans to RESIST the war and repression that has been loosed on the world by the Bush administration. It is unjust, immoral, and illegitimate. We choose to make common cause with the people of the world.

We too watched with shock the horrific events of September 11, 2001. We too mourned the thousands of innocent dead and shook our heads at the terrible scenes of carnage — even as we recalled similar scenes in Baghdad, Panama City, and, a generation ago, Vietnam. We too joined the anguished questioning of millions of Americans who asked why such a thing could happen.

But the mourning had barely begun, when the highest leaders of the land unleashed a spirit of revenge. They put out a simplistic script of "good vs. evil" that was taken up by a pliant and intimidated media. They told us that asking why these terrible events had happened verged on treason. There was to be no debate. There were by definition no valid political or moral questions. The only possible answer was to be war abroad and repression at home.

In our name, the Bush administration, with near unanimity from Congress, not only attacked Afghanistan but arrogated to itself and its allies the right to rain down military force anywhere and anytime. The brutal repercussions have been felt from the Philippines to Palestine, where Israeli tanks and bulldozers have left a terrible trail of death and destruction. The government now openly prepares to wage all-out war on Iraq — a country which has no connection to the horror of September 11. What kind of world will this become if the US government has a blank check to drop commandos, assassins, and bombs wherever it wants?

In our name, within the US, the government has created two classes of people: those to whom the basic rights of the US legal system are at least promised, and those who now seem to have no rights at all. The government rounded up over 1,000 immigrants and detained them in secret and indefinitely. Hundreds have been deported and hundreds of others still languish today in prison. This smacks of the infamous concentration camps for Japanese-Americans in World War 2. For the first time in decades, immigration procedures single out certain nationalities for unequal treatment.

In our name, the government has brought down a pall of repression over society. The President's spokesperson warns people to "watch what they say." Dissident artists, intellectuals, and professors find their views distorted, attacked, and suppressed. The so-called USA PATRIOT Act — along with a host of similar measures on the state level — gives police sweeping new powers of search and seizure, supervised if at all by secret proceedings before secret courts.

In our name, the executive has steadily usurped the roles and functions of the other branches of government. Military tribunals with lax rules of evidence and no right to appeal to the regular courts are put in place by executive order. Groups are declared "terrorist" at the stroke of a presidential pen.

We must take the highest officers of the land seriously when they talk of a war that will last a generation and when they speak of a new domestic order. We are confronting a new openly imperial policy towards the world and a domestic policy that manufactures and manipulates fear to curtail rights.

There is a deadly trajectory to the events of the past months that must be seen for what it is and resisted. Too many times in history people have waited until it was too late to resist. President Bush has declared: "you're either with us or against us." Here is our answer: We refuse to allow you to speak for all the American people. We will not give up our right to question. We will not hand over our consciences in return for a hollow promise of safety. We say NOT IN OUR NAME. We refuse to be party to

these wars and we repudiate any inference that they are being waged in our name or for our welfare. We extend a hand to those around the world suffering from these policies; we will show our solidarity in word and deed.

We who sign this statement call on all Americans to join together to rise to this challenge. We applaud and support the questioning and protest now going on, even as we recognize the need for much, much more to actually stop this juggernaut. We draw inspiration from the Israeli reservists who, at great personal risk, declare "there IS a limit" and refuse to serve in the occupation of the West Bank and Gaza.

We also draw on the many examples of resistance and conscience from the past of the United States: from those who fought slavery with rebellions and the underground railroad, to those who defied the Vietnam war by refusing orders, resisting the draft, and standing in solidarity with resisters.

Let us not allow the watching world today to despair of our silence and our failure to act. Instead, let the world hear our pledge: we will resist the machinery of war and repression and rally others to do everything possible to stop it.

http://www.notinourname.net/downloads/nion_NYT9-19.pdf.

According to Andrew Stroehlein, a critical observer of defunct independent US journalism, Rather's statement counts among "the most horrifying things ever said by a leading news person in the history of American journalism." The "Führer" would have been over the moon with newspaper editors like these, at any rate. And the CBS news director is far from being the most Goebbelsian of pundits – freethinking commentators and columnists have been sent packing everywhere by the united front of patriotism and censorship.

Admittedly, the fact that a "moral tramp" like Larry Flynt doesn't get put straight in the concentration camp but can file a complaint against the defense secretary does constitute one difference at least between Germany after the Reichstag fire and America after 9/11. On the other hand, that Flynt of all people should become a hero of the anti-Bush movement that refuses to be driven mad by a psychological operation like 9/11 and insists on autonomous development of the public unconscious – now that's as politically incorrect as it gets.

I think it's time to find a new term for the political style of Bush, who came to power as a "compassionate conservative," and his fellow propagandists. How does "compassionate fascism" sound?

When the decision as to how much "pubic hair" the public can take – let's say in the form of "obscene" images of victims in Afghanistan, in reports about the longstanding business connections of the Bush and bin Laden families, about the CIA's close complicity with the Pakistani ISI, the Taliban and local heroin lords, about the role of Unocal, Halliburton and other concerns in Pipelineistan – when research and publication decisions concerning facts like these are not the responsibility of independent reporters, but of directives from the propaganda ministry and its cheerleaders, then that is Bushism in its purest form.

When a national double standard in justice for nationals and foreigners, for "prisoners of war" and "combatants" is decided on, and legislators announce cheerily to the TV cameras that they didn't actually read the individual paragraphs of the "Patriot Act," but "naturally" approved it – that's Bushism.

When the "Freedom of Information Act" is put out of action by fiat, presidential documents from the era of Reagan/Bush and Iran-Contra affair are sealed forever, and the investigation into Enron corruption in the White House is blocked for "national security reasons" (by Dick Cheney in January 2002), then that is shady Bushist politics.

At this point Martin Luther King comes to mind: "We should never forget that everything Adolf Hitler did in Germany was 'legal.'" [26]

Now there are "no Republicans and Democrats, just Americans," according to Bush II in his "Axis of Evil" speech, just like Kaiser Wilhelm before the First World War. Since I have discovered anti-Bushism as a viewpoint I can now understand better why my breakfast threatens to make a return appearance at comments like these: as a German born in the former US zone in the mid-50's I am probably simply more American at heart than the empire in Washington currently permits. No wonder really – thanks to the Nuremberg trials and the Marshall Plan, Germany became the most faithful and grateful vassal state of the USA. That exemplary democrat Uncle Sam bestowed upon us our first chewing gums, cola, Levi's jeans – "cowboy pants" as my grandmother called them – and the GI's brought not just Camels and Marlboros, but later Jimmy Hendrix records and marijuana too. The Wolfman Jack Show played on AFN – who bothered listening to German broadcasts? Long hair, sit-ins, demos, happenings... all direct imports from the USA – a culture that drove the goose-step, the subservience to authority, the Führer mentality out of the militarized Teutons. Bob Dylan: "Don't follow leaders, watch the parking meters";

Timothy Leary: "Question authority! Think for yourself!"; Little Richard: "A Wop Bopa Loo Bop..." The new baptists, who made our bodies literate and taught our minds to dance, came from America; and they vaccinated the children of the Stalingrad Generation with a dose of American values – freedom, democracy, responsibility – to make them immune to any kind of fascism – or anti-Americanism. And so we were "On the Road" with Kerouac, cried with rage at the movies when the Bushists shot down "easy riders" Dennis Hopper and Peter Fonda – and became American patriots, without ever even setting foot in the country.

That behind the scenes back then a whole different political script was playing out, that with the Kennedy and Martin Luther King murders a Bushist putsch had set in, that American politics was drifting ever further from the values and culture that had just infected us in the West German colony – all this was still unknown to me at the time. The students' chant of "USA-SA-SS" at Vietnam demos, however, enlightened me: bombarding an impoverished population of rice farmers with napalm – surely it doesn't get much more Nazi than that. Yet the fact that the adored bringer of culture and liberator from fascism was itself now baring its "imperialistic teeth" could not shake the belief in American values. Under the motto "Come Together" Tim Leary competed for governorship of California against Ronald Reagan and lost; but the Beatles – who thanks to American spirit (and LSD) matured from British thrash and speed rockers to cosmopolitan cultureheads – turned his motto and program into a world hit. From a cultural point of view American values prevailed right across the board worldwide – while politically, conditions at home veered towards their opposite. What began with Kennedy's murder continued through Reagan and Bush I and is experiencing its premature climax with Bush II. 83 percent approval from the population – since Roosevelt in the Second World War presidents only achieved such numbers in totalitarian states.

"If a rational Fascist dictatorship were to exist, then it would choose the American system," as Noam Chomsky never tires of repeating.[27] Bush II is currently demonstrating the way the "American system" should look: "free elections," to which two thirds of the population don't even turn out; election financing and payment methods like in the last banana republic; monolithic solidification of public opinion and of the media by means of an unprecedented terrorist attack; proclamation of a state of emergency and mobilization; immediate identification of the enemy, of the enormous threat posed by him, and of the measures to be taken against him. What happened next had already been foreseen by Mark Twain, another wise man of the old American culture:

> Next the statesmen will invent cheap lies, putting the blame upon the nation that is attacked, and every man will be glad of those conscience-soothing falsities, and will diligently study them, and refuse to examine any refutations of them; and thus he will by and by convince himself that the war is just, and will thank God for the better sleep he enjoys after this process of grotesque self-deception.[28]

When football stars read out phrases from the Constitution before the Superbowl game, this will enable them and their millions-strong audience to sleep better too, while the "daisy cutters" of the air force are slaughtering more civilians in Afghanistan. The media and Congress no longer ponder why all air force squadrons remained on the ground on September 11 and allowed an aircraft to steer straight onto the Pentagon without a qualm. So while the criminal investigation into 9/11 – the investigation into the real course of events, culprits and string-pullers – disappears in the fog of war, the actual personification of evil in the form of Osama bin Laden is increasingly unimportant and abandoned in favor of an abstract world conspiracy of an "Axis of Evil," and "Terror" in general. Who, after the shock of 9/11, will not believe that a war against this nameless terror is justified? Meanwhile the most grotesque self-deception is that the war in Afghanistan and to follow against the "Axis of Evil" is even aimed at terror. Up to now at any rate none of the culprits of 9/11 has been caught, but thousands of innocent civilians have been killed in this cause.

Ah, those were the days, back in December 2000, when Dubya's jubilant political vision – "If this were a dictatorship, it'd be a heck of a lot easier, just so long as I'm the dictator" – cheered the crowd no end. In the face of the shock of 9/11 most of them now approve of him even if he has made "homeland security" a job for the military. And 91 percent of people surveyed on www.vote.com support the biggest boost to the weapons arsenal since the Second World War – and the most gigantic accumulation of debt since the fatal "Reaganomics" that transformed America from the world's biggest creditor into the world's biggest debtor. The Great Bankrupt USA had only just been set back on track to consolidation during the Clinton era; and now, thanks to the mega-fiend called "Terror," it can further encumber the world debt carousel – disastrous enough already – to the tune of billions with impunity, and paper over the recession with "war business" on credit. Every schoolchild knows that the Bushist economy – tax reductions here, armament there – cannot go up, but the psychological shock of the WTC crash is so deeply embedded that even using basic means of calculation only confuses the complexity still further; people prefer to perpetuate the grotesque self-deception and just follow the lead sheep instead. That Bush II rose from widely derided half-wit to wise leader of the civilized world overnight is due to the enduring impact of the catastrophe alone.

Yet there is no question: the man seems nice. That he sometimes gets his words mixed up and pronounces idiocies, that he bows to the military, looks as if he's imbibed and snorted a few and was an inveterate loser as a businessman – all this earns the president sympathy points as a Man of the People. That multi-tasking between TV, football, beer and pretzels gets a bit much for him at times – all this brings him closer to voters' hearts than his dry stick of a father ever was. His all-too-human qualities save him not only in the face of Enrongate – on this point his predecessor, the comparatively uncongenial Clinton, became the target of a pursuit of scandal proportions for similar trifles – they also make Bush II the ideal front man for the rock-hard geopolitical power politics scripted by clever CIA luminaries like Brzezinski (*The Only World Power*) and Huntington (*Clash of Civilizations*) – in a nod to their power theory models from Machiavelli to Carl Schmitt. The 9/11 plot, whoever was responsible for its execution, bestowed upon this little boy in shirtsleeves from next door a sovereignty that no *Imperator* in history could ever claim for himself.

Yet anti-Bushism is not entrenched in one little Gaul, but is a call to a struggle against the "Romans," even if it is all but hopeless for want of a miraculous magic potion. Both Emperor Bush and his hawk Wolfowitz have frequently made it clear that it's a case of "either with us or with the terrorists," simply either / or. However, if the aim here is a united effort against terror, the global community must make it clear to its world sheriff that he won't get far with "dead or alive" cowboy methods.

There must be independent international courts to monitor his police work. Terrorist havens like Saudi Arabia and Israel cannot continue to be spared just because the sheriff does business there. Heroin and cocaine production for the financing of deputy sheriffs can in future be as little tolerated as Koran schools and terror camps for training them. The notorious oil addiction that has turned the USA into a furious, violent junkie can be cured. In short: a global Pax Americana – instead of a Bushist New World Order – only has a lasting chance if it comes into being not through violence and in competition with the rest of the world, but in cooperation with it. The American values that drove fascism out of the Germans appear to be the best cultural and ethical platform for this, just like the economic and monetary principles that really did bring the western world something like "prosperity for all" from 1945 – 1965. Meanwhile the bottomless "junk bond" and "derivative" casino capitalism – to which the severance of the dollar from the gold standard in the 1970's opened the floodgates, and which now brings us the flabbergasting failure of arch-cheat Enron – this paradigm of the criminal, corrupt and asocial nature of Bushist economics can never become a model for the global economy.

Only the "Obelix Method" can help against robber baron activities like these, and even the most cowardly anti-Bushists agree: "We start with the pigs, move on to the Roman patrols and finish off with the wild boar."

Appendix 1.
9/11 FAQ – Frequently Asked Questions

The original German edition presented a catalogue of 100 questions compiled by 9/11 activist Nico Haupt on his website. As with the Richter scale, the questions on 9/11 are open ended. There is no maximum ranking for earthquakes and similarly the contradictions and inconsistencies before, during and after the attacks are countless. For the American edition we have settled on a more recent list by Ian Woods, publisher of Global Outlook magazine, of the 26 most egregious anomalies in the bin-Laden – al-Qaeda "official conspiracy theory version" of events, because otherwise, if you're not criminologically trained, it is too easy to lose track amid the jumble of names and details.[29]

To pursue these questions is actually the job of politics, the police, the secret services and the military. So please don't expect to get the answers from me, but from those institutions which are responsible and which are financed by your taxes.

On the Day of September 11, 2001

A. Bush's Puzzling Reaction – Why did Bush just sit there in the 2nd grade classroom reading for 25 minutes?

B. No Immediate Jet Scramble – Why was Flight 77 not intercepted after 1 hr 45 min of flying off course?

C. Collapse of the Twin Towers / Strength – Why has no steel skyscraper ever collapsed from fire before or since? How could structural steel disintegrate while magnetic hard drives remained intact?

D. Collapse of the Twin Towers / Speed – How can the 'Pancake Theory' account for the resistance of lower floor structures when 110 stories reached the ground at the free-fall speed of 10.4 seconds?

E. Collapse of the Twin Towers / Scientific – Why does the thermal data indicate 'hot spots' weeks after their collapse?

F. Flight 93 Crashed in Pennsylvania – Why was crash debris so small and spread out over a five-mile swath, if the plane was not shot down?

G. Mysterious Collapse of Building 7 – Why did Building 7 collapse straight down like in a controlled demolition, when no airplane hit it, nor any debris fell on it, only two small fires in the building which were left to burn?

H. Attack on the Pentagon / Flight 77 – Why was there so little damage and such a small amount of debris on the exterior, and what could penetrate through at least six heavy walls to the inner ring?

I. Attack on the Pentagon / Censored Evidence – Why has the Pentagon only released 4 frames out of all the video tapes?

The Background

J. Intelligence Warnings / Ignored – Why did Bush ignore an unprecedented number of intelligence warnings three months prior to 9/11?

K. Intelligence Warnings / Whistleblowers – Why did the FBI and CIA ignore agents Colleen Rowley, Kenneth Williams and Robert Wright?

L. Insider Trading / Cover-up – Why were there 1200% more 'puts' on United Airlines and American Airlines on 9/11?

M. The Roadmap to Empire / (PNAC) – What is the Project for a New American Century? (www.newamericancentury.org)

N. History of War / Pearl Harbor – Why did FDR knowingly let the Japanese attack Pearl Harbor (1941)?

O. History of War / Operation Northwoods – Has the military been planning another Operation Northwoods (1962)?

P. History of War / Kuwaiti Deception – Why was Bush Sr. not incarcerated for the 1991 Incubator Baby Scam?

Q. CIA Allies / Saudi Arabian Terrorists – Why was J. Michael Springmann issuing US visas to Saudi terrorists?

R. CIA Asset / Osama bin Laden – Why didn't the CIA arrest bin Laden in Dubai (July) or Rawalpindi (Sept. 10)?

S. CIA Buddy / General Mahmoud – Why was the 9/11 Money Man (Gen. Mahmoud) visiting DC on Sept. 4– 13?

T. CIA Connection / The ISI – Why did Pakistan's ISI airlift Al Qaeda to safety between November 2001 and January 2002?

U. The Bush and Bin Laden Family Ties – Why was Bush Sr. and the Carlyle Group meeting at the Ritz the morning of 9/11?

The Aftermath

V. Complicity / By the Media – How did anthrax from an American weapons lab end up on T. Daschle's desk?

W. Complicity / By Congress – Why would they pass the PATRIOT Act before everyone had a chance to read it?

X. Cover-up / By the US Government – Why was key evidence for the WTC site and Pentagon destroyed by the US Government?

Y. Cover-up / By the White House – Why did it take 411 days to form the 9/11 Commission when other commissions only took 7 days?

Z. The Motives / Who Benefited? – The CIA, the FBI and the military have all received budget increases, not reprimands.

Appendix 2.
A Short History of Foreknowledge

The "truth about the terror" of 9/11 includes a whole history of involvement and foreknowledge. Ever since two relevant FBI memos became known in mid-May 2002, this set of connections has moved into the public eye more and more.

The following outline is based on the "Timeline"[30] compiled by Mike Ruppert on his website *www.fromthewilderness.com*, which he published for the first time in November 2001 and regularly updates. The individual facts can be checked on this website.

1991 – 1997. Large US oil companies like Exxon Mobil, Texaco, Unocal, BP Amoco and Shell invest $3 billion to bribe the government of Kazakhstan to secure equity rights in the huge oil reserves in the region. The oil companies commit to future direct investments in Kazakhstan of $35 billion. The problem is, however, that the existing pipelines are in Russian hands and Moscow charges exorbitant prices for using them. The oil companies complain to the congressional "International Relations Committee" that they have no way of recouping their investments.

December 4, 1997. Taliban representatives are guests at Unocal's headquarters in Texas to negotiate the planned pipeline through Afghanistan. As different reports show, the negotiations failed because the Taliban demanded too much money.

February 12, 1998. Unocal Vice-President John J. Maresca, who was later to become a special envoy to Afghanistan, testifies before the House of Representatives that until a unified and US-friendly government is in place in Afghanistan, no pipeline can be built.

April 1998. The CIA ignores warnings by its own expert Robert Baer – according to Seymour Hersh of the *New Yorker* "perhaps the best on-the-ground field officer in the Middle East" – that Saudi Arabia is harboring an al-Qaeda cell led by two known terrorists. A detailed list of known terrorists is offered to Saudi intelligence in August but is refused.

Summer 1998 and 2000. Former President George Bush travels to Saudi Arabia on behalf of the privately-owned Carlyle Group, the 11th largest US defense contractor. There he also privately meets with members of the royal family and the bin Laden family.

January 2001. The Bush Administration orders the FBI and the intelligence agencies to "back off" from investigations involving the bin Laden family, including two of Osama's relatives (Abdullah and Omar), who lived in Falls Church, Virginia – close to CIA headquarters. This order was preceded by other restrictions dating back to 1996 that frustrated efforts to investigate the bin Ladens.

February 12, 2001. In a report about a trial of alleged al Qaeda members, news agency UPI's terrorism correspondent reveals that the National Security Agency (NSA) was able to intercept bin Laden's communications system. This does not mesh with the fact that the attacks had been planned for years without anyone finding out about it, as the government claims.

May 2001. Deputy Secretary of State Richard Armitage, a former career covert operative and Navy special forces member, and CIA Director George Tenet travel to India on an official mission. Tenet also discreetly drops in on Pakistani President Pervez Musharraf. Armitage has long and close ties to the Pakistani secret service ISI and has been awarded the country's highest civilian honor. It would be reasonable to assume that while in Islamabad Tenet also met with his Pakistani counterpart Mahmud Ahmed.

June 2001. The German intelligence service BND warns the CIA and Israel that Middle Eastern terrorists are planning "to hijack a commercial aircraft and use it as a weapon to attack important symbols of American and Israeli culture." At least that's what it said in German newspaper *Frankfurter Allgemeine Zeitung* on Sept. 14.

Summer 2001. Three US officials – Tom Simons (former US ambassador to Pakistan), Karl Inderfurth (former assistant secretary of state for South Asian affairs) and Lee Coldren (former State Department office head and expert on Asia) – meet with Pakistani and Russian envoys and intelligence officials between May and August. Berlin was the site of the last round of these secret talks, held under UN auspices and with the participation of all neighboring states, which had essayed to resolve the Afghan pipeline issue. Taliban representatives attended several of these sessions, but rejected American offers of participation in the pipeline profits as too low. At the last meeting in Berlin, the US delegates warned of a military operation against Afghanistan in October.

According to a story in Britain's *Guardian*, US Rangers are training special forces in Tajikistan. Tajik and Uzbek special forces supposedly are also being trained in Alaska and Montana, something the US Defense Department does not confirm.

The *Times of India* published the first truly hard lead to the backers of Mohamed Atta, the alleged leader of the "terror pilots." According to this report, Pakistani intelligence director General Mahmud Ahmad ordered the transfer of $100,000 to Mohamed Atta in July 2001. The transfer was allegedly made by Umar Sheikh, a covert ISI agent and radical Islamist of British origin, who was later charged with the kidnapping of *Wall Street Journal* reporter Pearl. Following the publication of the *Times of India* report, which cited Indian intelligence sources and FBI confirmation, General Ahmad resigned from his post as ISI director.

June 26, 2001. The Internet magazine "Indiareacts.com" writes that "India and Iran support US and Russian plans for 'limited military action' against the Taliban." According to the article, the fighting will be done by Russian and American troops with help from Uzbekistan and Tajikistan.

July 4-14, 2001. Osama bin Laden receives treatment for his kidney ailment in the American Hospital in Dubai, where he is visited by his family and high-ranking individuals from Saudi Arabia and the Emirates – as well as by CIA official Larry Mitchell, who is recalled from the Dubai office on July 15.

July 10, 2001. An FBI memorandum from its Phoenix, Arizona, office – and another one in August from Minneapolis – draw attention to the suspicion that al-Qaeda members are using US flight schools to acquire skills for hijacking aircraft. The July 10 memo recommends checking flight schools across the country and cites potential ties to Osama bin Laden. The Minneapolis FBI agents report the arrest of Zacharias Moussaoui, a French citizen of Moroccan origin, who only wanted to learn how to fly a Boeing 747 but not how to take off and land. In an email to headquarters, they describe him as someone who may plan to fly a jumbo jet into the World Trade Center. Both reports are ignored by FBI headquarters.

July 20-22, 2001. Prior to the G8 summit in Genoa, Italy receives warnings from several countries, including from Egyptian President Mubarak, of an attack on the conference building with hijacked airplanes that could be used as airborne missiles. As a result, the Italian government deploys anti-aircraft guns and closes off local airspace. As a precaution, George W. Bush spends the night on a US warship in the harbor.

August 6, 2001. A CIA briefing informs President Bush about the possible threat that attackers connected to Osama bin Laden might be planning to use airplanes as flying bombs. This warning from the intelligence services may have drawn on the FBI memos from Phoenix and Minneapolis. Yet neither air traffic control nor military air defenses are placed on high alert.

August 12, 2001. US Navy Lieutenant Delmart "Mike" Vreeland, jailed in Toronto on fraud charges, claims to be an officer of Navy intelligence with knowledge of impending attacks. As no one pays him any attention, he writes down the details on a note and hands it to the prison wardens for safekeeping.

August 20, 2001. Russian President Putin orders his intelligence service to convey a warning to US intelligence "in the strongest possible terms" of imminent attacks on government buildings and airports. The Russian newspaper *Izvestia* later specifies that the warning referred to 25 suicide pilots, who were planning an attack on prominent buildings.

August 20 – September 10, 2001. The Dow Jones Index on the New York Stock Exchange drops nearly 900 points in the three weeks prior to the attack. A major stock-market crash is imminent. Vice-President Cheney and other high-ranking government officials hold counsel behind closed doors about the foreseeable Enron bust, the biggest bankruptcy (and financial fraud) in US history.

September 1-10, 2001. In an exercise dubbed Operation "Swift Sword" and planned for four years, 23,000 British troops are redeployed to Oman. At the same time, two US carrier battle groups arrive off the coast of Pakistan, and another 17,000 US troops join the 23,000 NATO troops assembled in Egypt for Operation "Bright Star." All of these forces are in place before the first plane hits the WTC towers.

September 6-10, 2001. Dramatic increases in the volume of put options on United Airlines and American Airlines and other companies affected by the attacks, such as Merrill Lynch, Morgan Stanley, AXA Re and Munich Re, point to criminal insider trading on the stock markets.

September 10, 2001. The Federal Emergency Management Agency (FEMA) apparently was placed on alert in advance. In an interview with CBS News anchor Dan Rather, Tom Kenney, a leading member of the "Urban Search and Rescue Team," made the following odd remark: "We're currently one of the first teams that were deployed to support the city of New York for this disaster. We arrived on late Monday night [Sept. 10], and went into action on Tuesday morning."

September 11, 2001. General Ahmad, head of the Pakistani ISI (who "surprisingly" has to resign one month later over his money transfer to Mohamed Atta) arrives in Washington for talks on the Taliban.

Employees of Odigo Inc. in Israel, one of the world's largest "instant messaging" companies with offices in New York, receive threatening warnings of an imminent attack on the WTC less than two hours before the first plane hits the towers. The police and law enforcement authorities have gone silent about any investigation of this. The Odigo research and development offices in Israel are located in Herzliya, a ritzy suburb of Tel Aviv that is also home to the "Institute for Counter-terrorism," which reports early on about the insider trading that took place around 9/11.

In the space of 45 minutes four airplanes are hijacked and diverted from their flight path – the first one at 8:15 a.m. and the last one at 9:05 a.m. – but it's not until 9:30 a.m. that Air Force interception fighter jets take off, too late. The National Command Authority waits 75 minutes before taking counter-measures – a lapse unrivaled in history.

September 14, 2001. The prison authorities in Toronto open the envelope that was sealed by Mike Vreeland in August and find that it mentions the "WTC" and the "Pentagon." The US Navy subsequently claims Vreeland was discharged as a seaman in 1986 for unsatisfactory performance and has never worked for its intelligence service.

September 15, 2001. The *New York Times* reports that the head of Alex Brown Bank, Mayo Shattuck III, has resigned effective immediately only a short while after receiving a three-year contract (paying $30 million annually). Many of the UAL put options were bought through Alex Brown, which is owned by Deutsche Bank. Its former chief executive, "Buzzy" Krongard, left in 1998 to work for the CIA, where he is now the third highest ranking director.

September 29, 2001. The *San Francisco Chronicle* reports that $2.5 million of profits on put options on American Airlines and United Airlines have not been claimed with the banks. After the four-day suspension of trade the owners probably no longer dared to cash in their "hot" profits.

October 10, 2001. The Pakistani newspaper *The Frontier Post* reports that US Ambassador Wendy Chamberlain has paid a call on the Pakistani oil minister. A previously abandoned Unocal pipeline through Afghanistan is now back on the agenda "in view of recent geopolitical developments." (In February, negotiations took place, and at the start of May the BBC reported that the $2 billion project, the "largest foreign investment in Afghanistan," was a done deal.)

October 2001. The Dow Jones Index, which was already on a downward trend before the attacks, has recovered most of its losses. A stock-market crash has been averted thanks to a massive injection of government spending on defense programs, subsidies for the airline industry and planned corporate tax cuts. The companies benefiting most from these measures are defense contractors and military suppliers.

Appendix 3.
An Interview with Andreas von Bülow

What does the CIA know about 9/11? The former German Minister for
Research and Technology and Parliamentary State Secretary of the
Ministry of Defense Andreas von Bülow was not able to air his dissident
and unwelcome answers to this question in leading German magazines
like *Spiegel* or *Stern*, but he found refuge with *Konkret*. The following
interview that German author and journalist Jürgen Elsässer conducted
with him appeared in its December 2001 issue.

Elsässer: *There is much that remains to be explained with regard to the
terror attack on the World Trade Center. For example, there were
warnings prior to Sept. 11 by French intelligence, as well as Mossad.
Nevertheless, the US authorities' response totally lacked preparation –
security alert levels were not raised at airports, the response of airspace
control and air defense was wholly unprofessional and slow.*

Von Bülow: What is strange is that the Americans were totally unsuspecting until the attack, yet afterwards it took them no more than 48
hours to present the perpetrator – bin Laden and his legendary terror
network – to the world public. As for the Mossad warnings, it would be
nice to know what they knew and what they passed on. That isn't
necessarily one and the same. For example, with the Islamic suicide
attack on the US barracks in Beirut in the early 1980's, Mossad knew
beforehand the exact color and type of truck later used by the attackers.
Yet they only passed on a general warning to the CIA without the details.

Why?

One reason for the intelligence services' reserve is the protection of
sources. If you reveal the details then this might give clues to the identity
of the informer or informers. Besides that, of course, secret services, that
includes Western ones, often play a sometimes bizarre power game.

So maybe this time round the CIA also didn't know all that much?

That is not what I meant to say. Think back to the first attack on the
World Trade Center in 1993. Back then, the whole Islamist gang that had
carried out the operation was caught. Meanwhile, it has emerged that that
bunch had long before been infiltrated by the CIA and FBI. The bomb
maker was an agent provocateur of the FBI whose commanding officer
had promised to switch the explosives with harmless chemicals so that

the attackers could be lured into the trap yet harm could be prevented. The FBI, however, failed to honor its promise. Several fatalities and 1,000 injured were the result. Another strange fact… the members of the terror group had actually been barred from entering the United States and were on an FBI, State Department list. The CIA, however, made sure this ban was circumvented. The horror of 9/11 is a core meltdown of the American intelligence services. Altogether there are 26 and they compete with one another. It's understandable that someone who isn't cynical would despair amid all this confusion and chaos. Those who want to help their government in preventing terror attacks find themselves mired in a morass beyond compare.

So, all against all, and it's the terrorists who benefit?

After all, the crucial question is who are the terrorists. The former head of a strategic unit for combating international drug trafficking at the highest levels said in a Congressional hearing that in 30 years of working for the Drug Enforcement Agency he has never come across any major investigation in which the CIA didn't wrest control away from him.

But 9/11 wasn't about a drug offense.

Bin Laden is a product of the CIA, first created as part of the fight against the Soviet Union. It wasn't just a matter of fending off the Soviet intervention in Afghanistan. It was about the destabilization of the USSR via its republics with a Muslim population. Even before the Communists came to power in Afghanistan in 1978, the CIA had fomented unrest in Afghanistan. The central government couldn't control the situation. The Communists took the helm, also failed and called in Soviet troops, thereby stumbling into the trap laid by then US Security Advisor Brzezinski, with which he wanted to create a Russian Vietnam. Then in a single operation, mounted by the CIA together with the Saudi and Pakistani intelligence services and heavily dependent on financing from the drug trade, around 100,000 freedom fighters from Muslim countries in North Africa and the Middle East were enlisted as mercenaries for the fight against the godless Soviets.

Freedom fighters in quotation marks. In reality, these men were the good-for-nothings and roughnecks of the entire Islamic world. Wherever a black sheep of the family or the village was up to no good, the call of the Mujahideen lured them to the Hindu Kush where you could make yourself useful in exchange for oil and drug money. The Taliban themselves were plucked from the koranically strict orphanages of

Pakistan. Osama bin Laden was one of the organizers of the fundamentalist advertising campaign, and he was certainly allowed to draw his roughly 10,000 mercenaries from militant, anti-Western, anti-American circles. Some of his troops were specifically trained in CIA camps for special assignments. Thus, we are dealing with desperados rather than with deeply religious individuals. It's as if we enlisted our soccer hooligans for a holy war against Islam. But they are ideally suited for brainwashing a Western audience with the aim of hammering home the concept of a "clash of civilizations" with Islam as the new enemy.

You were a member of the German government at the time of the Soviet invasion of Afghanistan. How did German Chancellor Schmidt's cabinet discuss the issue?

Hardly. I only remember that Washington put a lot of pressure on us to boycott the Olympic Games in Moscow because of Afghanistan. The intensity of this pressure is also illustrated by another episode. At the start of the 1980's, American four-star General and NATO Commander Haig pushed with all his might for all national maneuvers, no matter how small, to be declared part of his large NATO fall maneuver. That's how on one weekend from Norway to Turkey a good million NATO troops in all were on the move from West to East.

As state secretary I took the liberty to remark that I found this to be problematic, particularly because in the West, all warning lamps would start flashing if the Warsaw Pact were to stage a similar East-West moving scenario. This small criticism resounded worldwide, in the US and all the way to Hawaii. When I visited the White House shortly after, Brzezinski and I ran into each other by what appeared to be coincidence and he asked me: "Are you the guy talking about maneuvers in Europe?" From today's point of view, the man was already kindling the fires back then, from the European as well as the Asian side. At present, the geopolitical game is being continued by expanding NATO at the same time as establishing military positions in the independent Asian successor states of the Soviet Union.

I recall moreover, given the contacts between Germany's socialist SPD party and the Communist party in the Soviet Union, that the Soviets clearly indicated on numerous occasions that they would be only too happy to withdraw from Afghanistan but that they feared the security chaos that was likely to ensue, with rival Afghan and Pakistani warlords and drug lords fighting each other. They tried to win over the Americans for a joint initiative, but Washington remained deaf to these overtures.

Didn't the German intelligence service BND also participate in the CIA's Afghanistan operation?

At most in a supporting role. At times, the Germans develop sentimental ties to the bitterly tested peoples of the region. In the case of Jürgen Todenhöfer, the German CDU party's unofficial envoy to Afghanistan, I can imagine him sitting around the campfire with the Mujahideen, singing freedom songs. The CIA's covert operatives pursue the covert, not democratically-legitimized goals of their country with an iron fist. Henry Kissinger, Brzezinski's predecessor, once said covert operations should please not be confused with missionary work. This was at a time when the CIA turned off the money tap – the drug trade – for the 30,000 Kurdish fighters battling Saddam Hussein, after decades of using them covertly in the interests of the Shah's Iran, and abandoned the leaders, as well as the rank and file, to face destruction by the dictator.

Back to 9/11. It seems remarkable to me that President Bush did not want to come to New York on the day of the attack out of fear that an attack was also planned on him, that is on Air Force One. William Safire pursued this matter further in the Sept. 15 issue of the New York Times *with reports that the terrorists had cracked the US government's secret codes, so the threat seemed plausible. Safire concludes that "the terrorists may have a mole in the White House – that, or informants in the secret services, FBI, FAA or CIA."*

That is absolutely possible. Even more interesting, I believe, is the theory of one British flight engineer, who claims that the scheduled flights were not hijacked on 9/11 but that they were steered into their targets by remote control from the ground via a backdoor feature in the on-board computers that overrides the pilots' control.

It would be easy to prove the contrary if the investigating authorities released the data from the flight recorders and the voice recorders of the third and fourth airplanes – one was flown into the Pentagon, the other crashed. But this isn't happening.

There are a number of unresolved crashes on the American East Coast. Like the Swissair plane or the Egypt Air flight. You could also argue that the British flight engineer's version is also backed up by the fact that the alleged hijackers were apparently not capable of steering an airplane. Newspapers in Florida reported that these people had totally failed in their flight training. The flight school said about one of the suspects that after 600 hours of flying they couldn't even entrust him with a Cessna.

Another one was described as so stupid that doubts arose whether he was even capable of driving a car.

In this regard, it has to be kept in mind that at least flight number three carried out an extremely complicated flight maneuver.

First, it was heading towards the White House in Washington and then it changed its course with a 270-degree loop over the telephone poles towards the Pentagon. This requires skill and plenty of flight experience. By the way, I'm not adopting the theory of the British flight engineer as my own. I'm only saying that the doubts and questions that he and others are voicing should be debated in public and investigated by experts.

No more questions are being asked about the insider trading either.

Indeed, in the week before the attacks, the trading volumes of shares that would later suffer drastic falls as a result of the events rose by 1,200%. The shares were sold at the high price before the event but would only be transferred some time afterwards so that the seller was able to buy the shares subsequently at the rock bottom rate, allowing him to rake in the difference as profit. This happened with the shares of the two airlines, as well as with the shares of financial institutions Morgan Stanley and Merrill Lynch, each of which had offices across 22 floors of the World Trade Center. In addition, the insiders bought US Treasury bills worth $5 billion in anticipation of a sharp rise as a result of the national catastrophe. Who were these insiders and through which channels did they arrive at their information? And where are the findings of the American financial investigators who routinely monitor unusual speculation involving future terror events in order to glean clues to attacks?

Bush Sr. works for the bin Laden family in Saudi Arabia through the Carlyle Group, an international investment firm. "The idea of the president's father, an ex-president himself, doing business with a company under investigation by the FBI in the terror attacks of September 11 is horrible," said the US anti-corruption NGO "Judicial Watch."

Bush Sr. is an old CIA hand. He was the agency's director in 1976-77. It is known that he had connections to Panamanian President Noriega, who allowed his country to be used for the transshipment of drugs to the United States, as well as the landing of aircraft full of drug money for the purpose of international money laundering. His extra $200,000-a-year income funded by CIA sources temporarily even exceeded the salary of the American president.

There are reports that the war against Afghanistan was not a US reaction to the terror of 9/11, but that it was planned beforehand. "Evidence suggests that Washington had planned to move against bin Laden in the summer," wrote Britain's Guardian.

For years, an American oil and gas company has been wanting to transport oil from the Caspian Basin to the Indian Ocean through a pipeline in Afghanistan worth billions of dollars. The CIA hoped to use the Taliban to protect the investment and simultaneously prevent a stretch of it being built across the territory of "rogue state" Iran. It's possible the war will now lead to a new government in Kabul that is sympathetic to the project. All in all, it can be assumed that the strategy heads at the CIA generally follow the geopolitical ideas of the afore-mentioned Brzezinski in *The Grand Chessboard: American Primacy and Its Geostrategic Imperatives*. This book, together with Huntington's *Clash of Civilizations*, is the blueprint for the covert and ultimately definitive US foreign policy over the next few years and decades. One by one, Brzezinski goes through the most important states that could rise up as opponents to US dominance. He looks for approaches as to how these potential opponents can be weakened. He sees the whole thing like a game of chess in which states as the main pieces are played against each other and within states ethnic minorities are used as pawns. The agitators among the leaders of the ethnic minorities are promoted, the peaceful ones are disavowed, passions are fanned, weapons are traded and it's all financed with drugs. Should the respective central government find it necessary to intervene more forcefully to uphold national peace, then public accusations of human rights violations will follow. Brzezinski is as if possessed by the issue of dominating the Eurasian region between the Pacific and the Atlantic, for him the key to global dominance. And given that Man, fallible as he is, wants to hate and must hate, Harvard professor Huntington presents Islam as the new enemy of the West, throwing in Orthodox Christianity while he's at it.

What contacts have there been in the recent past between bin Laden and the CIA?

Le Figaro said bin Laden met with the CIA head in Dubai as recently as July of that year. The CIA man apparently boasted about the meeting to his acquaintances.

When you point to the involvement of the CIA and other Western intelligence services with 9/11, surely you are reproached with adhering to conspiracy theories.

I'm not the one expounding a conspiracy theory. On the contrary, those who see a bin Laden conspiracy at work without producing any solid evidence – at least none has been forthcoming – should be upbraided. Here the media are again used to spread disinformation. For example, you could read in the *New York Times* that bin Laden welcomed the attacks in a statement and praised the attackers as "heroes." The comment was conveyed by a Palestinian living in Afghanistan, who passed on what a friend from the circle around bin Laden claimed to have heard about the latter's reaction. At the same time, the German local newspaper *Bonner Generalanzeiger* translated the BBC report on bin Laden's statement in which he deplored the death of innocents on 9/11. Why does the *New York Times* pick a news item that is most likely fake?

I certainly don't claim to have the answers to all the questions which the media are not even asking, which means those responsible aren't pushed to come up with convincing answers. Instead, images are conveyed that show bin Laden riding through a sand storm, the horseman of the Apocalypse, the unpredictable, treacherous, gruesome new enemy!

Why do the media, in Germany too, respond by toeing the line?

Only France seems to somewhat defy this hysteria and unqualified allegiance. In politics, as well as in the media, I have experienced the waves of conformity many times already. In the case of the neutron bomb it didn't quite work yet, but when it came to stationing 100 medium-range ballistic missiles conformity was plain to see. Then with the suppression of all comment regarding the supposedly rapid pace towards the "thriving landscapes" [a much-cited phrase coined by Chancellor Helmut Kohl at the time of German reunification to describe the prosperity that Eastern Germany was supposedly going to enjoy].

I felt that one of the worst instances of manipulation was the Gulf War. After years of being armed to the teeth by the West among others, Saddam Hussein walked into the trap laid by the American ambassador, who had assured him that the US did not care about border disputes with Kuwait. In the case of Star Wars under Reagan and now under Bush the same tendency is discernible, in our media landscape as well.

You have aptly described the phenomenon, but you still haven't explained it.

I know from an informant in the US that a person trusted by **the CIA is present in all the larger editorial offices and news agencies**, a person who can remove critical items from the news agenda or ensure silence on matters when needed. I don't know whether Germany's BND has similar powers. The most important US media czars sit on the advisory boards of the secret services. The CIA helps foreign journalists and news agencies with money to get started.

Apart from that, journalists often have a dependent relationship with the intelligence services, which hand out the big stories where they will be appropriately handled. Should the journalist take a tack away from the mainstream, the sources dry up. If he stays on course, he is invited to background briefings and conferences, often in the world's most beautiful locations and in the best hotels with prominent people to talk to.

Those who are considered "defense intellectuals" have a good life and exclusive information – nobody likes to mention corruption in this context. But there is a considerable difference from a journalist who, for example, sits behind a desk in Frankfurt-Bockenheim and has to dig up his own information every day.

I would also like to add that the most important task of the intelligence services is to deceive the public. The actual chain of causality must remain a secret. It's not difficult to win over a 30,000-man mountain tribe in Burma for the fight against the Vietcong, supplying money and weapons is enough. It's much more difficult to arrange the whole thing in such a way that the CIA does not appear as the instigator and the one giving the orders. So the CIA shrewdly manages and finances the activities in roundabout ways. The Central American Contras received weapons and money via drug dealers, who in turn were allowed to sell their wares in the US and Europe without fear of prosecution.

The laundering of drug money is covert so that the secret cycle works. **Everything is organized in such a complicated way that anyone suspecting or describing the true connections can be declared insane.**

Things are all the more cozy for journalists who sit in the lap of the intelligence services waiting for the disinformation with which to fill their columns.

You were state secretary and minister. How do the Social Democrats of your generation – people like Bahr and Schmidt – react to your research?

There is no reaction. Those who agree with my analysis should swim against the tide. Those who think it's wrong should be able to argue their case.

47th floor, going down. The sudden, apparently unprovoked collapse of WTC 7 is for many 9/11 skeptics the smoking gun *non plus ultra* of 9/11. This tower was never hit by any plane. There are no photographs of large fires, but there *are* photos showing only two small ones that the fire department is not bothering to fight – and without a single broken window from the ground to the 47th floor. The FEMA report was obliged to discuss WTC 7, but could draw no conclusions about it.

For the 9/11 commission report, the collapse is no part of the Al Qaeda myth, so it simply did not happen. The corporate media studiously ignore it. Public opinion is effectively manipulated by focusing attention on the drama of the Twin Towers, obfuscating the issues around that incident, and hushing up the unexplainable of Bldg. 7. See text *REDUCTIO AD ABSURDUM: WTC 7* on **page 241 ff.** and video clips of the smoothly gliding collapse at wtc7.net or www.hugequestions.com. Compare also www.controlled-demolition.com.

Cuttings & Confetti

"The only alternative to American power is global anarchy."
– Zbigniew Brzezinski, quoted in "Like it or not, U.S. in charge,"
Chicago Tribune, April 12, 1998

"We have no wish to hurt you, the innocent people of Afghanistan. Stay away from roads, factories, or bridges. If you are near these places, then you must move away from them." *– US Army pamphlet*

A-bombin'able Bushman, in his own words:

"Our enemies are innovative and resourceful, and so are we. They never stop thinking about new ways to harm our country and our people, and neither do we." *Bush, Aug. 5, 2004*

"Had I known that the enemy was going to use airplanes to kill on that fateful morning, I would have done everything in my power to protect the American people.... We're in for a long struggle. It's a tough war. This is an enemy that's not going to quit."
http://www.whitehouse.gov/news/releases/2002/05/20020517-1.html

"Terrorist attacks can shake the foundations of our biggest buildings, but they cannot touch the foundation of America. These acts shattered steel, but they cannot dent the steel of American resolve.
America was targeted for attack because we're the brightest beacon for freedom and opportunity in the world."
http://www.whitehouse.gov/news/releases/2001/09/20010911-16.html

"The attack on the Pentagon, on that day, was more symbolic than they knew. It was on another September 11th – September 11th, 1941 – that construction on this building first began."
Bush at Pentagon Memorial Service, October 11, 2001, 11:55 a.m.
http://www.september11news.com/PresidentBushPentagon.htm

Abu Mazen, Palestinian Prime Minister, and Nabil Shaath, his Foreign Minister, describe their first meeting with President Bush in June 2003. "President Bush said to all of us: 'I'm driven with a mission from God. God would tell me, "George, go and fight those terrorists in Afghanistan." And I did, and then God would tell me, "George, go and end the tyranny in Iraq ..." And I did.'"
– www.bbb.co.uk

"See in my line of work you got to keep repeating things over and over and over again for the truth to sink in, to kind of catapult the propaganda." *Bush, May 24, 2005.* (Cited in *Nazi Hydra in America* by Glen Yeadon.)

Washington Post: Why do you think bin Laden has not been caught?
Bush: Because he's hiding.
http://www.dubyaspeak.com/war.phtml

"It's in our country's interests to find those who would do harm to us and get them out of harm's way...."
"I've been to war. I've raised twins. If I had a choice, I'd rather go to war."
"I am mindful not only of preserving executive powers for myself, but for predecessors as well."
http://www.dubyaspeak.com/war.phtml

New White House Order on Secrecy of Historical Presidential Records Is Unlawful

Bush Administration Officials Should Be Made to Explain Actions to Congress, Public Citizen Says – Nov. 5, 2001.

Under the Presidential Records Act, an outgoing president can impose a 12-year restriction on public access to documents that involve confidential communications between the president and his advisors – communications subject to the so-called "executive privilege." After the 12 years are up, the law provides that such documents be made available to members of the public upon request.

The 12-year restriction on Reagan presidential documents housed at the National Archives' Reagan Presidential Library expired earlier this year. When the Archives informed the White House that it intended to release the documents to the public, the White House first directed the Archives to wait eight months while it studied the issue, and then promulgated the new executive order.

Under the new executive order, both a former president and the incumbent president have an unlimited amount of time to review any documents the Archives proposes to release after the 12-year restriction period expires. If the former president objects to the release of any materials, the executive order provides that the incumbent president will concur with the former president's wishes unless there are "compelling circumstances" that favor disclosure. But even if the sitting president finds that there are "compelling circumstances" and disagrees with the former president, the order requires that the Archives abide by the direction of the former president and keep the documents secret.
http://www.citizen.org/pressroom/release.cfm?ID=896

The 9/11 (C)Omission Report, Best-Selling Summer Fiction of 2004

The "official" bin Laden Conspiracy theory was issued with media fanfare in July 2004 as a bulky, cut-price paperback that went straight to the #1 slot on Amazon.com. Amazon's online customer reviews were all lavish in their praise, much to the despair of 9/11 activists who had viewed or heard about the book online, and were bombarding Amazon with critical reviews of the whitewash from Washington. Try as we might, we couldn't post a single pan. After a couple weeks, I finally spent several hours polishing a review in light of all the rules that could give Amazon's vetting wizards the least excuse to throw it out – and was thrilled to have the text published which you see below.

But even this turned out to be an interesting aside on how subtly effective US media censorship is. Uncomfortable facts are only allowed a fleeting existence in the limbo that Broeckers calls "elusive information." By the time Amazon allowed this first hostile review, the book had enjoyed 26 raves – and had already slipped from the top sales ranking. Posting it even gave them a chance to make it look like there is no censorship in America.

Now the Omission Report is mostly getting the bashing and trashing it deserves from one-star Amazon customer reviews – but it's long gone from the best-seller list. It's no longer "prime time." The controllers have other priorities. The corporatist monster is thick-skinned, and 5% of the reading public – who in turn are only a minority – isn't enough to bother it much.

70 people voted my review was helpful, 120 voted against it – by far the most brickbats of any review. Presumably from the paying public, although this is not certain. At that time, Amazon used to invite viewers to recommend related books, often leading to lively competition on political titles. 9/11 activists were able to take the high ground on the Commission Report page, with over a hundred votes recommending to buy David Ray Griffin's 9/11 exposé *New Pearl Harbor* instead of the Omission Report. Until the boom swung, and out of the blue, 300 "customers" recommended a completely unrelated, inane, obscure title, wiping Griffin off the page... and back under the radar again.

– John Leonard

More Shortcomings than Forthcomings

Reviewer: J. Leonard (USA), August 8, 2004.

The commission report tables almost all the issues raised by independent researchers about the anomalies of 9/11 by omitting them entirely. The most poignant result of books like The New Pearl Harbor, The War on Freedom, or Inside Job, is the suspicion that elements within our own government were complicit in 9/11. Many lay experts on 9/11 will take the government report's silence on these charges as a tacit admission of guilt.

The major exception is the failure to intercept, which the report explains with a new timeline, claiming 3 out of 4 planes had crashed before the military was notified of the hijackings – while blaming no one for the delay. The report's first chapter also gives some new details about the alleged hijackings, but doesn't explain why the new evidence it cites has never been made public, why the hijackers never showed up on the passenger lists, why black boxes didn't survive, why the government reportedly had war games going on 9/11 involving military planes masquerading as hijacked airliners, nor many other embarrassing questions by independent researchers.

That done, the report's succeeding chapters are less concerned with the events on the day of 9/11 than with buttressing the government's own Al-Qaeda conspiracy theory about the atrocity, and the government's own plans to use 9/11 as a pretext for more war, more incursions on civil liberties, more centralization of power, and more building the government-media myth of the Arab nemesis, much as was done with the lies about WMD to "justify" invading Iraq.

The account of what happened inside the Twin Towers after the impacts is a distraction, mostly a recital of the heroic efforts of firemen, police and survivors, followed by a laconic "The North Tower collapsed at 10:25:28 a.m." The authors omit to say how the buildings collapsed. They take part in the media blackout of the sudden collapse of building WTC 7 (or "7 WTC") by not even mentioning it ever happened.

Yet the newer 9/11 books by independents, especially Painful Questions, seize on the WTC 7 collapse as the most explosive smoking gun showing that 9/11 was an inside job, and with reason: WTC 7 was completely undamaged by the air crashes, yet collapsed instantaneously on the afternoon of 9/11. (By contrast, the government's FEMA report was obliged to "explain" the free-fall collapse of the Towers by the novel "pancake" theory, but was unable to come to any conclusion at all about WTC 7.)

With all respect, one must conclude with more regret than surprise that the 9/11 Commission Report is merely part of the government's cover-up of its own role.

I sincerely hope someone at Amazon will care enough about our country and our freedom to resist the censors and print this review.
http://www.amazon.com/exec/obidos/tg/detail/-/0393326713

5/28/2004
Update: Prosecuting 9/11

A Lecture by Mathias Broeckers at the
International Citizens Inquiry into 9/11,
Toronto, May 28th, 2004

In his famous "parable of the cave," the Greek philosopher Plato gives us a metaphor of our knowledge of the world. We are enchained in a huge cave, and only able to look in one direction; a fire at our backs casts a light, in front of which some jugglers are bearing objects, which throw shadows on the walls. Since all we are able to perceive is these shadows, we take them for the only "truthful and real" reality.

What would happen, Plato asks, if one of the inmates of the cave should become unchained and turn around to look in the opposite direction? First he would be dazzled by the fire, but then he would recognize the objects of the shadow play – and wouldn't understand it. If he were to come out of the cave into daylight, he would be dazzled even more – but after adjusting to the light he would finally become able to recognize the sun, the seasons and the whole world.

Generally this parable has been read as standing for Plato's idealism, the ascent to the realm of ideas, its wholeness and lucidity, of which the material world is only a shadow image. Yet this tale is embedded in Plato's *Republic* or *Politeia*, a treatise on politics. So we may take this story, which is 2,500 years old, as an example for the current information age – with all of us being inmates of a huge cave, which is no longer operating with archaic shadow plays, but with the technological advantages of multi-media – a cable TV cave with a multitude of channels and displays. And there are still those "jugglers," as Plato named them, producing a light-show of phantoms and simulations…

But before we come to the phantoms of September 11th, we should hear briefly what happens to the lucky one who is liberated from Plato's cognition-cave: out in the sunshine he starts worrying about his miserable chained companions and considers going back down to liberate them from their awkward predicament. At this point Plato utters an obvious warning: If he goes back down, he could be blinded in the darkness, and be mocked and scoffed at. Those still down in the darkness would say that he returned blind from his ascent, that it certainly wouldn't be worthwhile to leave the cave.

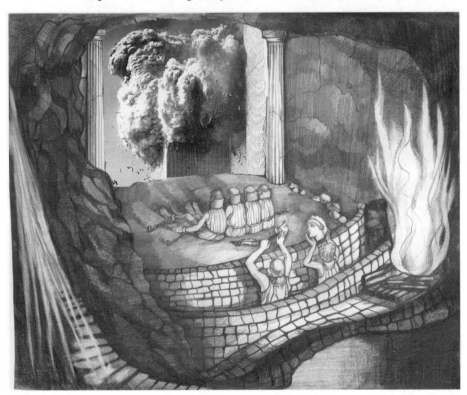

From *9/11 Synthetic Terror*, p. 348, ch. 13: "The 9/11 Myth: Collective Schizophrenia"

But this is not the only difficulty facing him. Socrates, who is telling the cave-story, asks: "If he frees them and tries to lead them upward, and if they lay hands on him, won't they kill him?" (Plato, *Republic* VII, 514)

This is not only a most ancient warning, that messengers can be killed for their message – which is exactly what happened to Socrates. It is also good advice for whistle-blowers of all kinds, and I think a good description of the post-9/11 situation. I think most of the speakers and participants at this conference have been mocked and scoffed at – as un-patriotic un-American conspiracy-nuts and whatnots. The good news is: we are alive; the bad news is: that's only because none of us really knows the whole truth about 9/11.

From the history of science we are familiar with the problem of prejudice in research: researchers tend to be more "theory-driven" than "data-driven." This means that researchers are uncomfortable with "facts" unless a suitable theory can explain them – and fail to see data that contradict their theoretical expectations. Not because the data are invisible, but they have a strong tendency literally not to perceive the offending data, as we know from a lot of psychological experiments on perception and cognition.

Our minds tend to construct models of the world which are consistent and coherent – which do not threaten our expectations and beliefs. And when we are inevitably confronted with offending data, we still try to avoid it by all means – like the pope and his advisors who kept a stiff upper lip and refused to look through Galileo's telescope. Even an enlightened genius like Albert Einstein balked to accept the new data of his colleague Heisenberg in the 1920's proving that in the quantum world, it's always the observer who decides what becomes manifest as "reality."

This uncertainty, the role of the observer and the conditioned bias of our cognition are things we should always bear in mind when it comes to perceiving, testing and judging reality – not only while researching the micro-world of particles, but in the macro-world of politics too. Especially in the realms of crime, secrecy and intelligence: like in the quantum world, we enter here the Hall of Mirrors, and instead of hard matter, we are confronted with what Heisenberg once called "possibility clouds." Unfortunately this kind of feasibility fog is not a piece of evidence that will lead to a court indictment, bring the perpetrators to justice and make officials take responsibility. And that is exactly what is urgently needed in the case of 9/11, because nearly three years have passed since the murder of 3,000 innocent people… with no one brought to justice or taking responsibility for anything at all.

So what this conference should focus on, in my opinion, is not the possibility clouds, but the allocable particles. That means the ones that would enable a courageous attorney general – like Jim Garrison in the JFK case – to indict the suspects; because a regular court proceeding, a law suit, is the only way to come forward and finally dig out what really happened. One need not be a prophet to predict that the 9/11-commission will fail to do this – it's a classic white-wash institution designed by an administration to shift blame away from the ones in power – and the corporate media won't do it either.

But it isn't enough if the "truth of 911" is posted everywhere on the Internet – we have to employ the remnant of the last constitutional power which might still work: Justice. If our inquiry is not able to bring some restless homicide detectives on the right track and an attorney to bring an indictment, it will be quite useless in the end.

The court cases in Hamburg against the two so-called "20th Hijackers" didn't meet any legal standard – there wasn't any evidence against the defendants – and the higher courts were consistent in overturning these judgments. We are not yet so far gone that all judges rule guilty only on the hearsay of intelligence agencies. And this might indeed be the reason why until this day no indictment has been brought against the alleged perpetrators of the attacks: Osama bin Laden and the 19 hijackers. There doesn't seem to be enough evidence against them, only some intel-hearsay, not enough to convince a jury…

Imagine any murder case with even one percent of the number of victims of 9/11, that is 30 people killed – and after 30 months of large-scale police investigation, no hard evidence, no clues, no background at all is found. And try now to imagine a press conference where the police chief admits just that – wouldn't he be grilled by the reporters immediately? Wouldn't that raise the painstaking question, whether the police had done their job right – or had they been following the wrong leads, the wrong suspects all the time? It sure would – and the fact that this hasn't happened with 9/11, that nobody questioned or scrutinized and tried to get to the bottom of the story, shows us in a nutshell the decline of the media.

Let's look at a few examples: about 48 hours after the attacks the FBI published a list of the 19 suspected hijackers. In the following week it turned out that at least six of these 19 suicide-bombers were still alive. Four of them were interviewed by reporters – and they wondered and complained, how their names, pictures and birth dates happened to get onto this "most wanted" list. They had nothing to do with the attacks, were not in the US around the time of 9/11 and were at home, at their regular jobs instead: at a telecommunications company, an oil refinery or the Saudi Airlines office. Two other suspected "hijackers" turned out to be pilots on a training-course, one in Morocco and the other in Tunisia, and these men also complained about being presented as mass murderers. The BBC, *The Guardian* and other leading "newspapers of record" reported in the weeks following Sep. 11th, 2001 that what occurred with the names of these "suicide-hijackers" was a case of mistaken identities – and the real hijackers must have stolen them.

So far no problem: criminals or terrorists use fake identities quite regularly. But what do you find when you take a look at the FBI website today? Even 30 months later, you still find those names and pictures of the same "19 suspected Hijackers" – and no mention of the fact that at least six of these people cannot be the real terrorists.

The first chapter of my second book on 9/11 takes a closer look at these dubious identities, and the fact that the original passenger lists of the four flights were never published, that no video-footage exists of their boarding at Boston airport, no fingerprints were found on the boarding cards, no proof that these 19 people even were on these planes. *Der Spiegel*, Germany's leading newsmagazine, took this part of my book to brand me as wacko researcher and crook, saying that the doubtful names and pictures on the suspects-list were all cleared up when the FBI published a corrected version on Sept. 27th.

But this is not the case at all – there are still hard and reasonable doubts about the real identities of the hijackers – and there are still nine skeletons in the closet. Nine dead bodies from the Pentagon and the Pennsylvania flights are still "on the rocks" at a military base in Maryland, all with the same name: John Doe... they are not identified. Why? If the hotels, bars and rental cars these guys used in the days before are known – and they are according to the FBI – why then is there not a single piece of evidence, not a hair, no piece of fingernail, no little booger to identify these alleged terrorists?

While writing this the news agencies report that the Mexican airforce videotaped something looking like UFOs – and once again it depends on the observer's belief system which "reality" he is going to extract from these luminous "possibility clouds." For a proper 9/11 inquiry – to avoid becoming marginalized into a kind of flying saucer sect, discussing shadows on dubious video-footage – we should look at first things first, and that means at the Unidentified Flying Subjects of 9/11: the 19 hijackers – and the smoking gun on ice: the nine unidentified bodies.

Since it is the very basic question of every crime investigation – Who dunnit?? – and it is still unanswered, we have to start here – the "How's?" and "Why's?" and "for what purposes?" and "Cui Bonos," all these questions are important, but they are secondary, in the intrinsic sense of the word. The answers to them remain speculative as long as the very first step – the identification of the actual perpetrators – is not done.

We have at least two dozen anomalies of 9/11 and every one of them with quite good evidence, any of them worth a whole book... I don't dispute these anomalies ... But where does it lead, to discuss – let's say the inner explosion of the twin towers, the rockets slung underneath the

Boeings or the size of the Pentagon-hole… ? Who can be brought to an indictment with this photoshop-evidence? Nobody, I think, and therefore I plea for the simple method, to take the first step first and look at the 19 alleged perpetrators, the main suspects.

What I have found about them in the published records and reports broadly amounts to two categories – the ghosts and the agents. From the first we know little to nothing. From the beginning they remain in their ghostly existence and partly dubious identity. From the second half – Atta, Al Midhar, Al Shehi et al – we know a lot more. Like Atta they were on the watch-list of at least five secret agencies – including American, German, and Israeli intelligence – and as we know from the history of terrorism and intelligence, the border between "watch list" and "payroll" is kind of evasive…. In Hamburg where Atta and his cadre lived, their flat in Marienstrasse was besieged by spooks who were even quarreling about who is whose asset….

And what investigative reporter Daniel Hopsicker dug up in his recent book *Welcome to Terrorland* about Atta's life and connections in Florida seems to add up to a new version of an Elvis song: "He walked like an agent, he talked like an agent." And he even sniffed cocaine like an agent… a real devil in disguise. Atta's comrades in Florida – no bearded Taliban but smart pilots from Germany, Austria, Holland – his American girlfriend, his liking for striptease clubs and Beasty Boys music – all this seems not to match the pure Islamist fundamentalist he is supposed to be.

But this information never became part of the official record, these witnesses – friends, neighbors, house managers – were not asked by the 9/11 commission. Instead they were silenced by the FBI. Why? Is it for the same reason the FBI directors shut down their own agents' investigations of suspected flight students ?

However – they walked and talked and moved and behaved indeed as if they had some protection. Once Atta flew into the US without a visa – and got two valid visas from the border inspectors. Khalid Al Midhar was on the terrorist suspect list since 1998, when the CIA wiretapped the home of his father-in-law – a safehouse for bin Laden supporters in Yemen. Al Midhar was provided with a fresh visa for the US until July 2001, even after he was suspected of being part of the group which bombed the USS *Cole* in October 2000, and was videotaped as a participant of an Al Qaeda meeting in Malaysia.

Forty years ago, when the Warren Commission investigated the JFK-assassination, the public were at least provided with backgrounds and whereabouts of the so-called "lone nut" Lee Harvey Oswald – but with 9/11 the situation seems much worse. Not only because any investigation at all was blocked by the Bush regime for more than a year – but also because the public is kept in the dark even on the very basic facts about the main suspect: his arrival in the US, his movements and contacts in Florida, the flight school he chose, and the amazing activities of its owners.

That the lone nut and pretended "Communist" Oswald in fact was trained at a secret CIA camp with right-wing Cubans – this came out only 15 years later, after the "House Select Committee on Assassinations" inquiry – and had to be covered up again. So time is not on our side with 9/11, and we should have an urgent look at the question whether the pretended "Islamist" Atta and his comrades were possibly trained at a secret CIA-front company, too.

What Daniel Hopsicker has found on "Huffman Aviation" points strongly in this direction – the real owner, retired millionaire Wally Hilliard, has different aviation companies which attracted attention – beside being a training camp for terror pilots – for two things only: not selling a single airline ticket and losing money on a permanent scale – and the trafficking of 40 pounds of heroin in one of their rental jets. Oops...

This time the background of the "lone nut" evildoers must not be labeled "Anti-Castro" as with Oswald; instead "Iran-Contra" for example seems more appropriate. That kind of long-running, secret drug, weapons, and money laundering-operation – with one end of the business chain in Florida and the other in Afghanistan, with Osama bin Laden in control of the world's main source of raw material – this seems to me the most realistic background for what happened on 9/11, and for the non-investigation and cover-ups before and after.

One whistleblower, the former FBI-translator Sibel Edmonds, points in the same direction – money-laundering and drug business – and said in a recent interview: "If they were to do real investigations, we would see several significant high level criminal prosecutions in this country. And that is something that they are not going to let out. And, believe me; they will do everything to cover this up."

http://baltimorechronicle.com/050704SibelEdmonds.shtml

Mrs. Edmonds has been silenced by the Department of Justice from speaking in public on what the FBI knew about the business partners and foreign countries involved in the background – she told it to the 9/11 commission, but since it was not a public statement, we have to fear it will not come out in the commission's report. However, if we look at what we know about Agent Atta in Florida, we might name those countries that seem to be involved: Saudi-Arabia and Pakistan. From the latter, a top agent of the Pakistan secret service ISI – Saeed Omar Sheik – whose director General Mahmud Ahmed happened to be in Washington on Sept. 11th and who was later indicted in the murder of journalist Daniel Pearl – wired $100,000 to an account of Atta in August 2001.

The months before, Atta and Al-Shehi had received similar large sums from an account in the Arabian Emirates. So far the FBI investigated the money trail of Atta very fast – but since then it has stopped, and turned around to cover up these and other connections of the supposed gang leader. CNN even blanked out the name of General Mahmud Ahmed in a transcript of Condoleezza Rice's press conference, where she was asked about his meetings in Washington on the days around Sept.11th.

In a similar way the Saudi background of 9/11 is covered up – a recent book *House of Saud, House of Bush* and Michael Moore's praised documentary have shed some light on this, and it's already discussed in many mainstream media. I can add a small detail here confirming the ongoing cover-up:

In my last book – documenting the dubious identities of the hijackers – I quoted from the press release of a Meeting of Minister of Foreign Affairs, Prince Saud Al-Faisal and President Bush on Sept. 20th, 2001:

> Regarding the inclusion of Saudi names in the published list of the suspects, Prince Saud commented that haste in publishing the names of suspects has been acknowledged, and that it has been proven that five of the people listed had nothing to do with what happened... We very much hope that before being published, information, names and pictures will be verified. (http://www.saudiembassy.net/press_release/01-spa/09-20-Saud2.htm)

This press release was published on the website of the Saudi Embassy – but you will not find it there anymore, it's now a dead link.

When our book *Facts, Forgeries and the Suppressed Evidence of 9/11* came out in August 2003 in Germany – and *Der Spiegel* Magazine tried to ridicule my claim of the highly dubious hijackers' identities, they asked the Saudi Embassy in Berlin about this quote from the Foreign Minister. Since the guys at *Der Spiegel* aren't cooperating with me, they didn't provide me with the answers; but instead they supported their friends, the TV-Magazine *Panorama*, for a smear of the books of Andreas von Bülow, Gerhard Wisnewski and me, so incredible that I sued them for defamation. To convince the judge what a bad journalist I am they sent in a huge pile of paper, and in this I found the document with the official answer of the Saudi Embassy to *Der Spiegel*:

> Regarding your request from Aug. 27th 2003 on the alleged press-release of HRH Foreign Minister Prince Saud Al Faisal after his meeting with US-President George W. Bush on Sept 20th 2001, in which he is supposed to have said that five names on the FBI's suspects list had nothing to do with what happened, the Embassy of the Saudi Arabian Kingdom intimates, that HRH the Foreign Minister never gave such a statement and this means, that what is written in the book *Facts, Forgeries and the Suppressed Evidence of 9/11* lacks any foundation.
>
> (Copy of the letter: http://www.broeckers.com/sb.html)

Thanks to the excellent memory of the Internet we can prove the opposite: the Saudi Foreign Minister indeed gave out the statement "that five of the people listed had nothing to do with what happened" on Sept. 20th – and thanks to the involuntary help of *Der Spiegel,* we can prove now, that two years later they officially deny it entirely. Needless to say that this was not seen to be a reason for the formerly leading news-magazine *Der Spiegel* to look a bit closer at this mysterious denial.

Why does the Saudi Secretary two years later deny that there had been errors in naming the suspects, after he had discussed this with President Bush, who had acknowledged a certain "haste in publishing"? If errors happened in "haste" and would have been corrected properly with the second FBI-list published a week later – why not simply say so? Why eradicate press releases and deny given statements ? – Because until today, the question of the true identity of the 19 hijackers is still totally unsolved – and the Bush administration and the officials of the other countries involved do everything they can to keep it that way. If they succeed these 19 will stay there for ever and become history.

How can this happen, since we have a free press scrutinizing and checking the statements, allegations and actions of our governments ? If you only look at this tiny example of the very basic question about the individuals who committed this crime you recognize that such a media doesn't exist anymore. With the collapse of the twin towers we have not only to be in mourning at the death of 3,000 innocent citizens, but also of the nearly total breakdown of the media's constitutional function in democratic societies as an instrument of a check on power and of critical investigation. The coverage of 9/11 shows that the mass media do a perfect job if it comes to grave criminal activities like presidential sex with White House trainees, but if it comes to small sins like the 9/11-events and letting them happen, there has been (and still is) no investigative journalism at all. The mainstream media has gone to rack and ruin, and became a brothel of propaganda. Welcome to Brainwashington D.C.

How could this happen ? Here we enter a phenomenon of the ongoing brainwashing operation which one could call "elusive information" – information that appears briefly – and reports some fragments of reality – and then disappears out of the media focus forever. There is no suppression of any news or report, no old-style censorship with Gestapo controllers on every editorial desk blacking out unwanted news – everything might be released. In this sense we still have a "free press."

But the simple appearance of a news-report does not mean that it really becomes "news." Becoming news – that is, becoming part of the reality picture the media paints – means being repeated over and over again! Only the endless repetition of a report or a statement makes them accepted "news," and it is this repetition above all that gains them wider public attention. But what finally gains that public attention through steady repetition – contrary to the simple, one-time appearance of a news report – is strictly controlled, and the more important, wider-reaching the media are, the stricter is their control.

So nobody prevented articles on the dubious hijackers, but after they were printed or broadcast the first time, they never passed the bouncer at the door any more. No permanent repetition, no announcement on CNN or the radio news every 10 minutes, no headline in the papers, no editorials by the editors – and so those bits of news were gone for good. No one asked further questions except a handful of journalists on the Internet, even though the official version turned out to have all the ingredients of an exemplary conspiracy theory: a simple-minded claim, a lousy proof and a loud call to action.

But instead of scrutinizing the incredible tale that Osama and 19 bandits from their Afghan caves conducted this deadly strike against the world's superpower out of the blue and all alone, the trombone orchestra of corporate media repeated this legend over and over and over again. And at the same time the media is promoting this conspiracy theory *ad nauseam*, it is spitting blame on any critical question to be just that: a conspiracy theory.

Why are alternative viewpoints immediately branded as "conspiracy theories"? Is it the lack of evidence? Certainly not, because there is a lot of evidence, and compared with the proof for the official version, for the Bin Laden conspiracy theory, there is quite a convincing case. Convincing enough at least to lead to further and deeper investigations. So these alternative viewpoints are not made worthless by logic or rationality, but by definition, *ex cathedra*, by a medieval banishment as "outrageous," by a kind of new inquisition defining every non-believer as "unpatriotic," "un-American," "undemocratic" and lately even as a "terrorist." This mechanism of declaring certain viewpoints as taboo in public opinion is at the core of this media manipulation – so the system works, like it did in the Middle Ages. With the difference that – thanks to mass media – the new inquisition possesses more powerful tools to spread the dogma and to burn it into the brains of the public.

As one of the pioneers of broadcast propaganda and mass brain-washing, Hitler's secretary for propaganda, Joseph Goebbels, once said: you can turn every lie into truth – you only have to repeat it often enough. So the legend that Osama and his 19 bandits plotted and conducted the attacks became self-evident truth, while remaining under control of the Bush administration to be adapted for changes as needed. While it seemed clear from Sept 13th, 2001 that 15 of the alleged hijackers were Saudi nationals, the brainwashers turned that spin significantly in the following 15 months. In February 2003, polls showed the majority of the American people were convinced that the hijackers were Iraqis – and that Saddam Hussein was behind the attacks. So we might expect they will turn to Syrians, Iranians or whatever Arab scapegoat is needed for a war…

Once more this shows to me the importance of investigating these hijackers, their true identity and their schedule in the days and months before the attacks; second their moneymen and backers; third their capacity to hijack these planes with box-cutters simultaneously, to sneak past the air defenses of FAA (Federal Aviation Administration) and NORAD (North American Aerospace Defense Command) and conduct these highly professional aviation tasks – if serious investigations of these three basic questions do not lead to a sufficient amount of evidence to indict these men – we would have to rehabilitate them posthumously and start a whole new search, now for the ones who used them as patsies.

I am not a lawyer or a legal expert, but in my opinion the only way is to stick with the 19 alleged plotters and make them accountable, with the courts pressing the FBI, CIA and White House to put on the table everything they have against them, and a jury deciding if this is sufficient to judge them guilty or not. I believe that we would have seen such a court case already if they had real evidence – and if it happens, I presume it would end like the cases against the two "20th Hijackers" in Hamburg. But this is the point to start. It makes no sense to blame entities like "The CIA," "The Military," "The Illuminati," "Big Oil" or whatever sinister groups as long as we have no individual persons to make them accountable.

Since I plead for simple steps it might be a contradiction that I brought a new "Unknown" into my lecture, suggesting that an Iran-Contra-style drug operation might be the background for the mysterious cover-up and non-investigation of the hijackers in Florida. But it seems to make sense: these Arabs were allowed to move freely in and out the USA not because they were known Islamic terrorists preparing an attack, but they had a free pass as agents and handlers of a covert operation, an official wildcard, which overrode any suspicions of honest border inspectors or FBI field agents. Like the 140 prominent Saudis who received a free pass to fly out despite the grounding of all air traffic.

If it were a regular business connection between the Bushies and the Saudies only – oil, defense, Carlyle Group investments – there would be no real chance for a successful cover-up, for the very reason that the Democrats would have made it a partisan issue. So there must be some irregular business in the closet, from which both parties profit – as with the Iran-Contra drug money – making camouflage a bi-partisan task. We are not talking about peanuts like the investments of some Saudis in G. W. Bush's failing companies, but of an annual volume of $400 billion, as General Wesley Clark recently estimated the flow of drug money on the Balkans route, which he opened with the Yugoslavia war in coalition with Osama's Al Qaeda fighters and NATO. If it's always best to "follow the money," this seems like the real jackpot we should look at.

The complexity of 9/11 is huge, and it's important to keep track and not to get lost in the hall of mirrors. So "Keep it Simple" seems like good advice to me, and I tried to follow it in my remarks here. There can be no doubt at all that the Bush regime exploited 9/11 for their long-planned wars and their cronies' profits – and at the same time did everything to prevent any reasonable investigation.

There is little doubt that the administration had foreknowledge. If this could lead to an impeachment and kick Bush and his gang out of this office – wonderful! But this will not solve the case of 9/11 !!… and Bush's possible successor and Skull and Bones-brother John Kerry should not be expected to make strong efforts in this direction either, as we already know from his role in the former "Iran-Contra" Commission. So we depend further on public pressure of the victims' families and the citizens to reach a full-blown prosecution by a courageous attorney general. Thanks to the Cannes Film Festival last week and Michael Moore, the 9/11 skeptics are now finally becoming really mainstream – the cover of Brainwashington is starting to be blown.

If we take Plato's advice, we have to be careful: with teaching the fools down in the cave – and with the dangers of self-delusion outside. Since we are still in the phase of adjusting we should behave more like detectives than as self-assured politicians – at least for me, observing and researching since the attacks happened, the puzzle of 9/11 is far from solved. If we are not driven by pre-fabricated theory, but by all the available data – then we have to put everything on the table, even if it gets complex and seemingly contradictory parts appear.

These parts mark the points where deeper investigation is needed – and as long as no attorney, no court, no state commission is willing to do it, so long it depends on us as citizens to conduct it – and on the alternative media to communicate it. But as the polls in Europe and now in Canada show, we have the *vox populi* behind us. Not the politicians, not the media, not the corporate state but – the huge majority of the people. They know that they have been lied to into this "war on terror," have been lied to on 9/11 – and they are tired of it. The contradictions and inconsistencies of the "official version" are already obvious to almost everybody. So I have some hope that it will last not half a century – like the last time – to reveal the truth of the New Pearl Harbor. And that this conference may lay out the necessary steps to reach this goal. Thank you.

Mathias Bröckers,

Toronto, May 25, 2004

http://www.broeckers.com/toronto.html

Notes

A live list of links in the notes is also at
www.zweitausendeins.de/broeckers.html

Part 1

[1] Freeman Dyson, "Time Without End: Physics and Biology in an Open Universe," Review of Modern Physics, Vol. 51 (1979), p. 447-460.

[2] Peter Kropotkin, *Mutual Aid: A Factor of Evolution* , (Porter Sargent, 1976).

[3] Lynn Margulis, Dorion Sagen, *Leben: Vom Ursprung zur Vielfalt* [Life: from Origin to Diversity] (Heidelberg 1997).

[4] Emerson Puigh, *BrainTech: Mind Machines and Consciousness* (Lutz Berger and Werner Pieper, Löhrbach 1989).

[5] Howard Bloom, *Global Brain: The Evolution of Mass Mind from the Big Bang to the 21st Century* (Wiley, 2001).

[6] Thomas Pynchon, *Gravity's Rainbow* (Penguin, 1974), p. 255.

[7] Robert A. Wilson, Robert Shea, *The Illuminatus Trilogy: the Eye in the Pyramid, The Golden Apple, Leviathan* (Dell, 1998).

[8] Robert A. Wilson, *Everything Is Under Control: Conspiracies, Cults, and Cover-ups* (HarperCollins, 1998).

[9] Andreas von Bülow, *Im Namen des Staates: CIA, BND und die kriminellen Machenschaften der Geheimdienste* [In the Name of the State: The CIA, BND and the Criminal Intrigues of the Secret Services] (Munich 1998), p. 102.

[10] Robin Blackburn, *The Making of New World Slavery, From the Baroque to the Modern 1492 – 1800* (London 1997).

[11] H. P. Willmott, *The Great Crusade: A New Complete History of the Second World War* (New York, 1990), p. 144, cited in Daniel Pipes, *Conspiracy: How the Paranoid Style Flourishes and Where It Comes From* (New York, Free Press, 1997), p. 193.

[12] Adolf Hitler, *Mein Kampf* (Munich 1935), p. 337.

[13] Hannah Arendt, *The Origins of Totalitarianism* (Munich 1951), p. 595.

[14] Jan van Helsing, *Geheimgesellschaften und ihre Macht im 20. Century* [Secret Societies and their Power in the 20th Century] (Lathen 1993).

[15] E.R. Carmin, *Das schwarze Reich: Geheimgesellschaften und Politik im 20. Jahrhundert* [The Black Reich: Secret Societies and Politics in the 20th Century], 4th Edition (Munich 1999), Introduction.

[16] http://www.uni-muenster.de/PeaCon/conspiracy/Weishaupt.htm

[17] Adolph Freiherr von Knigge, *Freimaurer- und Illuminatischriften, Sämtliche Werke* [Freemasonic and Illuminati Writings, Complete Works], Vol. 12 and 13 (Paul Raabe, Munich 1993), facsim. of 1781-1873 eds.

[18] Albert G. Mackey, *A Lexicon of Freemasonry – 1869* (Kila, Montana, 1997).

[19] Max Weber, *Economy and Society: An Outline of Interpretive Sociology*

[20] Helmut Creutz, *Das Geldsyndrom: Wege zu einer krisenfreien Marktwirtschaft* [The Money Syndrome: Ways to a Crisis-free Market Economy] (Frankfurt 1995) complete German text online, http://userpage.fu-berlin.de/~roehrigw/creutz/ geldsyndrom/; Bernard Lietaer, *Das Geld der Zukunft* [The Money of the Future] (Munich 2000); Bernd Senf, *Der Nebel um das Geld: Zinsproblematik – Währungssysteme – Wirtschaftskrisen* [The Money Fog: The Problem of Interest, Currencies and Economic Crisis] (Frankfurt 1996).

[21] All citations from Jacques Le Goff, *Höllenzins und Wucherqual: Ökonomie and Religion im Mittelalter* [Hell's Interest and Usury's Agony in the Middle Ages] (Stuttgart 1988), p. 28 f.

[22] Robert A. Wilson interview in *Lexikon der Verschwörungstheorien* [Dictionary of Conspiracy Theories, German edition of *Everything is Under Control*] (Frankfurt 2000), p. 379.

[23] http://www.pgpi.org/

[24] Jürgen Roth, *Die Mitternachtsregierung* [The Midnight Government] (Hamburg 1990).

[25] Andreas von Bülow, *Im Namen des Staates, op. cit.*, p. 12.

Part 2

[1] Only the Jan. 26, 2002, piece on media manipulation was left out because I integrated it into the long "anti-Bush" postscript of the Nov. 11, 2001, article. http://www.heise.de/tp/deutsch/special/wtc/11661/1.html

[2] http://www.thedubyareport.com/family.html#prescott

[3] Sun Tze, *The Art of War*, http://www.chinapage.com/sunzi-e.html

[4] Doug Cirignano, "FDR and Pearl Harbor: the FOIA Revelations," http://www.disinfo.com/archive/pages/article/id1488/pg1/

[5] "President Bush Holds Town Hall Meeting," CNN, 12/4/2001, http://www.cnn.com/TRANSCRIPTS/0112/04/se.04.html

[6] "Questionable Ties: Tracking bin Laden's Money Flow leads back to Midland Texas," http://www.globalresearch.ca/articles/MAD202B.html

[7] "The October Surprise Mystery," http://www.consortiumnews.com/archive/xfile.html

[8] "Why the Real Name is Osama bin London," http://www.larouchepub.com/other/2001/2838bin-london.html

[9] Charles A. Beard, *President Roosevelt and the Coming of the War*, p. 517.

[10] Robert B. Stinnett, *Day of Deceit: The Truth About FDR and Pearl Harbor* (Carmichael, Calif., 2001).

[11] New York Times, 9/23/1990,
http://www.whatreallyhappened.com/ARTICLE5/april.html

[12] http://cjonline.com/stories/091201/ter_binladen.shtml (registration required)

[13] "Wife of Solicitor General alerted him of hijacking from plane,"
http://www.cnn.com/2001/US/09/11/pentagon.olson/index.html

[14] "The Mother of All Lies About 9/11,"
http://www.geocities.com/subliminalsuggestion/olson.html

[15] "How Did United Flight 93 Crash?" http://www.flight93crash.com/

[16] "Elkhorn Manifesto: U.S. Corporations and the Nazis,"
http://www.wealth4freedom.com/Elkhorn2.html

[17] "Shadow of the Swastika," http://wealth4freedom.com/Elkhorn.html

[18] http://www.thirdworldtraveler.com/George_Seldes/Facts_and_Fascism.html

[19] *Der Spiegel*, 9/15/2001.

[20] Ulrich Völklein, *Geschäfte mit dem Feind. Die geheime Allianz des großen Geldes während des Zweiten Weltkriegs auf beiden Seiten der Front* [Trading with the Enemy: The Secret Alliance of Big Money on both Sides during WWII] (Hamburg 2002).

[21] Webster Tarpley, Anton Chaitkin (EIR 1992, Reprinted 2004, Progressive Press, Joshua Tree, Calif.), online at http://www.tarpley.net/bushb.htm

[22] www.henryk-broder.com

[23] http://www.cnn.com/SPECIALS/2001/trade.center/victims/main.html

[24] http://www.fbi.gov/pressrel/pressrel01/092701hjpic.htm

[25] "Alleged Hijackers Alive and Well (updated from 2001 archives),"
http://www.worldmessenger.20m.com/alive.html

[26] Fred Hoyle, *The Origin of the Universe and the Origin of Religion* (1993).

[27] Gunnar Heinsohn, *Die Erschaffung der Götter: Das Opfer als Ursprung der Religion* [The Creation of Gods: Sacrifice as the Origin of Religion] (Reinbek 1997).

[28] *FAZ (Frankfurter Allgemeine Zeitung)*, 9/18/2002.

[29] http://www.spiegel.de/politik/ausland/0,1518,157979,00.html

[30] Michel Chossudovsky, *The Globalization of Poverty and the New World Order* (Global Research, Canada, 1997-2005), Ch. 17.

[31] "FBI fails to find terror trail," http://
news.bbc.co.uk/hi/english/world/americas/newsid_1961000/1961476.stm

[32] Antony C. Sutton, *America's Secret Establishment: An Introduction to the Order of Skull and Bones* (Billings, Montana, 1986); Interview with Sutton:
http://www.freedomdomain.com/secretsocieties/suttoninterview.html

[33] Cited in Tarpley & Chaitkin, *George Bush: The Unauthorized Biography*.

[34] *Ibid*. http://www.tarpley.net/bush2.htm, Ch. 2: "The Hitler Project."

[35] Henry L. Stimson, *Diaries 1909-1945* (McGraw-Hill, 1976).

[36] Paul Goldstein, Jeffrey Steinberg, "George Bush, Skull & Bones and the New World Order" (April 1991)
http://www.parascope.com/articles/0997/whitepaper.htm

[37] *Ibid.*

[38] Atlantic Monthly on Bush und S&B: http://www.theatlantic.com/issues/2000/ 05/robbins.htm (registration required); Ron Rosenbaum, Esquire Magazine: http://www.freedomdomain.com/secretsocieties/skull02.html

[39] "GW Bush, Jesus and the Manhattan Institute," www.hartford-hwp.com/archives/ 45c/180.html

[40] Robert Lederman, "A Jewish Perspective on GW Bush," lederman.911review.org/nazi-bush-1-28-01.html

[41] Antony C. Sutton, *Western Technology and Soviet Economic Development*, 3 vols. (Stanford, Calif., 1968-1973).

[42] www.whatreallyhappened.com

[43] Goldstein & Steinberg, *George Bush, Skull & Bones, NWO (op. cit)*.

[44] http://www.spiegel.de/kultur/literatur/0,1518,157874,00.html

[45] T. Pynchon, *Gravity's Rainbow, (op. cit.)*, p. 268, p. 441.

[46] http://www.br-online.de/geld/plusminus/beitrag/20010925/thema_2.html

[47] Karl Laske, *Ein Leben zwischen Hitler und Carlos: François Genoud* [A Life between Hitler and Carlos] (Zürich 1996).

[48] *"Berlusconi – Die Entgleisungen in Wortlaut"* [Train of Words Derailed], http://www.spiegel.de/politik/ausland/0,1518,159688,00.html

[49] "Burden of Dreams" (blog), http://www.guerrillanews.com/users/user.php?id=40

[50] Penny Lernoux, *In Banks We Trust* (Garden City, NJ, 1984)

[51] E.R. Carmin, *Das schwarze Reich. Geheimgesellschaften und Politik im 20. Jahrhundert* [The Black Kingdom: Secret Societies and Politics in the 20th Century], (Munich 1999), p.273 ff. http://www.explorate.de/Forum/showpost.php?p=70054&postcount=4

[52] http://www.spiegel.de/spiegel/0,1518,160075,00.html

[53] Bernard Lewis, *The Assassins: A Radical Sect in Islam* (Basic Books, 2002), incl. following quotations.

[54] Antony Sutton, *Best Enemy Money Can Buy* (Liberty House, Billings, Montana 1986), online-edition http://reformed-theology.org/html/books/best_enemy/

[55] http://emperors-clothes.com/analysis/creat.htm

[56] Ahmed Rashid, *Taliban: Militant Islam, Oil & Fundamentalism in Central Asia,* Yale University Press, 2001, p. 130.

[57] http://emperors-clothes.com/news/albu.htm

[58] http://www.dhm.de/lemo/html/dokumente/wilhelm00/

[59] Tilmann Holzer, *Globalisierte Drogenpolitik. Die protestantische Ethik und die Geschichte des Drogenverbots* [Globalized Drug Politics: the Protestant Ethic and the History of Drug Prohibition], Berlin 2002; *Die Geschichte des O. Opiumfreuden – Opiumkriege* [The Story of O: The Joys and Wars of Opium], Löhrbach 1998.

[60] http://www.thirdworldtraveler.com/CIA/CIAdrug_fallout.html

[61] B. Raman, "Heroinisation of the Pakistani Economy," 4/30/2000, http://www.subcontinent.com/sapra/regional/regional20000430a.html

[62] *Rolling Stone*, Vol. 10/2001.

[63] Andreas von Bülow, *Im Namen des Staates*, op. cit., p. 273 ff.

[64] "Afghan opium production grows," http:// news.bbc.co.uk/hi/english/world/south_asia/newsid_1843000/1843726.stm

[65] Robert Fisk, "What Muslim would write: 'The time of fun and waste is gone'?" http://www.geocities.com/WestHollywood/Park/6443/WTC/fbi1.html

[66] Bob Woodward, "In Hijacker's Bags, a Call to Planning, Prayer and Death," http://www.washingtonpost.com/wp-dyn/articles/A37629-2001Sep27.html

[67] http://www.spiegel.de/politik/deutschland/0,1518,161124,00.html

[68] Carol A. Valentine, "Operation 911: No Suicide Pilots," http://www.eionews.addr.com/psyops/news/carolvalentine.htm

[69] Jon Dougherty, "McVeigh, Nichols 'did not act alone,'" http://www.worldnetdaily.com/news/article.asp?ARTICLE_ID=22684

[70] Zbigniew Brzezinski, *The Grand Chessboard: American Primacy and Its Geostrategic Imperatives*, Basic Books, 1998.

[71] Samuel Huntington, *The Clash of Civilizations and the Remaking of World Order*, 1996, 1998.

[72] "Suspicious profits sit uncollected," http://www.sfgate.com/cgi-bin/article.cgi?file=/chronicle/archive/ 2001/09/29/MN186128.DTL

[73] "Suppressed Details of Criminal Insider Trading Lead Directly into the CIA's Highest Ranks," http://www.fromthewilderness.com/free/ww3/10_09_01_krongard.html

[74] http://www.eionews.addr.com/psyops/news/passenger_list_puzzle.htm

[75] Gary North's Reality Check, "The Perplexing Puzzle of the Published Passenger Lists," http://eionews.addr.com/psyops/news/wtc_unanswered_questions.htm

[76] Adam Hamilton, "The Inflation Tsunami," http://www.zeallc.com/commentary/tsunami.htm

[77] James Petras, "'Dirty Money' Foundation of US Growth and Empire," http://www.fromthewilderness.com/free/economy/053101_banks.html

[78] "House and Senate Leaders Clash on Banking Measure," http:// www.nytimes.com/2001/10/17/national/17MONE.html?todaysheadlines

[79] Manoj Joshi, "India helped FBI trace ISI-terrorist links," http://www.timesofindia.com/articleshow.asp?art_id=1454238160

[80] "Bush asks Daschle to limit Sept. 11 probes," http://www.cnn.com/2002/ALLPOLITICS/01/29/inv.terror.probe/

[81] "Daschle: Bush, Cheney Urged No Sept. 11 Inquiry," http://www.newsfrombabylon.com/index.php?q=node/1680

[82] "Making a Killing: The Business of War," http://www.public-i.org/bow

[83] www.fromthewilderness.com

[84] http://www.fromthewilderness.com/free/ciadrugs/bush-cheney-drugs.html

[85] www.debka.com

[86] "New rules in Chechnya,"
http://news.bbc.co.uk/hi/english/world/europe/newsid_1569000/1569249.stm

[87] George Monbiot, "America's pipe dream,"
http://www.guardian.co.uk/waronterror/story/0,1361,579169,00.html

[88] Rahul Bedi, "India joins anti-Taliban coalition," http://
www.janes.com/security/international_security/news/jir/jir010315_1_n.shtml

[89] "Warum ließen die Geheimdienste Atta laufen?" [Why did the secret services
let Atta go?] http://www.spiegel.de/politik/ausland/0,1518,164902,00.html

[90] Douglas Valentine, "The CIA and Poison Letters: Black Valentines?"
www.counterpunch.org/valentine3.html

[91] http://en.wikipedia.org/wiki/MKULTRA

[92] Matthew Rothschild, "Iraq, Anthrax, and the Hawks,"
http://www.commondreams.org/views01/1022-08.htm

[93] Arundhati Roy, "Why America must stop the war now,"
http://globalresearch.ca/articles/ROY110A.html

[94] http://www.spiegel.de/kultur/literatur/0,1518,165236,00.html
Arundhati Roy, "War Is Peace," http://www.zmag.org/roywarpeace.htm

[95] John Pilger, "This War is a Fraud," http://
www.mirror.co.uk/news/allnews/page.cfm?objectid=11392430&method=full

[96] http://whatreallyhappened.com

[97] "Delmart Edward Joseph "Mike" Vreeland – Spy or Con?"
http://www3.sympatico.ca/ron666/vreeland.html

[98] *Le Figaro*, 10/11/2001, http://www.globalresearch.ca/articles/RIC111B.html

[99] "Air Force One," http://www.boeing.com/defense-space/military/af1/

[100] Webster Tarpley, *9/11 Synthetic Terror: Made in USA,* Ch. IX, "Angel is
Next – The Invisible Government Speaks," p. 272-310 (Progressive Press,
2005).

[101] Michel Chossudovsky, "Cover-up or Complicity of the Bush
Administration?" http://globalresearch.ca/articles/CHO111A.html

[102] Michel Chossudovsky, *America's "War On Terrorism,"* Global Research,
2005.

[103] Arnaud de Borchgrave, "Interview with Hamid Gul, former chief of ISI,"
http://www.pakistan-
facts.com/staticpages/index.php?page=2002122312295195

[104] Seymour Hersh, "Watching The Warheads: The risks to Pakistan's nuclear
arsenal," http://www.bintjbeil.com/articles/en/011029_hersh.html

[105] "Reaction of ordinary people in Northern Afghanistan," BBC Newsnight
transcript, http://
news.bbc.co.uk/hi/english/events/newsnight/newsid_1591000/1591530.stm

[106] Chossudovsky, "Cover-up or Complicity."

[107] Arnaud de Borchgrave, "Interview with Hamid Gul."

[108] Mike Ruppert, "'Oh Lucy! – You Gotta Lotta 'Splainin To Do' – A Timeline around September 11th," http://www.fromthewilderness.com/free/ww3/02_11_02_lucy.html

[109] William D. Hartung, "The Carlyle Group: Crony Capitalism without Borders," www.thirdworldtraveler.com/Corporate_Welfare/CarlyleGroup_HMOWD%3F.html

[110] "Bush Sr. in Business with Bin Laden Family Conglomerate through Carlyle Group," WSJ / Judicial Watch, http://www.globalpolicy.org/wtc/analysis/0928bushsr.htm

[111] "Has someone been sitting on the FBI?" Greg Palast, Joe Trento, M. Springman, http://news.bbc.co.uk/hi/english/events/newsnight/newsid_1645000/1645527.stm

[112] Rashmee Z Ahmed, "Bush took FBI agents off Laden family trail," http://www.timesofindia.com/articleshow.asp?art_id=1030259305

[113] Greg Palast, David Pallister, "FBI claims Bin Laden inquiry was frustrated," http://www.guardian.co.uk/Archive/Article/0,4273,4293682,00.html

[114] Greg Palast et al., "Has someone been sitting on the FBI?" op. cit., audio file, http://www.informationclearinghouse.info/article6589.htm

[115] "Has someone been sitting on the FBI?" Greg Palast et. al., op. cit.

[116] "The Arming of Saudi Arabia," Transcript of PBS *Frontline*, 2/16/1993, http://emperors-clothes.com/news/arming-i.htm

[117] The GW Bush – Osama Bin Ladin Connection," http://lundissimo.info/wtc/bushbinladen.html

[118] "U.S. Was Foiled Multiple Times in Efforts To Capture Bin Laden or Have Him Killed; Sudan's Offer to Arrest Militant Fell Through After Saudis Said No" http://www.washingtonpost.com/ac2/wp-dyn?pagename=article&node=&contentId=A61251-2001Oct2

[119] "Bin Laden in the Balkans," from the The Washington Times June 22, 2001, http://emperors-clothes.com/news/binl.htm

[120] James Bissett, "War on terrorism skipped the KLA," National Post, 11/13/2001, http://globalresearch.ca/articles/BIS111A.html

[121] Michael C. Ruppert, "If CIA and Government Weren't Involved in the September 11 Attacks what were they Doing?" http://home.earthlink.net/~berniew1/911sum.html

[122] Jean-Charles Brisard, Guillaume Dasquié, Wayne Madsen, *The Forbidden Truth.*

[123] End Game, The Daily Brew, 5/19/2002,.http://democrats.com/view.cfm?id=7352

[124] Julio Godoy, "U.S. Taliban Policy influenced by Oil," http://globalresearch.ca/articles/GOD111A.html

[125] "The Accidental Operative: Richard Helms's Afghani Niece Leads Corps of Taliban Reps," 6/6/2001, http://www.villagevoice.com/issues/0124/ridgeway.php

[126] Godoy, "U.S. Taliban Policy influenced by Oil," op. cit.

[127] http://www.blythe.org/nytransfer-subs/2001mid/Guerrilla_of_the_Week

[128] http://www.washingtonpost.com/ac2/wp-dyn?pagename=article&node= &contentId= A61251-2001Oct2

[129] Rupert Cornwell, The Independent, "John O'Neill and the Oil Connection He Died Trying to Expose," http://www.rense.com/general25/fkf.htm

[130] "F.B.I. Is Investigating a Senior Counterterrorism Agent," http:// www.nytimes.com/2001/08/19/national/19FBI.html?searchpv=nytToday

[131] Lawrence Wright, "The Counter-Terrorist: John O'Neill was an F.B.I. agent with an obsession: the growing threat of Al Qaeda," 1/14/2002, http://www.newyorker.com/fact/content/?020114fa_FACT1

[132] www.rememberjohn.com

[133] http://www.pbs.org/wgbh/pages/frontline/shows/binladen/interviews/al-fagih.html

[134] "Transition of Power: President-Elect Bush Meets With Congressional Leaders on Capitol Hil ," http://www.cnn.com/TRANSCRIPTS/0012/18/nd.01.html

[135] www.rawilson.com

[136] "Bio-ID," http://www.spiegel.de/politik/deutschland/0,1518,163867,00.html

[137] Frank Rich, "Wait Until Dark," http://www.nytimes.com/2001/11/24/opinion/24RICH.html?todaysheadlines

[138] Professor Francis Boyle, "No War against Afghanistan!" http://www.globalresearch.ca/articles/BOY111C.html

[139] Patrick Martin, "Iran-Contra gangsters resurface in Bush administration," http://www.wsws.org/articles/2001/aug2001/cont-a01.shtml

[140] Zbigniew Brzezinski, The Grand Chessboard.

[141] http://www.councilonforeignrelations.net/ ; http://www.cfr.org/

[142] http://www.trilateral.org/

[143] Stephen Gowans, "Getting the Pipeline Map and Politics Right," http://www.swans.com/library/art7/gowans10.html

[144] Zbigniew Brzezinski, op. cit.

[145] Andreas von Bülow, Im Namen des Staates, op. cit., p. 489.

[146] Robert Fisk, "We are the war criminals now," www.zmag.org/fiskcrim.htm

[147] "UNOCAL Statement," http://www.globalresearch.ca/articles/UNO111A.html

[148] http://pilger.carlton.com

[149] John Pilger, "The Truths they never tell us: Behind the jargon about failed states and humanitarian interventions lie thousands of dead," http://www.globalresearch.ca/articles/PIL111D.html

[150] Brisard, Dasquié, and Madsen, The Forbidden Truth.

[151] "Unocal's People Lead Afghanistan," www.indymedia.ie/newswire.php?id=674

[152] http://www.afghanistan-seiten.de/afghanistan/bios_mujagilkar.html

[153] "Ashcroft Defends Antiterror Plan,"
http://www.nytimes.com/2001/12/07/politics/07CIVI.html?todaysheadlines

[154] http://www.bushwatch.org/bushmoney.htm ; http://germany.indymedia.org/2001/09/8042.html

[155] Hearing on "Oversight of the Presidential Records Act,"
http://www.fas.org/sgp/congress/2001/110601_snelson.html

[156] http://www.jihadunspun.com/articles/04302002-Questions.Of.Liberty/

[157] John Dean, "Hiding Past and Present Presidencies,"
http://www.geocities.com/justicewell/dean.htm

[158] http://www.thirdworldtraveler.com/Chomsky/Noam_Chomsky.html

[159] "The Man Who Knows Too Much," http://www.almartinraw.com/uri1.html

[160] "The BCCI Affair: A Report to the Committee on Foreign Relations,"
http://www.fas.org/irp/congress/1992_rpt/bcci/

[161] http://www.bushwatch.net/bushmoney.htm

[162] "Peter Dale Scott's Website," http://socrates.berkeley.edu/~pdscott/q.html

[163] *"Große Knüppel, kleine Geister"* [Big Sticks, Small Spirits],
http://www.spiegel.de/spiegel/0,1518,170665,00.html

[164] Stefan Aust, *11. September 2001. Geschichte eines Terrorangriffs* [History of a Terror Attack], Cordt Schnibben, Stuttgart 2001.

[165] Uwe Galle, *"Was alles zu Beweisen werden kann"* [Everything that can be proven] http://www.zeit-fragen.ch/ARCHIV/ZF_85d/T04.HTM

[166] http://www.forteantimes.com/

[167] Mike Ruppert, "Government Complicity in the WTC, Pentagon Attacks,"
http://www.fromthewilderness.com/free/ww3/12_05_01_portland.html

[168] Wilhelm Reich, *Die Massenpsychologie des Faschismus* (1933), *The Mass Psychology of Fascism,* (Farrar, Straus and Giroux, 1980).

[169] www.convar.de

[170] http://convar.de/de/presse/presse_echo_15_11_2001.htm; *"Das Geheimnis der verkohlten Festplatten"* [The Secret of the Burnt Hard Drives],
http://www.spiegel.de/wirtschaft/0,1518,173404,00.html

[171] Jim Hoffman, "Black Boxes: Contents of Flight Data and Cockpit Voice Recorders Are Missing,"
http://911research.wtc7.net/planes/evidence/blackboxes.html

[172] The World Trade Center Demolition and the So-Called War on Terrorism,
http://www.serendipity.li/wtc.htm

[173] Tom Flocco, "Profits of Death – Insider Trading and 9-11," http://www.fromthewilderness.com/free/ww3/12_06_01_death_profits_pt1.html

[174] Roberto J. Gonzalez, "Ignorance is Not Bliss: Lack of Reporting Civilian Casualties from the War in Afghanistan is Keeping Americans in the Dark – and Endangering Their Future,"
http://www.commondreams.org/views02/0102-02.htm

[175] "General Myers Confirmation Hearing," Senate Armed Services Committee, 9/13/01, http://emperors-clothes.com/9-11backups/mycon.htm

[176] http://emperors-clothes.com

[177] 9/11 FAQ, http://emperors-clothes.com/indict/faq1.htm

[178] Gonzalez, "Ignorance is Not Bliss," op. cit.

[179] Walden Bello, "The American Way of War," http://globalresearch.ca/articles/BEL201A.html

[180] Lonnie Wolfe, "Americans Target of Largest Media Brainwashing Campaign in History," Executive Intelligence Review, http://www.rense.com/general15/tr.htm

[181] "Petition to the Senate to Investigate Oddities Involving 9/11 Terrorist Attacks," http://www.petitiononline.com/11601TFS/petition.html

[182] "Questions About What Bush Administration Was Willing to Do in Pursuit of Oil," CNN transcript, http://billstclair.com/911timeline/2002/cnn010902.html

[183] *Le Monde*, Dec. 5, 2001

[184] Kim Sengupta, "New US envoy to Kabul lobbied for Taliban oil rights," http://www.ariannaonline.com/forums/archive/index.php/t-1427.html

[185] "Afghan Roots Keep Advisor Firmly in the Inner Circle," http://www.spongobongo.com/her9937.htm

[186] *"US-Regierung verheddert sich in Widersprüchen,"* [US government entangles itself in contradictions], http://www.spiegel.de/wirtschaft/0,1518,176467,00.html

[187] "Deutschebank and Harken Energy, W's Own 1991 Insider Trading Scam," http://www.fromthewilderness.com/free/ww3/01_09_02_death_profits_pt3.html

[188] http://www.sfgate.com/cgi-bin/article.cgi?f=/chronicle/archive/ 2002/01/06/ED125108.DTL

[189] Michael Ruppert, "Enron Exploding – May Connect to Money Laundering," http://www.fromthewilderness.com/free/ww3/enron_money_laundering.html

[190] Tom Flocco, "Connecting The Dots: Insider Trading and 911," http://www.scoop.co.nz/stories/HL0207/S00229.htm

[191] "On the Public's Right to Know: The day Ashcroft censored Freedom of Information," San Francisco Chronicle, Jan. 6, 2002, http://www.sfgate.com/cgi-bin/article.cgi?f=/chronicle/archive/ 2002/01/06/ED125108.DTL

[192] *"Zur Ökonomie des Kriegs* (No business like war business)," http://www.heise.de/tp/deutsch/inhalt/co/11619/1.html

[193] http://www.skolnicksreport.com/

[194] Sherman H. Skolnick, "The Enron Black Magic, Part 4: The Swindlers and their Victims," http://www.rense.com/general19/swind.htm

[195] "Rat Line," http://lexikon.idgr.de/r/r_a/rat-line/ratline.php

[196] Sherman H. Skolnick, "Corrupt IRS Officials Face Exposure in Dope Bust," http://www.skolnicksreport.com/corruptirs.html

[197] http://www.arthurandersen.com

[198] "The man who knew too much – Clifford Baxter, former vice-chairman of Enron," http://www.telegraph.co.uk/news/main.jhtml?xml=/news/2002/01/27/wenron27.xml

[199] Skolnick, "The Enron Black Magic 4," http://www.skolnicksreport.com/tebm4.html

[200] "Mafia in Russia," http://www.ulfsbo.nu/ussr/mafia.html

[201] Pepe Escobar, "Pipelineistan, Part 2: The games nations play," http://www.atimes.com/c-asia/DA26Ag01.html

[202] "Spy Case in Canadian Courts Suggests US Naval Officer had Foreknowledge of 9-11," http://www.copvcia.com/free/ww3/01_25_02_revised_012802_vreeland.html

[203] Letter, http://www.fromthewilderness.com/free/ww3/01_28_02_vreeland.jpg

[204] Jean-Charles Brisard, Guillaume Dasquié, Wayne Madsen, *Forbidden Truth: U.S.-Taliban Secret Oil Diplomacy, Saudi Arabia and the Failed Search for Bin Laden* (Nation Books, 2002).

[205] http://www.alternatenews.com/archives/00000304.shtml

[206] Jean-Charles Brisard, Guillaume Dasquié, Wayne Madsen, op. cit.

[207] George Szamuely, "Nothing Urgent," New York Press, Vol. 15 No. 2, http://www.globalresearch.ca/articles/SZA202A.html

[208] "The President's Story," 60 Minutes, http://www.cbsnews.com/stories/2002/09/11/60II/main521718.shtml

[209] "America's Chaotic Road to War – Bush's Global Strategy Began to Take Shape in First Frantic Hours After Attack," Dan Balz and Bob Woodward, Washington Post, January 27, 2002, http://www.washingtonpost.com/wp-dyn/articles/A42754-2002Jan26.html

[210] "'We Will Rally the World' Bush and His Advisors Set Objectives, but Struggled With How to Achieve Them." http://www.washingtonpost.com/ac2/wp-dyn?pagename=article&node=&contentId=A46879-2002Jan27&notFound=true

[211] Raman, "Heroinisation of the Pakistani Economy," op. cit.

[212] Adam Porter, "The Secret Heroin War," http://www.agitprop.org.au/nowar/20011023_porter_the_secret_heroin_war.php

[213] Peter Dale Scott, "Heroin, drug warlords reappear on Afghan scene," http://www.finalcall.com/perspectives/afghan_drugs01-01-2002.htm

[214] "Drug Control Agency in Kabul is Evicted," by Patrick Cockburn in Kabul, http://www.counterpunch.org/pcockburnopium.html

[215] "Crackdown Hurts Afghan Opium Market," AP, http://nucnews.net/nucnews/2002nn/0202nn/020211nn.htm

[216] "Bush Anti-Drug Strategy Stresses Community," http://www.cannabisnews.com/news/thread11992.shtml

[217] Philip Smith, "Opium Dealers Cheer Ban on Afghan Poppy Cultivation," http://www.alternet.org/story.html?StoryID=12329

[218] "White House Airing Super Bowl Ads,"
http://www.cannabisnews.com/news/thread11882.shtml

[219] Office of Inspector General, Investigations Staff, "Report of Investigation –
Allegations of Connections Between CIA and the Contras in Cocaine
Trafficking," January 29, 1998,
http://www.cia.gov/cia/reports/cocaine/report/

[220] Philip Smith, "Noam Chomsky on the Drug-Terror Link,"
http://www.alternet.org/story.html?StoryID=12420

[221] *Drug War: Covert Money, Power & Policy*, excerpted at:
http://www.drugwar.com/dwindex.shtm

[222] *Ibid.*, "CIA Syndicate," http://www.drugwar.com/ciasyndicate.shtm

[223] "Cannabis as an illicit narcotic crop: a review of the global situation,"
http://www.undcp.org/bulletin/bulletin_1997-01-01_1_page004.html

[224] http://www.newstatesman.co.uk

[225] *"Rumsfeld: Pentagon lügt nicht"* [The Pentagon isn't lying],
http://www.heise.de/tp/deutsch/special/info/11895/1.html

[226] John Sutherland, "No more Mr Scrupulous Guy: How one of the two brains
behind the Iran-Contra scandal this week became one of America's most
powerful men,"
http://www.guardian.co.uk/Columnists/Column/0,5673,651975,00.html

[227] "Daschle Says Bush and Cheney Urged No 911 Inquiry,"
http://www.rense.com/general25/ggg.htm

[228] "The Israeli Spy Ring," http://whatreallyhappened.com/spyring.html

[229] Michael Rivero, "Fox News Pulls Its Four-Part Israeli US Phone Spying
Series," 12/22/2001, http://www.rense.com/general18/spypull.htm

[230] "This Story No Longer Available, by Carl Cameron, 12/21/2001"
http://www.foxnews.com/story/0,2933,40679,00.html

[231] "The Israeli Spy Ring," *op. cit.*,
http://www.whatreallyhappened.com/spyring.html

[232] Charles R. Smith, "FBI Investigates Foreign Spy Ring – US Companies
Deny Involvement," 1/16/2002, http://www.rense.com/general19/spy.htm

[233] Richard H. Curtiss, "Report of Israeli Eavesdropping On White House
Telephones," Washington Report, 12/15/2001,
http://www.rense.com/general18/report.htm

[234] "Israeli Press – Sharon to Peres: 'Don't worry about American pressure; we
control America,' "Infopal, http://www.wrmea.com/html/newsitem_s.htm

[235] Hannah Arendt, *Origins of Totalitarianism* (Harcourt, 1973).

[236] Suzanne Goldenberg, "Furious Bush hits back at Sharon," 10/06/2001,
http://www.guardian.co.uk/israel/Story/0,2763,564379,00.html

[237] http://www.petitiononline.com/warcrime/

[238] Robert Fisk, "Another war on terror…the truth at last...," The Independent,
London, 11/28/2001, http://www.zmag.org/fisksabra.htm

[239] "The Israeli Spy Ring," *op. cit.*,
http://www.whatreallyhappened.com/spyring.html
[240] Holger Jensen, "Articles on the Middle East,"
http://www.angelfire.com/co3/alaqsaintifada/Holger/articles.html
[241] Holger Jensen, Letter, http://www.broeckers.com/jensen.htm
[242] Amos Oz, "About the Soft and the Delicate – Interview with Ariel Sharon,"
12/17/1982, http://www.jerusalem.indymedia.org/news/2002/04/6506.php
[243] "Usama bin Laden Says the Al-Qa'idah Group had Nothing to Do with the
11 September Attacks," Interview, Ummat, Karachi, 9/28/2001,
http://www.robert-fisk.com/usama_interview_ummat.htm
[244] Carl Schmitt, *The Concept of the Political* (University of Chicago, 1996).
[245] "Police Follow Lead On Pearl's Body, MSNBC, 5/16/2002, http://www.
stevequayle.com/News.alert/Terrorism/020516.lead.on.Pearls.body.html
[246] "Pentagon: Hunt the Boeing! And test your perceptions!"
http://www.asile.org/citoyens/numero13/pentagone/erreurs_en.htm
[247] http://www.angelfire.com/ego/steveseymour/mirror/uj/pentagon.htm
[248] http://www.EricHufschmid.net/ThePainfulDeceptionsVideo.html
[249] "In pictures: Pentagon crash," http://
news.bbc.co.uk/hi/english/world/americas/newsid_1861000/1861977.stm
[250] "The Claim that the Pentagon was not Struck by a Plane is Deliberate
Disinformation," http://www.whatreallyhappened.com/hunthoax.html
[251] www.worldbank.org
[252] www.imf.org
[253] www.gregpalast.com
[254] http://judicialwatch.org/
[255] Wes Vernon, "Scandal Inside the FBI: Did G-Men Miss the Boat on 9-11?"
3/14/2002, http://www.newsmax.com/archives/articles/
2002/3/13/94339.shtml
[256] "World Bank Secret Documents Consumes Argentina: Alex Jones
Interviews Reporter Greg Palast,"
http://www.gregpalast.com/detail.cfm?artid=125&row=1
[257] *Ibid.*
[258] *Ibid.*
[259] Greg Palast, *The Best Democracy Money Can Buy*, London 2002

Part 3

[1] Peter Dale Scott, *Deep Politics and the Death of JFK*, Berkeley and Los
Angeles 1996 – also as e-book at: http://www.netlibrary.com/index.asp
[2] Robert A. Wilson, *Lexikon*, p. 8 f.
[3] Ummat, *op. cit.*, http://www.robert-fisk.com/usama_interview_ummat.htm
[4] "Text of President Bush's address to the UN,"
http://www.washingtonpost.com/wp-
srv/nation/specials/attacked/transcripts/bushtext_111001.html

[5] Mathias Kepplinger, *Die Kunst der Skandalierung und die Illusion der Wahrheit* [The Art of Scandal-Mongering and the Illusion of Truth] (Munich 2001), p. 87.

[6] Dan Rather, Barry Petersen, CBS News, "Bin Laden Whereabouts Before 9/11," http://globalresearch.ca/articles/CBS203A.html

[7] Heinz von Foerster, Bernhard Poerksen, *Wahrheit ist die Erfindung eines Lügners* [Truth is the Invention of a Liar] (Heidelberg 1998), p. 29.

[8] Sen. Frank Church, cited in *"Mordreport"* [Murder Report], Ossietzky, Dec. 2001 (retranslated to English).

[9] "Poll Shocker: Nearly Half Support McKinney's 9/11 Conspiracy Theory," Newsmax, 4/17/2002, www.globalresearch.ca/articles/GRI505A.html

[10] "Fear and Learning in America," The Independent, 16.4.02, http://www.counterpunch.org/fisk0416.html

[11] Michael Davidson, "Conspiracy Theorist Immune to the Widespread Support for War on Terror," www.globalresearch.ca/articles/DAV205A.html

[12] "Musharraf, Karzai Agree Major Oil Pipeline in Co-operation Pact," Irish Times, 2/9/2002, http://billstclair.com/911timeline/2002/irishtimes020902.html

[13] "Vreeland Challenges Solomon and Corn Directly – Requests a Pacifica Interview," http://www.fromthewilderness.com/free/ww3/04_09_02_vreeland_letter.html

[14] "What the CIA Doesn't Want You to Know – Interview with Delmart Vreeland," *Ibid.*

[15] "Foreknowledge of 9-11," http://globalresearch.ca/articles/CRG204A.html

[16] Joshi, "India helped FBI," *op. cit.,* http://www.timesofindia.com

[17] "Friendly Fire – Book: U.S. Military Drafted Plans to Terrorize U.S. Cities to Provoke War With Cuba," http://www.ratical.org/ratville/CAH/JCS1962abc.html

[18] L. L. Lemnitzer, Chairman JCS, "Justification for US Military Intervention in Cuba," 3/13/1962, http://www.fromthewilderness.com/free/ww3/11_20_01_northwoods.pdf

[19] Daniel Hopsicker, "Did Terrorist Pilots Train at U.S. Military Schools?" http://www.madcowprod.com/issue05.html

[20] BBC, "FBI fails to find terror trail," 5/1/2002, *op. cit.*

[21] Robert S. Mueller, III, http://www.fbi.gov/pressrel/speeches/speech041902.htm

[22] *"Passagierlisten,"* http://www.medienanalyse-international.de/paxeaa11.html

[23] Eric Lichtblau, Josh Meyer, "FBI fails to uncover key clues into 9-11, Lack of hard evidence, paper trail hurts efforts to ward off new attacks," LA Times, 4/30/2002, http://www.detnews.com/2002/nation/0204/30/a05-477843.htm

[24] "The Independence of the Press,"
http://www.constitution.org/pub/swinton_press.htm
[25] Michael Massing, "Press Watch," 9/27/2001,
http://www.thenation.com/doc/20011015/massing
[26] "Martin Luther King,"
http://www.spartacus.schoolnet.co.uk/USAkingML.htm
[27] Noam Chomsky, *9-11*, Seven Stories Press, Nov. 2001.
[28] Mark Twain, *The Mysterious Stranger* (posthumous, 1916).
[29] Nico Haupt's site is www.911skeptics.blogspot.com. List of anomalies
adapted from Ian Woods, 4/2/2004,
http://www.globalresearch.ca/articles/WOO404A.html
[30] Ruppert, "Oh Lucy! – You Gotta Lotta 'Splainin To Do," *op. cit.*

Index of Names

Subject Index